THE WORLD OF ANCIENT ROME

Text by:

VINCENZO ARANGIO RUIZ
Vice President of the Accademia dei Lincei

PAOLO EMILIO ARIAS
of the University of Pisa

JEROME CARCOPINO
of the Académie Française

LUCA DE REGIBUS
of the University of Genoa

GIULIO GIANNELLI
Rector of the Scuola Normale Superiore of Pisa

PIERRE GRIMAL
of the Sorbonne

GIUSEPPE LUGLI
of the University of Rome

ALDO NEPPI MODONA
of the University of Genoa

GIOVANNI PUGLIESE CARRATELLI
of the University of Florence

PIETRO ROMANELLI
of the University of Rome

CESARE VASOLI
of the University of Cagliari

FRANK W. WALBANK
of the University of Liverpool

General Advisers:

GIULIO GIANNELLI - UGO ENRICO PAOLI

The help of the following is acknowledged — in the chapter on family life, MARIA PAOLI and GIANFRANCO MADDOLI; ANTONIO LUGLI on the « Roman Chronicles » and J. R. VIEILLEFOND for his contribution on music and dancing to the chapter on art.

Editors: ITALO SALVAN *and* RENATO CAPORALI

Layout Artists: ATTILIO ROSSI *and* GIANFRANCO BULLETTI

Photographic Advisers: SCALA of Florence.

THE WORLD OF
ANCIENT
ROME

edited by GIULIO GIANNELLI

333 illustrations in colour

PUTNAM - NEW YORK

FIRST AMERICAN EDITION 1967

Library of Congress Catalog Card Number: 67-15663

This translation edited by Joan White

First published in Italy in 1963
as TUTTO SU ROMA ANTICA
by BEMPORAD MARZOCCO, Florence
© 1963 BEMPORAD MARZOCCO, Florence

This translation
© 1967 MACDONALD & Co. (Publishers) Ltd.

Printed in Italy

The reader will find a vast panorama of life in the pages of The World of Ancient Rome. *An epoch and its ambience have been clearly and precisely recreated. The editors have taken full advantage of modern production techniques for intimately relating text and illustrations — which were chosen each to complement the other — so as to present the most complete account consistent with scientific standards of exactitude.*

Distinguished authors from Italy, France and England worked together to give an authentic sense of daily life in Rome, of the problems of the metropolis, and to portray in all its light and shade a civilization which gave its name to twelve centuries of the history of mankind. Some way had to be found to give a comparable sense of authenticity in terms of the illustrations since it was felt that the commonplace views of ruined forums and lifeless archaeological finds would be entirely inappropriate. On the contrary, houses and temples, streets and bridges, weapons and household utensils, all had to take on a dimension of reality that would be capable of suggesting « Rome as it was » so that the illustrations would give point and immediacy to the grand sweep of the text.

At the same time, the individual articles had to be coordinated with each other; documents had to be checked; the countless photographs from the great museums had to be ruthlessly sifted to ensure as far as possible that only material was used that could be dated within the chronological limits set by the overall framework, that is, from the decline of the Republic to the rise of the Empire.

This « Rome without ruins » is thus the product of intricate organization and rigorous editorial commitment. It has been dependent on the help given by scholars and experts, by centres of learning and by well-known technical organizations: to all these, the editors extend their warmest thanks.

CONTENTS

2

THE METROPOLIS IN THE AUGUSTAN AGE

The elder Pliny and Martial stated proudly that no city in the world could compare with Rome. It certainly was an immense city, with its twelve-and-a-half-mile long boundary and two million inhabitants, but it was not so much these factors of area, size or population density that made it unique, as the grandeur of its monuments and public buildings.

The great building revolution in Rome began under Augustus (63 B.C.-A.D. 14). The political changes of the time seemed to demand material changes too and the brick, wood and stone of old Rome were replaced by other materials. The grandiose plan to make the city a worthy setting for a new and greater Rome belonged to Julius Caesar, but it was Augustus who brought the white marble from the Luni quarries to decorate the great new buildings and to give increased lustre to those already existing. The main roads were widened and straightened, old aqueducts were repaired and new ones built, existing public works were enlarged and new undertakings were launched. It was a vast plan of activity, embarked upon with determination and a wide vision, and destined to continue down the centuries until the fortunes of Rome herself declined, and her incomparable heritage of civilisation fell before the ignorance and ferocity of the barbarian invaders.

« I found a city of bricks and I left it marble », were the words Suetonius put in the mouth of Augustus, and they do summarize the vast building revolution which began in Rome at the end of the first century B. C.

Up to that time sun-baked bricks, with a thin facing of plaster had been used. Once the habit of using sawn marble had established itself, the big marble quarries at Luni in Tuscany were worked and gradually this white Luni marble began to replace the peperino stone from the Alban Hills and the travertine stone quarried near the sulphur baths on the way to Tivoli. It was used for facing public buildings and even private persons began to use it more and more in their building projects.

Augustus found the city untidy and neglected. The Romans were attached to their old stone temples, to the noisy Forum and its constant crowds of all sorts of people, to the dark, narrow streets where women chattered and men drank in low taverns. It was important to live in the centre of the city because on the hills water, food supplies and even security were lacking. All this made the city grow haphazardly; the lath and plaster houses went on adding storey after storey, sadly diminishing both stability and daylight.

In comparison to the hellenistic cities that had been built in Egypt and the East, all regularly planned, and with new architectural forms, Rome looked like an old town, hardly worthy of the dominion she now held over most of the known world. Sulla (138 B.C.-78 B.C.) and his son had repaired many of the cities of Latium (Praeneste, Tibur, Tarracina, Cora) which had suffered in the civil war against Marius the Younger, but had done nothing in Rome, except for completely rebuilding in stone the temple of the Most Excellent and Almighty Jupiter (*Optimus Maximus*), the Senate House and the Tabularium on the Capitoline hill.

Caesar was the first to conceive a large-scale plan for reconstructing the town. The course of the Tiber was to be diverted along the foot of the Vatican

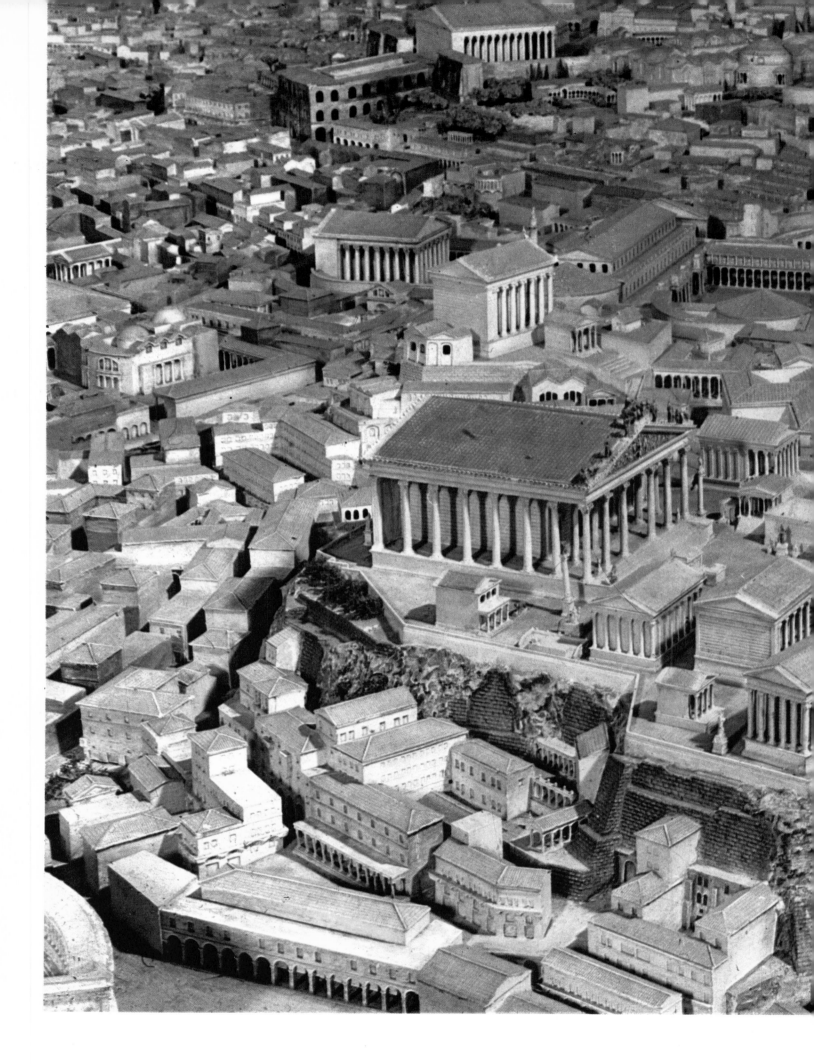

A view of the great elevated model of Imperial Rome made by the architect Halo Gismondi on the basis of Rodolfo Lanciani's « Forma Urbis » and brought up to date in the light of the most recent archaeological research. (Museum of Roman Civilisation, Rome).

hills; the old river-bed was to be drained and filled in; the Campus Martius joined to the centre of the city and a new army exercise ground constructed on the outskirts. By way of a start he built a new Forum (the Julian Forum) adjoining the old one, with a temple to *Venus genetrix* in the centre, just like the old Italic forums, and he restored many buildings in the old Forum. At the same time Pompey drained the Campus Martius and built the first stone theatre with a splendid portico, which was still much admired in the latter days of the empire.

THE TOWN PLAN OF AUGUSTUS

Augustus had two possibilities: either to continue Caesar's plan or to be content with restoring and improving the old town as far as possible without changing its basic appearance. He decided on the second course for three reasons: the huge cost and the difficulties involved in an almost total renewal of the traditional structure of the city; the tenacious conservatism of the populace which preferred its ancestral way of life; and lastly, his own personal aversion to big innovations, overbold plans and excessive expenditure.

Augustus was above all immensely thorough and even the limited plan demanded a basic re-planning of the city by means of its division into new districts and wards. It was not easy to impose this partition on a city whose growth had been a question of successive waves of settlement rather than the result of a predetermined plan, but it was necessary to do so. He created fourteen numbered wards (*regiones*), each in turn divided into districts (*vici*). In order to achieve this, the city was taken as being circular in shape: two concentric lines were then drawn around the Palatine Hill, one along the Servian walls and the other around the toll-gates. Inside this area the city was divided into districts, the boundaries of which were radial lines following the chief routes out of the city from the Forum to the wall gates. Thirteen of these districts were on the left bank of the Tiber and the fourteenth — the modern Trastevere — on the right. The break with tradition was made greater by setting only five of the districts within the ancient circuit of the city, five others were partly within and partly without and four were completely outside. A

noticeable difference quickly became apparent between the two principal sets of districts, for those within the walls could not be enlarged and much of the space available for private residence was taken up by new public buildings, while the outer districts had no such limitations and might therefore expand out of all proportion to the inner area. This problem grew more acute in succeeding centuries, as imposing imperial buildings went up round the Forum, on the Palatine, in the Campus Martius and on parts of the Esquiline Hill. Augustus placed the districts under the control of magistrates, chosen annually by lot, and the wards under supervisors (*vicomagistri*) locally elected and chosen for their civic virtues. Each ward had four supervisors and their municipal duties included responsibility for the street shrines (*lares compitales*), assistance

Another view of the great reconstructed model of Rome, intersected by the solemn procession of the arches of Nero's aqueduct. To the left the Colosseum. (Museum of Roman Civilisation, Rome).

with the census, and until A.D. 6, responsibility for the fire brigade.

But all public offices have a habit of multiplying, and Pliny the Elder tells us that in A.D. 73 the number of districts had grown to 265 and the number of *vicomagistri* to 1060. In Constantine's reign (A.D. 306-337) there were 423 districts.

But Augustus did far more than this for the comfort and convenience of the city. As the city was constantly menaced by outbreaks of fire, he created a public corps of *vigiles* or fire-fighting nightwatchmen; as la protection against floods he cleared the Tiber channel which had been checked with an accumulation of rubbish and narrowed by projecting houses. He increased the number of public fountains, bakeries and food shops, reorganised the food warehouses and the

city's cleansing services which were handed over to the special soldiers called *urbaniciani*. And for the protection of the public, squads of nightwatchmen carrying torches patrolled the streets.

The supply of water for Rome had become quite inadequate for the greatly increased needs of the growing population. The old aqueducts of the Appian Way, of the Marcia, Aniene and Tepula waters, were put into working order again by Augustus and Agrippa, and three new sources were found to supply the new buildings they had put up, especially in the Campus Martius: the Julia to increase the Tepula supplies: the Vergine at the eighth mile on the Via Collatina for the pool and the Thermae in the Campus Martius; the Alsietina from the lake of the same name (today Martignano) served the amphitheatre on the far side

15

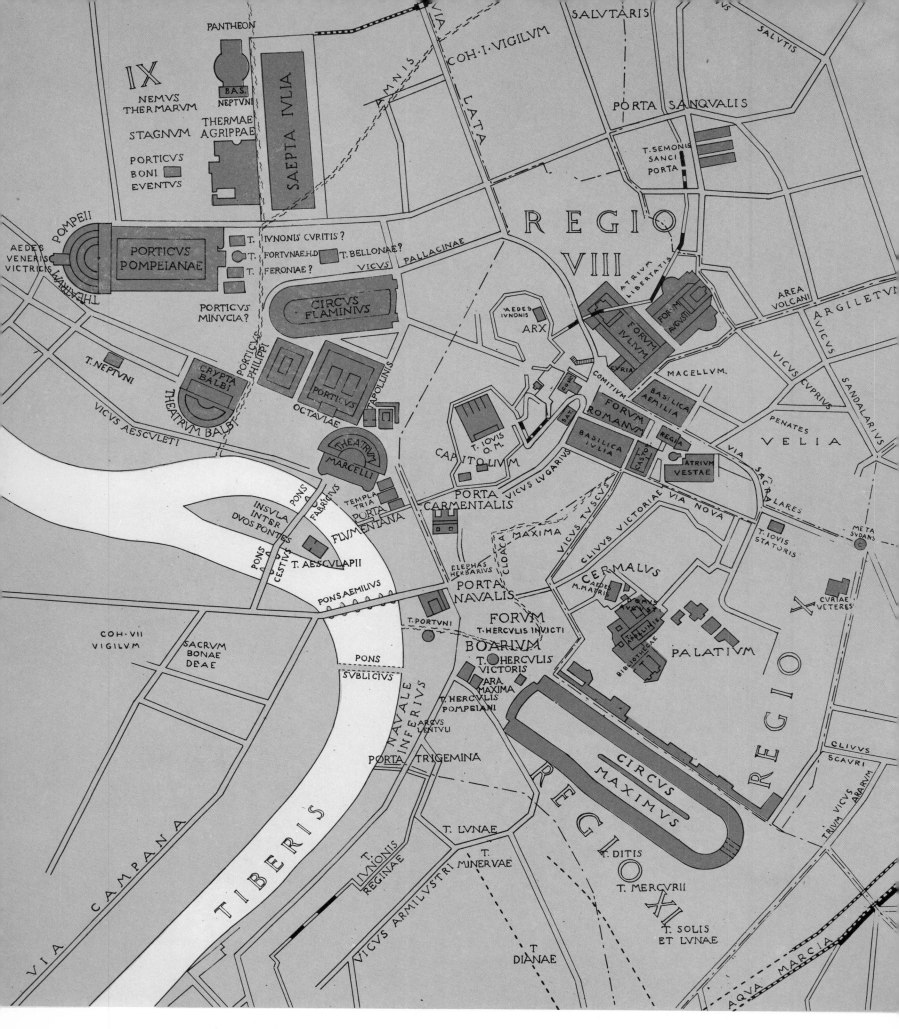

Topographical reconstruction of the central area of Rome as it was at the time of Augustus, drawn by Professor Lugli in 1952. In this plan, which is probably the best documented of all existing plans, the position of the Theatre of Balbus and of the Circus Maximus may have to be corrected later. (By courtesy of Professor Giuseppe Lugli).

Rome. Arch erected in honour of the Flavian Emperor Titus at the top of the Via Sacra, the Sacred Way.

of the Tiber where mock naval battles were staged. In the year of his aedileship in 33 B.C., Agrippa repaired the entire drainage system of Rome and covered the whole course of the Great Sewer (*Cloaca Maxima*).

The banks of the Tiber too were reinforced, and buildings too close to the river's edge were pulled down so that the embankments could be used once more by the barge-drawing cattle to bring the cargo ships up to the Navalia. A large area marked by travertine was reserved for their berthing on both sides of the river. Some of the blocks of travertine are preserved in the National Roman Museum in the baths of Diocletian, in Rome. In the reign of Tiberius (reigning A.D. 14-37) a permanent committee of five senators was charged with the responsibility of caring for the Tiber, and this lasted to the time of Domitian (reigning A.D. 81-96), when the job was entrusted to a magistrate and two assistants.

The building boom and the concurrent growth of trade gave rise to the usual urban problems. To cope with these, Augustus put in hand an overall plan for street repair in the inner town, on similar lines to a programme he had already initiated in the suburbs. The work on new drains in many roads, like the Via Lata-Flaminia, provided the opportunity to raise and level these roads. Pavements were often widened and at crossings small votive statues and altars went up, largely financed by *sportula* (« little gifts »), given by the people to the emperor on his birthday.

Some bridges like the Pons Sublicius and the Pons Mulvius were also repaired and where the Farnese Palace now stands Agrippa built a new bridge of which no trace remains today. Access to the city along the main arterial roads like the Appian, Flaminian and Cassian ways was improved. Arches were erected in honour of the emperor and the young imperial princes Drusus, Germanicus and Tiberius, and innu-

17

Rome. The solid Corinthian columns, remains of the façade of the Temple of Minerva.

merable temples, porticos, baths and fountains were repaired.

The buildings begun by Caesar, the law basilica, the new Forum, the Curia and the Saepta (the voting-halls), were finished, and the Temple of the Divine Julius was dedicated to Caesar to mark his deification: its site was the very spot in the Forum where he had been cremated. Augustus, grateful for Apollo's protection over his first enterprise, built a sumptuous temple and portico to this god next to his own residence on the Palatine; another temple near by was dedicated to Vesta, because as chief dignitary of the State religion,

The model of the city at the time of Constantine in the Museum of Roman Civilisation showing some of the monuments put up after the Augustan Age. Among these, on the left of the Sacred Way, the so-called round Temple of the Divine Romulus, the Basilica of Maxentius, the ten-columned Temple of Venus and Roma, and the Thermae of Trajan up on the Oppian hill.

Augustus had to live close to the divinity which stood as a symbol for the State.

Part of Augustus's plan for the new organisation of Rome included the encouragement of a religious revival, and to this end he paid much attention to the archaic temples in the Forum Romanum, the chief public square of Rome. Under his influence the temples of Saturn, Castor, Vesta and Concord were restored. Suetonius tells us that he often urged leading citizens to embellish the city with new public monuments, and in response to his urging, other temples were built, notably those of Hercules and the Muses, Diana and Saturn.

19

Perhaps his new Forum was his greatest architectural achievement. It was built because the two already in existence were not large enough to cope with the demands of legal business: in it, public prosecutions and the casting of lots for jury service took place. Its greatest monument was the superb temple of *Mars Ultor*, Mars the Avenger, which stood in the centre, its giant columns of Luni marble soaring towards the sky. Augustus had vowed to build this temple during the campaign at Philippi against Caesar's assassins. For sheer mass, prodigal use of marble and luxury of decoration, the conception of the Forum went beyond anything Rome had ever seen.

But it was in connexion with the Campus Martius that both Augustus and his close friend and adviser Agrippa conceived a plan destined to make that area one of the finest in the world. Augustus concentrated on the area to the left of the Via Flaminia, from what is today Piazza Colonna to the then extreme northern limits of the city, and there he built the shrine to Peace (the *Ara Pacis*), small in size, but exquisite in conception and style. Here too he built his own Mausoleum, which he surrounded with gardens in the manner of the main cemeteries situated along the consular highways, and his own crematorium. In the centre he erected a giant obelisk (the obelisk of Montecitorio) to serve as a huge sundial whose shadow would mark the hours on the marble pavement below.

AGRIPPA'S LABOURS

Agrippa used his great riches to improve a more southern area that had always been noted for its oppressive, bad air. Even today the area is one of the most low-lying in the city, and in the Middle Ages it was known as the *Valle*. Agrippa's chief monument was the Pantheon or temple of all the gods, particularly sacred to the memory of Julius Caesar's clan, or family, the Julian Gens, to which Augustus of course belonged; but little is left of the building of the Augustan Age; for what we now see was entirely due to the reconstruction of Hadrian. The near by Thermae, the first conceived with hygiene in mind, were surrounded by gardens and a lake from which a covered canal led down to the Tiber. Agrippa also built a part of the Via Lata-Flaminia and the Saepta, the great voting hall of the Roman people and originally planned by Julius

Caesar. Its two porticoes were called Meleager and The Argonauts, because of the decoration on them.

While Agrippa was reclaiming the Campus Martius and allotting large tracts of it for public use, Maecenas, another friend and counsellor of Augustus, reclaimed the Esquiline, an area that had been neglected and disease-ridden because for centuries it had served as a burial ground for the poor of Rome. Maecenas levelled the whole area and adorned it with pleasant gardens.

At the same time private individuals were building sumptuous villas (known as *horti*) on the Palatine, Pincian and Esquiline hills, and on the far side of the Tiber. Taking their name from the *horti*, the three hills were known as *colles hortulorum*. Augustus himself purchased the villa of the orator Hortensius (now known as the House of Livia), on the Palatine, to restore and embellish it as a private dwelling for himself.

AUGUSTUS THE RESTORER

The list of all the buildings erected or restored by Augustus in his reign, and mostly with his money, would be long indeed. The Senate conferred on him the apt title of *Restitutor aedium sacrarum et operum publicorum*, but he restored more than bricks and mortar; Augustus also restored the state, the ancient traditions of Rome and internal peace. Under Tiberius the people of Rome erected temples to his deified memory, associating it with the goddess Roma, whom he had raised to such power and splendour.

But in spite of the many buildings and works that were undertaken by Augustus and his collaborators, the general aspect of the city did not change so very much: the hills and the valleys remained. Indeed today, while the Piazza Santa Maria Maggiore is practically on the level of the old tufa foundations, the near by Via Urbana is more than fifty-five feet above the ancient level of the Augustan city. The difference in level between the Temple of Jupiter Capitolinus and the pavement of the Forum, was more than ninety-eight feet.

The streets were closed in by three-or-four-storied houses, and their twists and turns were dictated by the variations of level. The only drains were in the main streets. Houses, craftsmen's shops and stables stood crammed close together, without plan. There was but one real centre, the Forum Romanum, which drew

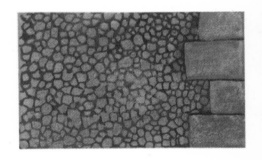

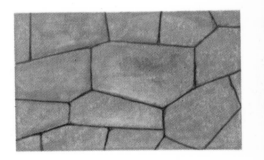

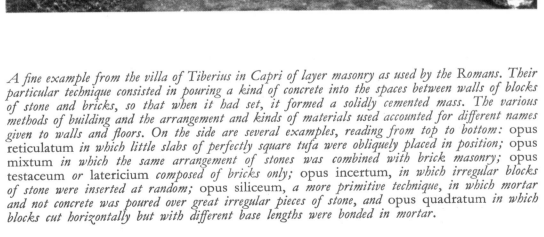

A fine example from the villa of Tiberius in Capri of layer masonry as used by the Romans. Their particular technique consisted in pouring a kind of concrete into the spaces between walls of blocks of stone and bricks, so that when it had set, it formed a solidly cemented mass. The various methods of building and the arrangement and kinds of materials used accounted for different names given to walls and floors. On the side are several examples, reading from top to bottom: opus reticulatum *in which little slabs of perfectly square tufa were obliquely placed in position;* opus mixtum *in which the same arrangement of stones was combined with brick masonry;* opus testaceum *or* latericium *composed of bricks only;* opus incertum, *in which irregular blocks of stone were inserted at random;* opus siliceum, *a more primitive technique, in which mortar and not concrete was poured over great irregular pieces of stone, and* opus quadratum *in which blocks cut horizontally but with different base lengths were bonded in mortar.*

the whole tumultuous populace to it for all the religious and political ceremonies, and to get to it they had to trudge up and down the difficult roads of the seven hills. The journeys were even more troublesome when they returned laden with food. This reason alone was enough to justify Caesar's plan to change the layout of the city, which by then was old and inadequate, and the chance to start re-building from scratch might well have given Nero a motive for setting fire to the city in A.D. 64.

Although the building revolution demanded new materials, many of the methods used by Augustus in building were traditional: the *opus reticulatum* of tufa for small buildings and for details of the larger ones, and the *opus quadratum* of parallel slanted blocks of stone and tufa mixed, or travertine and *peperino*, all used to cover a base of *opus caementicium*.

A typical example of this very traditional way of building can be seen in the great mausoleum Augustus built for himself in 27 B.C. almost immediately after he rose to power. He deliberately sought to conform to that ancient Italic style of building that had been inspired by Etruscan religious architecture, and he intended the monument to resemble the tumulus which covered the remains of the first kings and the early, glorious generals of Rome.

But a close examination of the plan and the internal structure of the building reveals the clumsiness of the architect who designed these substructures. The interior was sub-divided into tiers of compartments by a complex system of ring and radial concrete walls, rising up to the burial chamber. A central column cored the system and supported the statue of Augustus. A far better solution to the same problem was found a century and a half later for the Mausoleum of Hadrian. A half century before Augustus, in Sulla's time, architects had solved the problem by multiple arched terraces almost hanging from the hillsides, and by their bold bridges and aqueducts, built with an impressive technical skill. They had made careful studies of plane surfaces and had found brilliant solutions when dealing with enclosed spaces. Viewed from this angle, the Augustan architecture seems less advanced than that of Sulla's age.

But once marble had been introduced into temple architecture and into architectural sculpture, these criticisms no longer apply. The architects of Sulla knew nothing about marble lintels and entablatures,

and those of Caesar little more. The architects of the Augustan Age, however, were past-masters of its use. There was in fact a gap between the old style and the new. One only has to compare the decorative fragments of the *Regia Pontificis* in the Forum (36 B.C.) and of the Temple of the Palatine Apollo (30 B.C.), both roughly carved, irregular and quite unpolished, with the flowing, elegant and almost chiselled fragments of the Temple of Apollo in the Campus Martius (12 [?] B.C.) or of the Temple of Mars Ultor in the Forum of Augustus, or of the Temples of Concord and of Castor and Pollux in the Roman Forum, to see the progress or rather leap forward that Rome achieved in the space of a single generation. The new style cannot be entirely attributed to the craftsmen of Rome, who after all had been accustomed to carving stone, and who, when first confronted with the new material, had demonstrated the hard but uncertain line of Caesar's time. Clearly foreign craftsmen were involved, and these of course were Greeks, called to Rome by Augustus to teach an art in which they had been supreme for centuries.

Greeks carved the friezes on the *Ara Pacis*, even if the spirit and artistic expression of the story are Roman. Greeks decorated the Temples of Jupiter and Juno in the portico of Octavia, and the Tiberian temples in the Forum, and the sculptors who belong to the school which we usually call neo-Attic are in fact Greek. As for the painters of the third style, they come from Alexandria and their work clearly reflects the flora of the Nile.

Since the vault was not much used in architectural design at that time its place was taken by tall marble columns capped by immense architraves, carved from great blocks of marble. It needed great skill to put these blocks into position: the Greeks were past masters in the art — witness the Temple of Jupiter on Olympus and the Parthenon in Athens.

It is therefore to Augustus that credit must be given for the encouragement of this new art; it was he who showed his successors the architectural means which would make Rome the finest city of the world, with all the glory of huge buildings such as Hadrian's Pantheon, the Flavian amphitheatre, Domitian's palace on the Palatine, the Thermae of Trajan, Caracalla and Diocletian which were to remain down the centuries as witnesses to the constructive genius of Roman craftsmen and to the might of an empire.

HOUSES AND FURNISHINGS

The Roman house, the traditional domus *closed off from the outside world by external walls without windows, was a building typical of agricultural workers who had no need to worry about space. It was built round the* atrium *from which it received both light and air, and it was, as Cicero called it, the « sacred sanctuary » of each citizen, the repository of « his altars, his hearth, his family gods, his rites and his ceremonies », his temple in fact, as well as the home of that fundamental institution of Roman society, the family. Once Rome had grown into a metropolis, the* domus *became elegant and was much influenced by features of Greek importation such as colonnades, fountains and water grottoes; it became a privileged possession limited to the leisured class and the citizens inscribed on the census.*

Meanwhile, among the marble-covered temples, forums and circuses, the insulae *appeared — tall tenement blocks of three, four and five stories with flats to let, whose little cramped rooms housed most of the Roman populace and the immigrants from the countryside. The small dwellings, with little air or light, open to the hubbub of the shops and the noise of the streets, became a compulsory refuge at night and in bad weather, but were not — and could not be — a* domus *for a true Roman.*

Anyone who thinks that Rome at the time of the great Roman Empire was a collection of beautiful buildings only, would be wide of the mark. Just as the old cities of modern Europe have beautiful palaces in the centre, built by famous architects, and set alongside humble dwellings, so ancient Rome had its great houses where famous men and noble families lived alongside buildings occupied by poor people — and the latter were far more numerous than the former. Fifty thousand buildings were listed in the *Regionarii*, the official description of Rome, and of these, only 2,000 were patrician houses.

It was the patrician house that became known as a *domus*, while most Romans spent their lives in small uncomfortable flats in the *insulae*.

In fact, the *insulae* were the Romans' answer to their housing problem. The *domus* on the other hand was a house built to particular specifications. It might be simple or sumptuous, but to appreciate it one had to go inside. From outside all one saw was a blind un-broken wall, for the rooms received their light and air from the central courtyard.

Any attempt to reconstruct such a house from evidence in Rome would be difficult. As the Empire itself declined, so Rome lost its importance as the capital, and a turbulent succession of events began; pillaging by soldiers and barbarians, changes in government and in ways of living; the city was abandoned, then repopulated; the population grew and with it the need for new housing to which all great cities are subject. There was much new building, but also much destruction of the old houses in order to re-use whole areas in the centre of the city, and thus much of the past was swept away, save for a few great monuments.

The way the Latin writers describe life in Rome gives us some idea of what their houses were like and of the splendour or the poverty they witnessed.

The real information comes from the excavations at Pompeii and at Ostia. This is where we learn about how the Romans lived, and from these ruins archaeo-

23

The Street of Abundance in Pompeii, a typical example of a road with shops (tabernae) *running down it.*

logy has discovered material evidence of what these houses were really like.

Originally Pompeii was a city inhabited by patricians, landed proprietors living in handsome detached houses. As commerce and industry brought increased wealth to the city the patricians moved away from the centre into the suburbs, nearer to their land, and sold their houses to the new rich industrialists and traders. They in turn transformed these noble old buildings into workshops and storehouses till what little was left of the original *domus* would finally have disappeared, had it not been for that overwhelming eruption of Vesuvius which suddenly brought life to a halt. Whoever lived there was killed under the shower of ash and stones, but the *domus*, the noble patrician house the Romans knew, was preserved for posterity as a unique testimony.

Ostia had been founded some sixteen miles from Rome in the fourth century B.C., before the Empire. It had great importance as a naval base and as a commercial centre. Under the Empire it grew in importance, for the big ships laden with wares from the distant provinces came there and the cargoes were unloaded and stored in the city's warehouses. The city arranged the distribution of these cargoes. With increasing traffic

the population grew in number and more houses went up to accommodate all these people who needed to live as near as possible to their work. In order not to take up too much ground space, very many *insulae* went up in Ostia. When the capital of the Empire moved to Byzantium, the great maritime colony of Rome declined in importance; its population decreased, its buildings were abandoned and fell into gradual disrepair as maintenance became less and less worthwhile. Never again would Ostia's streets be thronged with people or the city regain its importance. But where the requirements of the new Rome necessarily destroyed the old, in Ostia, on the other hand, the old ruins still exist and offer precious evidence which has allowed scholars to recapture the nature of the *insulae*, not by imaginative reconstruction, but by a precise study of what the great tenements in which the Roman populace lived were really like.

THE PATRICIAN HOUSE

The original *domus* was not nearly so complicated as those illustrated by the layouts reproduced in the adjoining plans; these are later than the original *domus*, which consisted of only the front part of the plan.

The exterior of the house gives no indication of its interior. There is no door — entrance is directly into a corridor. This leads straight into the centre of the house. Half way down the corridor is a door which divides it in half; the first half is called the *vestibulum*, the second the *fauces*. Even in the *vestibulum* the nature of the house, patrician or otherwise, is clear from the objects around one: the statues, for instance, or the

Reconstruction from original materials of a northern Roman villa room. (Museum of Art and History, Brussels).

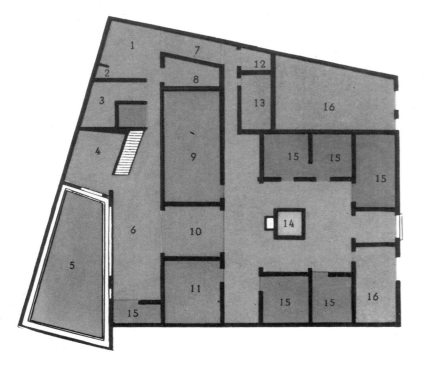

Plan of the Surgeon's House in Pompeii. 1. *Kitchen;* 2. *and* 3. *Lavatories;* 4. Triclinium *for summer use;* 5. *Garden;* 6. *Portico;* 7. *Corridor;* 8. *Pantry;* 9. Triclinium; 10. Tablinum; 11. Triclinium; 12. *Courtyard;* 13. *Storeroom;* 14. Atrium; 15. *Bedrooms;* 16. *Shops.*

Plan of Pansa's House in Pompeii. A. *Small letting quarters.* B. *Baker's Shop (b. oven).* C. *Shops.* - 1. *Vestibule.* 2. Fauces. 3. Atrium. 4. *Bedrooms.* 5. Triclinium. 6. Tablinum. 7. *Rooms opening on to the peristyle.* 8. *Peristyle.* 9. *Rooms.* 10. Triclinium. 11. *Stables.* 12. *Storeroom.* 13. *Kitchen.* 14. *Large* Triclinium (oecus). 15. *Bedroom.* 16. Cella. 17. *Portico.* 18. *Side door.*

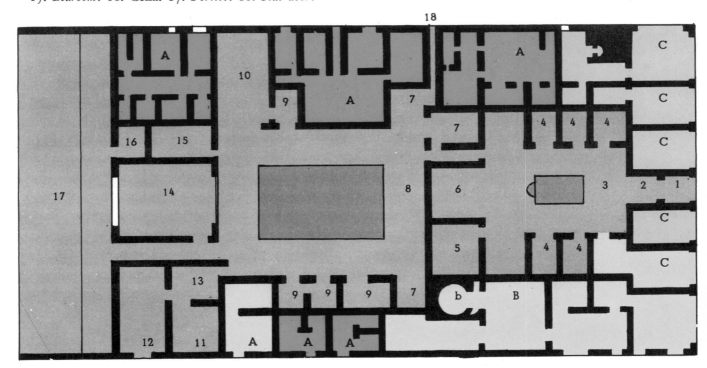

25

Reconstruction of the so-called House of the Tragic Poet in Pompeii (exterior). The House of the Tragic Poet is famous for its lavish wall decoration and for its pavement mosaic, both of superb workmanship. (Museum of Roman Civilisation, Rome).

Longitudinal cross-section of the House of the Tragic Poet in Pompeii. Access was gained through a narrow entrance paved with mosaic. The first room on the left was presumably a servant's room. The large atrium in the centre was surrounded by small rooms, probably bedrooms. Next to the atrium, the tablinum decorated with tragic and comic themes. From the tablinum into the peristyle, where the family altar was, looking rather like a booth, and then the triclinium, built in masonry, where family and friends took meals in the warm months. (Museum of Roman Civilisation, Rome).

columns. A secondary entrance (*posticum*) which lies in a side-wall of the house served as a tradesman's entrance and also gave the owner a means of escaping some boring visitor without being seen.

The second half of the corridor leads to a courtyard (*atrium*) which is partially covered. High up in the centre of the roof is a great rectangular aperture (the *compluvium*) exactly below which is a trough (the *impluvium*) which collects the rain water, and this drains away to a basement cistern.

In the earliest days the rooms of the house all opened off the *atrium*, the courtyard around which all family life revolved. It served as living-room, dining-room and work-room; there the family fire burned and guests were received. As the house became bigger with the development of the peristyle, the *atrium* became merely an antechamber housing the small chapel of the Lares (the gods who protected the family). Here, too, were to be found the family safe, any especially fine ornaments or precious possessions and occasionally a portrait bust of the owner of the house.

Several quarters traditionally gave on to the *atrium*. The two rooms on each side of the entrance were servants' quarters, but they often had no access to it and opened outwards, as they were sometimes used as shops (*tabernae*).

The rooms opening out from either side of the *atrium* were usually bedrooms (*cubicola*) and had characteristic features: the mosaic on the floor was white and the ceiling lower than elsewhere in order to make the room feel cosier. There were only two rooms opening out from the *atrium* which did not have the features of a *cubiculum*. They were called *alae*, and it is not clear what purpose they served. Directly facing the entrance to the *domus* is the *tablinum*, a large room wide open to the *atrium*. In early times this was where the main meal was eaten and often it also contained the bed of the master of the house, the *pater familias*. Once the *domus* was enlarged, this room became the principal passage through to the peristyle.

This was an open courtyard bordered on two or more sides with columns and surrounded with additional rooms. Both the portico and the garden it enclosed were usually much admired either for the beauty of the columns or for the rare plants growing there. These gardens were beautifully kept, with flowers and greenery arranged in symmetrical patterns, water playing everywhere, and in among the foliage, statuettes, tables, little colonnades: all objects designed to make the place more attractive, but tending rather to spoil the natural beauty of the garden. The best rooms in the house faced outwards, overlooking the garden.

In the atrium, *the framework of the* compluvium *might or might not be supported on columns which rested on the four corners of the* impluvium, *the natural reservoir for rain water for the Roman house.*

The House of the Red Walls and the House of Caius Secundus in Pompeii. On the page opposite: *Rome, House of Livia on the Palatine. Detail of the* tablinum *with large wall decoration.*

The end wall of the garden, the rooms without windows where light and air never had direct access, surely helped to give the inhabitants of these houses a sense of segregation, if not isolation. The Romans liked greenery: witness the great garden-villas they built in the country or on the immediate outskirts of the town. The best evidence for this liking is to be found in the very many gardens attached to city houses.

THE INNER ROOMS

In the earliest times the Romans ate in the *atrium* or in the *tablinum*, but once the Greek habit of eating in a reclining position caught on, a special dining-room was built, called the *triclinium*. In very grand houses there were more than one of these, and they were used according to the number of guests, so that a small gathering should not feel lost in too big a hall or a considerable number feel cramped in too small a room. Sometimes an astonishing number of people might be assembled.

However large the *triclinium*, the air was often heavy, especially as the great dinners could last for hours and hours. The host could satisfy his desire to hold large parties by having stone tables built in the garden, where feasts could be held as soon as the weather was warm enough. Dining comfortably in the open air meant that one avoided the inconveniences of steaming hot food and stinking torches which at times made the air unbreathable.

Food in Rome was plentiful and people enjoyed eating, but all cooking was done in small and smoky kitchens, heavy with the fumes from a hearth set in one wall; there was one oven and a miserable little sink. It is noticeable that while house plans give the precise position of a variety of rooms, they never indicate the location of the kitchen; this room had to fit in wherever it could, regardless of practical needs or hygiene. Baths and lavatories were always near the kitchen on account of heating and drainage requirements.

The rooms on the peristyle had no definite purpose as the rooms off the *atrium* had, but could be used equally well as bedrooms, as reception rooms or as *triclinia*.

There was no special provision for slaves' quarters: they slept wherever they found room, except for certain favoured ones who had a small antechamber attached to their master's bedroom to ensure his undisturbed rest.

The general layout of a Roman patrician house was as described here, but the builder's imagination or the master's tastes could modify the plan in detail or could build on an altogether more complex basis. Sometimes the peristyle would be only partly surrounded by a colonnade. In some houses there was no peristyle at all, in others there might be two, the one leading into the other. In some houses one very large room faced the peristyle and was on the opposite side from the *tablinum*. It was completely open to the garden and in

The peristyle of the House of the Vettii in Pompeii. The peristyle, a feature of the Greek house, became an essential part of the villa and then of the Roman patrician house. It was a courtyard decorated variously with fountains, statues and flowers beds, surrounded by a colonnaded portico.

the summer months the family would use it for relaxation and amusement. It was called the *exedra*.

WORKING-CLASS LIVING CONDITIONS

Few families could afford a *domus* all of their own. Most lived in a flat (*cenacula*) in the great tenement blocks called *insulae* because of their island-like appearance in a sea of streets. They were high, narrow houses on a foundation at most of 400 square yards, and about sixty feet high, which easily allowed for five floors. There were many large doors and windows. Wood and stone alternated on the façade in pleasing arrangements, or the house was faced with bricks in patterns of considerable art and good taste. On the upper floors there were terraces giving light and air to the rooms, but on the ground floor the walls were often opened up to form porticoes which housed lines of shops. Above the porticoes and between the rooms and the top terraces there were covered terraces like the loggias which the Renaissance architects used to give lightness to the upper parts of their buildings. On the façades of all the buildings and hanging from window sills were flowers and climbing plants, carefully chosen and tended, so that the streets of Rome looked gay and bright. This exterior beauty was by no means matched by the arrangements inside.

Detail of the peristyle in the House of the Vettii. Great attention was paid to plants, which were sometimes rare specimens.

Another detail of the Vettii peristyle. The rooms at the back of the house look out on to it.

Triclinium *in masonry in a Pompeian peristyle. People preferred to live in the open, weather permitting, to avoid the internal rooms which were generally poorly lit.*

Reconstruction of a building adjoining the « insula » of the Capitol, with the wide loggias and covered courtyards which opened in front of the storehouses and shops. (Museum of Roman Civilisation, Rome).

Five-storeyed house of the imperial age, at the foot of the Capitol (reconstruction by the architect Gismondi). This is a typical example of a house with flats to rent. On the ground floor vast shops face an open courtyard. The most spacious flats are on the third floor with a line of balconies. The remains of this building are actually buried up to the second floor today. (Museum of Roman Civilisation, Rome).

*Section of the great elevated model of imperial Rome made by the architect Gismondi for the Museum of Roman Civilisation. Several storied houses (*insulae*) are visible, for the lack of space forced building upwards.*

In some *insulae* the ground floor was arranged as a private apartment, and sometimes so luxuriously appointed as to merit the name of *domus*, but with the main difference that in a *domus* each room had its traditional place, whereas in the *insula* the tenant could use the rooms as he pleased. In other buildings the rooms attached to the entrance corridor, as sometimes in the *domus*, were used both as shops and living-rooms. The rooms were divided horizontally, the shop below and the shopkeeper's family above; access would be by means of a narrow winding staircase intended to take up as little room as possible. Sometimes the workers in the shop lived upstairs. This upper room was little more than a small box where one cooked, ate and slept. The rooms (*cenacula*) in the floors above were let to tenants of the *insula*, and in theory every flat was to be occupied by one family. But Rome at the time of the Empire had an ever-increasing population, and the demand for flats far exceeded the supply; rents rose constantly and the apartments deteriorated through lack of maintenance in spite of their high rentals. In the last years of the Republic, when prices had not yet reached their maximum, 2,000 sesterces were being paid for a very modest flat. The sum is difficult to convert today, but it was certainly excessive.

To meet these high rents many families were obliged to sublet one or more rooms; the results of this overcrowding can be imagined — instant deterioration in cleanliness, health, hygiene and the general peace of the building. Moreover, overcrowded families with poor living conditions and low pay could hardly be expected to form a quiet and balanced community, so that quarrels were frequent and everyone in the building suffered accordingly. Rents were not always paid on time and dealings with these unfortunate people, harassed by economic conditions, were not easy. The owner would sometimes make matters simpler for himself by granting a five-year lease to someone well able to make a profit from the rising rents, though the lessee would have to pay a considerable price for the privilege, as well as listen to the complaints of the tenants about their awful premises and put up with their many pretexts for delaying or avoiding payment of rents.

5

This brazier, used for heating bath water, comes from excavations at Stabia. (National Archaeological Museum, Naples).

Portable kitchen stove in two parts: in the smaller part with high surrounds, there is room for the big pans, in the larger lower and wider section, one could grill and keep wide-bottomed pans warm. (National Archaeological Museum, Naples).

The rooms themselves might often be paved with neat bricks or elegant mosaics, and the walls might be frescoed, but they possessed none of the simplest amenities common today: no light, no heating, no conveniences of any kind.

In theory, if the large windows were opened the rooms could enjoy fresh air, and if closed, they could offer protection against the cold, but in fact neither light nor air ever entered. It was only under the Empire that thin discs of mica or glass began to be fitted into the frames of these windows. Previously two wooden shutters, like those in mountain chalets today, filled in the window frame, and acted as blinds. Often these too were missing and people sheltered from the cold, the wind and the rain by hanging cloth or skins over the opening. Either way, no light could enter and one had to be grateful for the sight of a single sunbeam.

Heating was quite primitive. The Romans were familiar with central heating and made great use of it in certain rooms. It resembled our hot air systems in that the warm air circulated inside the walls. But no evidence has ever been found to show that the system was used in apartment houses. Besides, the Romans knew nothing of chimneys that draw up smoke, so there were no stoves or fireplaces. Braziers of all kinds abounded, in bronze and copper, some simple, some elaborate, some easily transportable by hand from one room to another, and some so big that wheels were fitted for moving them about. The only way not to die of cold was to light a brazier, and the price then paid for warm air included the inevitable fumes and gases given off by the poorly carbonized wood. Things often caught fire with so many braziers about, not to

mention the torches and oil lamps used for lighting, and a small fire would soon develop into a large one which might destroy the whole *insula*.

In this connection the emperor Augustus, instituted some practical reforms including local fire brigades, but outbreaks of fire continued to be a big worry on account of the lack of water inside the houses. There

Three-legged table in common use. (Museum of Roman Civilisation, Rome).

Round three-legged table used for very special dishes during a meal. Found at Herculaneum. (Museum of Roman Civilisation).

was even a law ordering citizens to have some water always handy for putting out fires, but when the need arose it would be found that the law often had not been observed, so that the flames rushed onward, destroying everything while everyone ran for water.

The emperors were so concerned with the lack of water in the city that no less than fourteen aqueducts were built, bringing thousands of gallons of water every day to the many fountains scattered all over the city. But this water was not carried into the houses themselves. There were great water mains, it is true, but as there was no pressure they never reached the upper floors. Moreover the right to take water from the mains was very costly, and if it was granted at all, it would be to an owner and not a tenant — and then for strictly personal use to be immediately withdrawn when the concessionaire died.

The inhabitants of the *insulae* had no lavatories. In the *domus* and on the ground floor of the *insula* the problem of drainage was easy, thanks to the sewers or *cloacae*, of which the first had been built in the fifth century B.C. These vast sewers became ever more numerous till they formed a whole network of great canals under the city. All kinds of rubbish were emptied into these canals, which flowed into the waters of the Tiber. Ground-floor dwellings could easily be attached to the main drain by pipes, but there were no such pipes on the upper floors and the Romans had to use public conveniences, or else some corner of the home and then throw the refuse out of the window. This mostly happened at night when in theory no one was about, but people going home late frequently received an unwelcome dousing as they passed. The ensuing quarrel often ended up in court with damages for the victim. Fines in these cases were very heavy.

FURNISHINGS

If fires were all too frequent and very difficult to put out, they were nevertheless accepted with a resigned cheerfulness when they destroyed an *insula*. The poor, it was said, suffered little except in so far as they had to find somewhere else to live, for their goods could be gathered in a sack and easily saved. This was all too true for many of them, who had little else besides a bed and a few cooking pots.

Even the rich did not possess a great variety of furniture, and the main difference between rich and poor, between the furnishings of a *domus* and an *insula*, consisted in the greater or lesser elegance of the few items of furniture, the beds, a table, a few chairs and stools. In fact quality, not quantity, determined the tone of the house.

The bed or couch was common to most houses, though there were some families too poor to possess one, and they would sleep on straw pallets on a raised stone like a large step. Whoever could afford a couch certainly had a wide choice among the many types created by the Romans. There was the common single bed called *lectulus* and the double bed for married couples called *lectus genialis*. There was the study couch for reading and writing (*lectus lucubratorius*) and the couch to eat from (*triclinium*). This latter was for three, but if you wanted to astonish your guests with your wealth or originality you provided a couch for six in your *triclinium*.

Oak, maple and terebinth were the main woods used in making couches, but there was also a rare and exotic wood with undulating grain and changing colours reminiscent of a peacock's tail. Couches made of this wood were called *lecti pavonini*, and were proof of wealth and luxury.

Then there were couches made of less noble wood, but nevertheless of considerable value on account of

Lantern carrier in bronze with four arms found in the so-called villa of Diomedes in Pompeii. (National Museum, Naples).

Cupboard with two doors of chestnut wood, reconstructed from remains of furniture in Pompeii.

Bronze lamps decorated with eagles and dolphins. (Museum of Roman Civilisation, Rome).

Cylinder shaped lantern used for home and outdoor lighting. From Pompeii. (National Archaeological Museum, Naples).

their wealth of ornament: they would have fine bronze legs, chiselled, or inlaid with tortoiseshell, gilt or silvered bronze, or — a sign of the highest wealth — solid silver legs.

The piece of furniture the Romans called *mensa* was not what we call a table, although it fulfilled something of the same function. In the dining-room, it was not only used to display the food but also to show off the rarest and most precious ornaments in the house.

There were tables with one, two, three and four legs, and some of the marble, bronze or ivory supports were of fine workmanship, as was the exquisite inlay work on the surface. It is interesting that only the three-legged tables were made with less valuable wood for people of more modest means.

The Romans did not feel the need for chairs much, since they ate and worked mostly reclining on one side, but there were several types of chairs, according to the use made of them and the occasions for which they were needed. The high-backed chair (*cathedra*) was reserved for matrons, priests in temples, and teachers giving lessons. The seat without a back but with arms

Lantern carrier. (Museum of Roman Civilisation).

(*sella*) was made so that it could fold and be easily transported like a camp stool. It was reserved for the magistracy (*sella curulis*) and the military (*sella castrensis*). The bench or stool (*scamnum*) which consisted of a piece of boarding on four legs was in most common use. As with other furniture, seats varied in their degree of simplicity according to the workmanship in them.

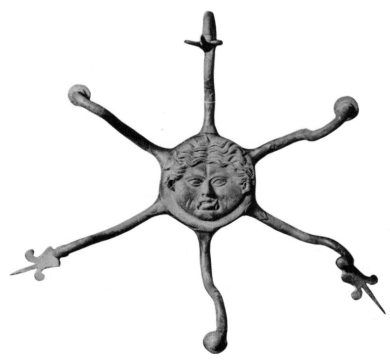

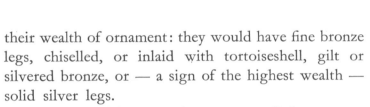

The *sella* used by Julius Caesar was of solid gold. But however rich and ornate the seats might be they were probably all rather uncomfortable, despite many cushions, for the Romans knew nothing of upholstery.

Cupboards very similar to our own were used mainly to store books, and the sacred vessels used on various special occasions and for religious festivals. The Romans stored money and particularly precious objects in low sturdy chests (*arcae*) decorated with bronze and furnished with stout locks.

In the end what distinguished the *domus* from the apartment in the *insula*, apart from the furniture and its workmanship, were its many ornaments, statues, vases, tripods, lamps, carpets and curtains — furnishings which were often of immense value. Dishes and plates might be entirely of silver, those of clay or earthenware being common among people of modest means. The silver was often chiselled by master craftsmen and sometimes enhanced with gold intaglio and precious stones.

Bed reconstructed from fragments preserved in the National Roman Museum. (Museum of Roman Civilisation, Rome).

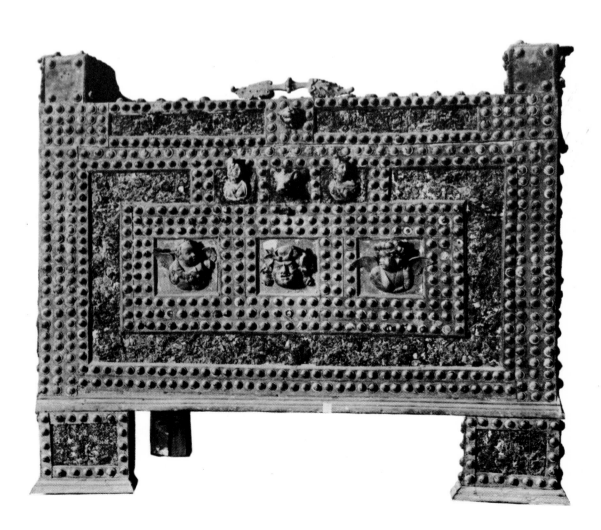

Iron chest, a veritable safe, embossed and decorated with little heads. Found at Pompeii. (National Archaeological Museum, Naples).

FAMILY LIFE

The term familia *cannot simply be translated by the word «family». The modern word conveys only a part of this entirely Roman concept — an institution which had effective juridical, economic, religious and social implications: a relationship which bound together father, mother, children, slaves and clients and, alongside the living, the spirits of the Lares and Penates. This compact nucleus was the basis of Roman society. The power of the father, the* patria potestas *was the legal foundation of the government. The three family virtues which Cicero gave as* gravitas, pietas *and* simplicitas *were the foundation of Roman ethics.* Gravitas *meant awareness of responsibility;* pietas *the recognition of divine and human rights; and* simplicitas *implied an exact estimation of things which was a peculiar virtue of the Roman. He sought out the* res, *the concrete, before anything else. The Roman family was a microcosm, an autonomous and spiritually complete world, and as such it was the great strength of the Republic. It survived the inevitable moral decline of more prosperous and more powerful times, when the emancipation of women seemed to threaten the very foundations of this most solid Roman institution.*

If Roman society is likened to a great mosaic, then the family represents the individual tessera; it was one of the highest forms of civilisation in the ancient world.

All Roman citizens, whether free by birth or freed, that is given their freedom, had three names, and this was a privilege that was highly prized. These were the *praenomen*, the *nomen* and the *cognomen*, each of which had its own precise significance.

The *praenomen* was the equivalent of our Christian name, and the male, but not the female, children received it from their parents, on the ninth day after birth. The name was chosen from a relatively limited list: the most frequent were Aulus, Appius, Gaius, Gnaeus, Decimus, Lucius, Marcus, Manius, Numerius, Publius, Quintus, Servius, Sextus, Spurius, Tiberius, Titus and Vibius. The first name was closely bound to the legal identity of the child and the man, and unlike the other two names, it was strictly personal. Usually the firstborn in a family always bore the same name. Inside the house, slaves called their master by this name, even if he was the emperor.

The *nomen* or family name indicated membership of a *gens* or clan and was borne by citizens descended from the same ancestor; for example, the *Iulii* claimed descent from Iulus, or Ascanius as the Greeks called him, the son of Aeneas. Each *gens* carefully preserved the memory of the more or less legendary head of the *gens* from whom it was descended. The *nomen* took the form of an adjective and frequently ended in *-ius*, because it implied belonging to a group. Marcus Iulius, for example, meant Marcus of the *Iulii* clan. The *nomen* also helped to classify a person in the social scale. Some names belonged specifically to members of the patrician clans, that is to the most ancient and noble Roman families; other names were used by those belonging to plebeian clans.

The *cognomen* was simply an extra name added to the group name. In the earliest times such a name was strictly personal, then it became hereditary and served

Pachyus Proculus and his wife: a moment of quiet in the family, from a fresco in Pompeii. (National Archaeological Museum, Naples).

to distinguish between various branches of a *gens*. Thus there were *Corneli Cethegi* as well as *Corneli Scipiones*. As the clans gradually got farther and farther away from an ancient and common origin, as they increased and scattered, *cognomina* also increased, and the same branch of a family might enjoy several *cognomina*. Sometimes the *cognomen* was a popular nickname; there is a whole series taken from the names of vegetables, like Lentulus. In this group the best known is Cicero, *cognomen* of the Tullian *gens*. It seems that once long ago, a member of the family was nicknamed « *Cicer* », for some mysterious reason as many nicknames are given in villages. Then there were *cognomina* to mark a victory gained by the bearer; Scipio was called *Africanus* after his Carthaginian triumph, and so on.

Women, who possessed no *praenomen*, were called by the name of the *gens* to which they belonged, sometimes softened to a diminutive name of endearment. Thus Cicero called his daughter *Tullia* or *Tulliola*.

Slaves had but one name. When they were freed they took the name and often the *praenomen* of the master who had freed them.

Inscriptions show the name of a citizen followed by a reference to one of the ancient divisions with whom he voted, and frequently by the father's name, to show that he was free by birth. If the citizen was a freedman, the former master's name stood instead of the father's, followed by the letters LIB, for *libertus*, meaning freed slave.

THE FAMILY AND THE *PATRIA POTESTAS*

In primitive Rome the life of each citizen, whether free or slave, was not subject to the state but to the father who presided over the group to which he belonged. The father was a man of authority, and was called *pater familias*. The very form of the phrase with its archaic genitive indicates the antiquity of the institution.

The *familia* was the whole body of people who lived under the same roof, and therefore under the rule of the same father. It included not only the sons of the house, the wife and the daughters, but also the sons-in-law, grandchildren and, what is astonishing today, the servants, slaves of both sexes and freed persons living in the house of the *pater familias* to whom they owed respect and, in some cases, obedience.

The *familia* differed from the *gens* in that it was transient. Its life depended strictly upon that of the ruling father. With his demise the family divided up into as many branches as there were heirs. Often the eldest son took the place of the father until such time as the sisters left the hearth to marry, while the other sons went away to found other families. The widowed mother also passed under the tutelage of the eldest son, as did children not yet « emancipated » and girls not yet married.

Originally the father had complete power over the family. He could, for example, sell one of his sons as a slave. But the law soon limited these rights by providing that a son who had been sold three times by his father would automatically be released from the *patria potestas* and become a free citizen.

In very serious cases the father had the right of life and death over his wife, his sons and, of course, his slaves. In fact this right was never exercised without some control. It was customary for a father who wanted to impose such a grave penalty to summon a kind of family tribunal which might include friends, relations and people renowned for their wisdom. Sentence could only be passed with their consent.

Another aspect of *patria potestas* gave the father the right of disowning at birth a child his wife had borne him. In such a case the father had the child « exposed », that is thrown out on the street, thus condemning it to death by starvation, or to slavery if the child should be rescued by a slave merchant who might bring it up in the hope of making a profitable sale later on.

It seems that fathers mostly exposed girls, because their education was a burden and ended with the provision of a dowry when they were of an age to marry. The practice was common only in early Rome. Gradually the Romans came to feel ashamed of exposing their own children and only the poor, driven by necessity, continued to do so. Already, under the Republic, patrician and middle-class families greeted the birth of a child with rejoicing. Augustus had a law passed which gave considerable privileges to fathers who had at least three children.

Examples of severity towards sons are rare and belong almost entirely to the early days of Rome. There was a consul who condemned his son to death because he had gone into battle against his father's express wish. This was the *imperator* acting to impose discipline, rather than the father exercising *patria potestas*.

A later example of a father exercising the power of life and death over his son occurred in the case of Aulus Fulvius, a member of the Catiline conspiracy, whose father, on discovering his son's guilt, asked the Senate's permission to deal with him himself, received it, and killed him in his own house. Here was an obvious case of an archaic survival, not of a normal everyday practice.

In Nero's day also, the wife of a senator was suspected of « foreign superstitions » and judged before a proper family tribunal presided over by her husband. The woman was found not guilty, but this too would seem to have been an exceptional case, and very probably a device of the husband to protect his wife, for if she had been tried by an ordinary court she would doubtless have run great risks.

The *patria potestas* lost its value with the passage of time. From the second century B.C. the jurists, with the support of public opinion, started modifying the

law. The father, according to ancient law, was the only one who could possess wealth and fortune. Other members of the family, including the sons, could not possess private means and this became intolerable as wealth increased. How, for example, could an ex-consul, returning from leading an army, suddenly become subject to the tutelage of his father again, if the latter was still alive?

Reasons such as this produced the general practice of « emancipation », or liberation from the *manus*, the power of the husband/father. Originally emancipation had been a kind of rejection of the son by the father, a punishment by which the victim's name was cancelled from the *familia*, so that he lost all the social advantages which membership of a group brought with it.

As customs became less severe it was inevitable that the older boys should enjoy greater independence. Emancipation offered a convenient solution, and from that time it was no longer a punishment, but a useful and legal way out. The tone of *patria potestas* was

The first lessons in reading and writing. Wall painting in the Villa of the Mysteries in Pompeii.

also reduced as regards the wife of the family; the means by which this was achieved are dealt with in the section on matrimony.

By the time of Cicero the family was united in much the same way as it is today, by the natural affection of husband and wife and their love for the children.

DAILY OCCUPATIONS

The day's occupations naturally varied according to social status and to the particular day in question. The Romans had many festival days and behaved differently then from the way they behaved on ordinary days. But festival or no festival, the day for the Romans always began at cockcrow. To them it seemed a waste to lose daylight, so they got up early.

Dressing was easy; they slept in a tunic, without sheets and wrapped in a blanket. Moreover they washed little because they took their baths in the evening after the day's work.

Breakfast was fairly frugal: bread, milk, fruit or cheese. No time was wasted in eating.

The first weekday duty of a patrician was to receive the people who enjoyed his protection — his *clientes*. This was a well-established Roman custom: in the earliest times it was customary for free men to entrust themselves to some wealthier person in return for protection and help, and in the time of Augustus the practice had been consecrated by usage; for instance, a freed man was automatically a *cliens* of his former master and neither he nor a free man could bear witness against their patrons. The custom was for the *cliens* to visit his patron every morning, very early; he would wait outside the house until the appropriate time, then hurry inside to ask for help or advice or just to pass the time of day. The patron helped where appropriate by gifts of food, usually placed in the small basket the client brought with him. In return, he could expect the client to give him what support he could in both public and private life. Clients might be parasites, but a patrician's reputation often stood or fell by the size of the mob waiting at his door every morning. Receiving clients was a necessity he could never shirk.

When all the visitors had finished greeting their patron, and had presented their various petitions, they gathered into a procession moving towards the Forum of the Curia. If their patron was a magistrate he would attend to his legal duties later in the morning, or in the early afternoon, seated upon a tribune, a kind of balcony, where he would rule on the questions submitted to him, or he might go to the Senate to take part in a debate.

Even without an official post, a Roman patrician would always have some business in the Forum, such as helping a client before a tribunal, or acting as a witness or a surety in some case or other. The Romans took considerable pleasure in litigation. Sometimes a patrician would sit alongside a judge, invited as private counsel, to give his opinion on some delicate point.

For rich Romans there were activities other than administering justice and discussing politics, the disposal and increase of their capital. Moneylending was a favourite occupation — there were immense concentrations of capital in Rome. It came from trade (Rome was, after all, the greatest centre of trade and commercial speculation) and from the huge revenues of the capitalists' vast estates. Most business, like all public affairs, was conducted in the Forum, where the whole population met as in some great office-cum-parlour, for this is where the bankers' quarters were. Attached to the Forum were spacious halls (*basilicae*) with long porticoes providing shelter from sun and rain. But as far as possible the Romans preferred being in the open air.

If time allowed there would be a hot meal at noon (the *prandium*). It was very simple and was taken without wine. There were, of course, no clocks at that time, only the meridian sundial in the Forum, but since this had not been built for Rome's latitude it was therefore fairly inaccurate. Not till 164 B.C. were the Romans able to use a sundial exactly constructed for the geographical position of Rome. Fifteen years later a water hourglass, a *clepsydra*, was put alongside the sundial and it told the time day and night.

In summer, after the *prandium*, the Romans sometimes took a siesta during the hottest hours of the day; then they worked for another two or three hours, the day's labours ending well before nightfall. At about 4 p.m. in winter and 7 or 8 p.m. in summer they went to dinner (*cena*), and this was by far the most important meal of the day.

Between the end of work and dinner there was a rest hour, which the Romans often spent in the baths. Under the Republic and during the first years of the Empire one paid for using the baths. If there was

The Forum in Pompeii at sunset, as it is today.

Portrait of a woman in mosaics. (National Archaeological Museum, Naples).

none at home — and only the very rich had private baths — one went to a privately owned establishment. The habit came from the East; in Greece it was very common after exercise and athletics. It was a kind of Turkish bath, being full of hot steam, where one sweated abundantly, splashing the body afterwards with cold water. A slave then scraped the body with a kind of wooden comb (a *strigilo*) which removed dirt and sweat.

The bath often ended with a dive into a pool of cool water, and a quick swim if the pool were large enough, as indeed it usually was under the Empire. Then it was the turn of the masseur.

The bath was a fine occasion for relaxing, and it was above all a community affair. Friends met there and conversed; surrounded by steam, the bathers exchanged the gossip of the day before splashing themselves with cold water.

We tend to be surprised at the idea of these collective baths, but it was commonplace to the Romans and nudity caused no embarrassment. Of course there were days reserved for the ladies in all the baths, though some of them preferred to bathe with the men. In Hadrian's reign (A.D. 117-138) however, mixed bathing was prohibited.

The women got up early and began the day by attending to household matters. Free women were exempted by tradition from all forms of housework: their only task was to spin wool, a noble activity in those days. They enjoyed a small army of slaves, from the small girl slaves right up to old freed slaves who acted as superintendents and housekeepers. The noblewomen of Rome often trusted these housekeepers so much that they handed over to them the administration

In the course of her day and in between visits to friends, the Roman matron sometimes found time to consult a fortune-teller. (Vatican Museum, Rome).

of the household, while they concentrated on making themselves beautiful. That indeed was the morning's main occupation. They had certain slaves for particular tasks: one to brush the hair, one to curl it with curling tongs, one to dress it, one to place the combs in the right place, and so on. Then the cosmetics were applied, which was another complicated procedure.

These ladies spent the day paying visits, as this was the fashionable thing to do. The matrons either visited each other in their homes or met in the street, where they were preceded by slaves if on foot, or carried in litters. Some held a salon where all kinds of subjects were discussed: politics, literature, sometimes philosophy. In olden days custom compelled the matrons to stay at home and weave the wool for their menfolk's clothes, but by the last days of the Republic the tradition had more or less disappeared. Augustus, however, always insisted that the women of his household, and especially Julia his daughter, should weave their own garments with their own hands.

The matrons went shopping in the late morning or early afternoon, frequently at the cloth merchants, but hardly ever for food. The purchase of foodstuffs was a matter for the slaves, or, especially in the poorer families, for the men, in order that they might control the family expenditure.

This was how the day was spent by people of some importance. But Rome contained many craftsmen, traders and minor officials who went out to work. They of course seldom went to the Forum; their day was largely spent in the shops and workshops. But when work was over, they too closed their shops and went to the baths or for a walk with friends.

A Roman lady at home, busy with household matters. Probably she is about to settle down to her daily work at the loom. She is wearing a simple tunic, gathered at the waist by a belt. The tunic allowed ample freedom of movement. (Wall painting from the Mansuelli Collection, Vatican Museum, Rome).

Slaves. A prisoner of war and a worker, from the frieze on Trajan's Arch at Benevento. (Museum of Roman Civilisation, Rome).

Everyday life in Rome was intensely social. Men were never overwhelmed by their work. There was always time for friends.

THE SLAVES

Roman society, like all societies in classical antiquity, was founded on slavery. There were men and women either born into that condition, or thrust into it after capture in war or after the fall of their cities. All of them had to work for the benefit of free citizens.

At first Rome had few slaves, and virtually all of them were prisoners of war, working on the land. Their master's life was very like their own: the same frugality, the same rough existence. But with ever-growing conquests and the growing wealth of the citizens, great hordes of slaves were brought into the city, and the slave merchants went on bringing in more and more.

Slaves were sold in a market near the Forum. They had to stand on a platform with a label round their necks stating their name, origin and capabilities. People walked round feeling their muscles, asking

Busts of Salvius and Sinnius, imperial slaves. The former looked after the silver, the latter was a bodyguard to Drusus. (In the Columbarium of the Codini Vineyard, Rome).

questions to see whether they were intelligent or stupid, while the merchant was at pains to extol the virtues or hide the blemishes in his wares.

Their fate depended on whether they were allotted to country or city work. In the countryside life was still primitive and the need for labour very great. A crushing discipline was enforced. Heavily built male slaves were sent there, and they had to work chained to each other and with shackles to prevent their running away. At night they were locked up in what was basically a prison.

These methods were inherited from the East and had become traditional by the first century B.C., but they never really satisfied the farmers or the intelligent landowners. Labour forces of this sort were ruinous; they worked badly and with poor results. It became obvious that country slaves should be freed from their shackles and allowed to lead a less restricted life; the companionship of a woman slave and the raising of children would help them to become attached to the land and enjoy their work.

Town slaves too had varied conditions of work according to the social standing of their masters.

Paradoxically slaves in less well-to-do families were happier than the others: true friendship often developed, slaves and master sharing in the good or ill fortune of the house. In richer families the administration was more impersonal: the highly specialised slaves were organised in groups, according to the nature of their work. If they were educated they would be put in charge of the accounts or the library, or they might become tutors to the children in the house. Of course, if they did secretarial work for their masters, their situation improved greatly.

The less gifted or less educated dealt with all the other household tasks, cooking, cleaning, caretaking, city errands, looking after the chariots. The porter-slave was often chained to the entrance during work hours, lest he slip off to the nearest tavern and leave the house unattended.

Women slaves were numerous and mostly in the service of the mistress of the house and her daughters. There were in addition public slaves who belonged to the community, to the state, or to the provincial cities, and sometimes to the temples. These were minor functionaries, municipal porters, maintenance workers on the aqueducts, or engaged in some minor trading activity or craft, the profits of which went to the city which owned them.

At first, the slaves had no rights. They were treated as things, objects one might buy, sell, beat, mutilate and kill, without anyone being able to prevent it. They could not marry, and those who had children were not allowed to bring them up. The master could take them away whenever he wanted to, for they too were slaves and therefore belonged to him.

But this legal barrier was soon removed and slaves were allowed to live as husband and wife, though they could not marry. Gradually rights grew up around this practice. Children born in slavery in a master's house (*vernae*) were surrounded by affection and played with the children of the master. They enjoyed closer ties with the family than the « imported » slaves. Historians recount instances of great devotion shown by slaves to their masters, although at the same time many masters, at least under the Empire, feared assassination at the hand of their slaves; there were examples of such crimes.

The slave, totally dependent upon the master, could be punished, often with the greatest cruelty. He could be beaten endlessly for the slightest fault, and in the

The teacher of gymnastics was often a slave or a freed man. (Lateran Museum, Rome).

larger households there were slaves delegated specially for this duty. If a slave escaped and was caught, he was subjected to heavy punishment. He would be branded with a hot iron, or fitted with an iron collar which could never be removed, so that he would be recognised if he ever fled again. Slaves found guilty of theft were also branded. In serious cases they were crucified, a penalty never inflicted on a free man. Sometimes the master gave the slave over to the magistrate in charge of the public games and then the wretched man was thrown to the wild animals in the arena. However, these executions must have been rare, for the master preferred to keep such expensive purchases alive and well and preferred to send the incorrigible delinquent to work in his fields as a convict.

The best slaves would be freed, or received permission to buy their freedom by paying to the master the price he had originally paid for them. The slaves were allowed to save the tips and the small earnings they received. More often they were freed in the will of their master, at his death. The freed man stayed on with the family of the master as a trusted man, a secretary or perhaps a bailiff. When the system spread, imperial freed men even became ministers, and occasionally abused their new powers.

BOYS' EDUCATION

The education of his sons was considered almost a sacred duty by the *pater familias*. The elder Cato even changed his sons' diapers and taught them their first steps. Usually the mother performed these duties and she fed her sons with her own milk. The practice of having wet-nurses, who were nearly always slaves, came in only in the last years of the Republic. Middle and working-class people were against the practice.

Tacitus tells us that children in patrician families were often handed over to the care of an older relative, such as a maiden aunt. Writers warn parents never to commit their sons to slaves of foreign origin, as this may permanently damage their speech habits. A future orator — and all aristocratic Romans must aim at being orators — should learn their language from wet-nurses who spoke the purest Latin.

Nevertheless one knows that several children of families related to Augustus were left to the care of the worst kind of slave. Even Nero was brought up by a groom for a time, but of course Nero's father was dead and his mother in exile.

Very early in her history Rome set up state schools which were open to children from the age of seven upward for instruction in the rudiments of knowledge. No exact date is known, but they certainly existed in the second century b.c. and were held under the porticoes in the Forum.

Elementary schools were directed by the *grammaticus* who taught the schoolboy to read classical authors and explained texts to him. The boys learnt the epic poems of Ennius by heart. These were believed to inculcate the boys with the foundations of ethics, love of country, love of glory and similar virtues. In this the Romans imitated the Greeks, for whom all teaching began with the reading of Homeric poems. Later, under the Empire, Ennius was replaced by Virgil.

There is little resemblance between Roman and modern methods of teaching arithmetic. The system was duodecimal, with no zero, so that the use of digits with separate identities was unknown. No problems were set: an abacus was used and the main answers were learnt by heart. Arithmetic lessons were therefore more like a catechism: the recitation of Pythagorian tables in a kind of tedious chant.

The school of the *grammaticus* was highly disciplined. The teacher held a cane and often rapped the knuckles of an inattentive pupil, while the disobedient were formally beaten.

In the classical period, young Romans learnt Greek at the same time as they learnt Latin, for Greek was considered the language of culture, indispensable for reading philosophy and the classics. There were also practical reasons for learning Greek, since many of the patricians' slaves and many traders were of Greek origin. Latin, moreover, from the third century b.c. onward, had become full of Greek technical terms. A Roman with no Greek would have felt a stranger in his own country.

When a Roman boy had learnt all he could from the *grammaticus*, which usually happened between the ages of twelve and fifteen, he would go the *rhetor's* school, to learn the theory and practice of eloquence. The rhetoricians, as their name implies, were Greek in origin. Their art had been born in Sicily. Some Latin rhetoricians opened schools of their own in imitation, but the Senate forced them to close in order to give the Greek schools greater scope.

These games show that children's pastimes change little down the centuries. Some of the children are rolling a hoop while others are engaged in battle, riding pick-a-back; others have piles of nuts and are tossing them in the air. (Lateran Museum, Rome).

Children's games often imitated adult pastimes. In this fresco from the House of the Vettii in Pompeii, a very small chariot drawn by deer is the plaything in question.

On the sarcophagus of M. Cornelius Statius, the pictures from a child's life: the mother suckling her child while the father is looking on; the father holding the child in his arms; the child, older now, in a little chariot harnessed to a goat. (The Louvre, Paris).

In Cicero's day, however, the Latin rhetoricians were allowed to open their schools again. While these had been closed, it had been the custom for young men destined for public service to accompany some prominent personage to the Forum, and being entrusted to him would model themselves upon him. In this way these young men also gained some practical experience in the law, and when they took up their first post as magistrates, they were quite familiar with public life.

In the latter days of the Republic and in the early days of the Empire, the young men no longer accompanied their « patron » into the Forum, but attended the rhetoricians' schools, by now well established. Here they learnt how to plead the least hopeful cases with immense skill, in contests of oratory organised by their teachers. These contests were based on *suasoriae*, speeches supposedly made to legendary or historical characters who were to be influenced (*suadere*) thereby at a critical moment in their careers; and there were *controversiae* or defence pleas in fictitious court cases, whose particulars were supplied by the teacher, and were often exaggeratedly sentimental. The rhetoricians' schools were also held under the colonnades of the city's squares. Sometimes famous orators condescended to be present when their young disciples were showing their skill.

The young received virtually no scientific training. This was reserved for a few specialists who worked in solitude. Frequently the young orators attended the schools of the philosophers who taught in rooms off the main squares. The Greek philosophers had been dismissed several times under the Republic and by some of the emperors (notably Domitian), but they always enjoyed a big audience and their influence was widespread. Aristocratic youths even made the journey to Athens or to Rhodes to listen to them. This Greek journey often completed the education of the young Roman in the classical age.

CHILDREN'S GAMES

Children in all ages have played with anything that came to hand, and Roman children were certainly no exception. A stick serves as a horse, a few nuts make a billiard game, and little bones thrown up in the air can score points just as well as dice.

Wax tablets and a stylus were indispensable to the Roman schoolchild. (National Archaeological Museum, Naples).

There were toys especially made for children; little clay dolls have been found in some excavations. Some have rudimentary shapes which vaguely resemble the human figure, but others are more life-like and some actually have articulated limbs and could be dressed. Wooden tops were favourite toys. Both boys and girls liked hoops, and some hoops were decorated with bells or metal chips to make them sparkle and ring as they rolled.

As in all generations, the Roman children loved playing with little carts. Very small children would fix mice to minute carts and have races, just like in a circus. Later on, the children might ride in carts pulled by dogs, goats or little ponies.

There were many party games. Pompeii frescoes show winged cupids playing at imitating grown-ups, pretending to be merchants, gladiators and soldiers. The girls organize imaginary households, do the cooking and rock small dolls. They are often seen on a swing being pushed by the boys. Frescoes show boys and girls playing ball and catching from all sorts of positions, even pick-a-back.

There were games with sticks, too, but even though we see them reproduced on Greek vases, the rules are unknown to us. Young Romans certainly played them too.

Among the pastimes originally imported from Greece, but surely reinvented on the banks of the Tiber by childish ingenuity, were kite-flying and blind-man's buff, called the « copper fly ». One child had his eyes covered with a scarf and went about crying « I'll catch the copper-fly », while the other children teased the blind man with long sticks.

There were doubtless all sorts of games with dice and counters, just as there were for the grown-ups, who played games similar to backgammon. Adolescents preferred more violent sports and trained for military exercises, which formed a part of their education.

GIRLS' EDUCATION

Roman ethics and the role of women in society influenced the kind of education given to girls. In ancient Rome girls were taught to obey, to be modest and to spin wool. This was once considered sufficient for the making of a good wife, but soon it became apparent that more was needed, and the young Roman girl began to receive an education more like that of her brothers.

Elementary schools were mixed. Boys and girls learned to read and write on the same benches and under the same disciplines. Livy's story of Virginia shows her at twelve years of age attending lessons in a school by the side of the Forum. The story is set in the fifth century B.C.

The girls did not stay at school right to the end of the course like the boys, and did not attend the schools of rhetoric. Daughters of the aristocracy received private tuition at home or attended private schools along with relations and friends. The teachers were Greek, more often than not, and the pupils studied the

Music was very important in a girl's education, for She had to be able to accompany songs or poetry reading. The cithera and the lyre, the most common stringed instruments, are here reconstructed after a fresco in the Villa of Boscoreale in Naples, and according to fragments found in a Roman tomb at Kerch in the Crimea. (Museum of Roman Civilisation, Rome).

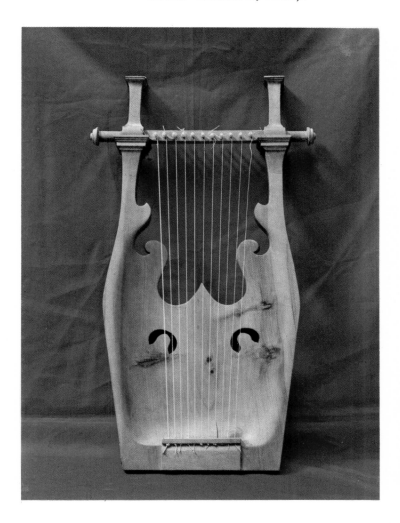

literature of both languages, concentrating particularly on poetry. As in the Hellenistic world, music had great importance in this kind of education. The girls learned to sing, and accompanied themselves on the lyre. Some learned composition, songs in the Aeolian modes, and, when elegies came into fashion under Augustus, they were set to composing them. Some of these compositions have survived. Other girls, of more serious disposition, took to the study of philosophy.

Generally speaking, these girls received a fairly liberal education, somewhat more so in fact than the boys, because being privately educated they escaped official control. All this smoothed the way for the entry of Hellenism into Rome, and it explains the part played by the great matrons in Roman society from the time of Scipio onward, and how they inspired it and kept their « salons » in Rome.

Sometimes young women of good Roman society who had received this sort of education looked down on the traditional duties of a matron; they preferred dancing and music and the company of other young people. The moralists of the time deplored this state of affairs, but their strictures need not be taken too seriously. The greater part of Rome's young women made excellent wives and were far from being stupid. In her day no woman was more cultivated or a better

mother than Cornelia, the mother of Gaius and Tiberius Gracchus.

Obviously such an education was available only to the daughters of great families; the others had to be content with much less. They learnt the rudiments of knowledge and no more; to complete their education, their mothers instructed them in the elements of domestic economy. No women at that time entered the professions or engaged in trading. There was no technical education for women. They were destined to become wives and mothers in adult life.

MARRIAGE

Marriage was the most solemn moment in Roman life, since the whole society was based on the family and its stability.

Thus fathers liked to choose their sons' fiancées and their future sons-in-law themselves, without consulting their children. Matrimony had social consequences and often formed an alliance between two families — an important point in political life. Yet the mother's wishes had to be taken into account, likewise those of the future mother-in-law, and those wishes might be on the side of sentiment rather than interest.

Nuptial procession. The betrothed on the extreme right are ritually shaking hands in front of witnesses representing Cybele, Juno Pronuba and Suada, the goddess of persuasion. In the centre one of the servants is carrying the hard cake of spelt which the couple will eat together in the symbolic communion which represents the supreme moment of the ceremony. (Church of San Lorenzo Fuori le Mura, Rome).

The father's right to choose a bride or bridegroom for his children was derived from the old *patria potestas*, but as customs changed, this right, too, became circumscribed, so much so that the young people acquired the privilege of refusing an allotted partner if they believed the choice to be altogether unacceptable.

Girls could be married at twelve years of age, youths after the age of fourteen. It was very young indeed to get married, in fact boys of that age hardly ever did. Girls, on the other hand, did marry very young.

A marriage was announced after a very long engagement, since the engaged couple were often promised to each other as children. The respective fathers made the betrothal in front of witnesses, binding their children. Often the engaged boy or his father would make a gift to the fiancée, which was given back if the engagement was broken. The engaged couple also exchanged rings.

There were several forms of marriage. Three of these placed the bride under the complete rule of her husband (*in manu mariti*). In the latter days of the Republic these forms fell into disuse and a fourth form of marriage came in, which gave the wife her independence.

The three ancient forms of marriage were the marriage by purchase (*coemptio*), the marriage by communion (*confarreatio*), and the marriage by co-habitation (*usus*). The first form was a marriage by acquisition of the wife in front of witnesses, so that the husband became the proprietor of the wife. The second and probably most ancient form was religious, in that it was performed in front of the *Pontifex Maximus* (High Priest) and the flame of Jove. The high moment of the ceremony was the cutting in half of a cake of spelt (an inferior kind of grain used in certain religious rites). This implied communion between the newly wed during the sacrifice, and their religious union.

This was the form used by the patricians and it was essential if the children of the newly wed were likely to take up certain priestly duties.

The third form was extremely simple: the marriage by co-habitation meant living together, and after one year the woman submitted to the *potestas* of the hus-

Juno in a bride's dress from a Pompeian fresco. The goddess wears the customary nuptial orange-coloured veil on her head, the flammeum. *(National Archaeological Museum, Naples).*

53

band, unless she had taken the precaution of absenting herself for three days and three nights before the end of the year. With this proviso, in common usage from the fourth century B.C. onward, certain categories of women were exempted from the *manus* or authority of their husbands, especially after the first marriages between patricians and plebeians. In such cases the woman remained under the guardianship of her father, and at his death, under a guardian chosen by the praetor.

In the classical period therefore marriages were genuinely free unions, founded on mutual consent and affection. Nevertheless the first steps of the marriage ritual were surrounded by picturesque ceremonies which were largely traditional and went back a very long way. The significance of these had been lost, but they were continued because they brought good luck.

The wedding day was carefully chosen among feast days of specially good portent. The bride was dressed on the previous evening. Her hair was parted to form six plaits which were wound round the head and fixed with narrow bands of wool. She was clad in a tunic woven all in one piece, with a belt at the waist that was ceremonially fastened in a ritual « knot of Hercules ». During the rite, the bride wore an orange veil, the *flammeum*. That night the bride said farewell to her childhood toys and presented them to the Lares.

The following day parents and guests went to the bride's house in the morning and a sacrifice was made in the *atrium*. A sow or sheep was sacrificed and its entrails kept for the augurs to inspect, but this practice was discontinued in the classical period. The contract documents were then exchanged in front of ten witnesses, who affixed their seals to them. In front of the sacrifice, the bride and groom gave their mutual consent and the bride pronounced the famous formula: *Ubi tu Gaius, ego Gaia*, which blended their wills and their lives together (« Where you are master I am mistress »), after which those present applauded heartily and cried « *Feliciter* », for good luck.

Then everyone sat down to the banquet which went on late into the evening. When the first star, the evening star, began to shine in the sky, the moment came for the bride to go to the groom's house. She had to appear frightened and take refuge in her mother's arms, from which the bridegroom had to wrest her, though not usually with any difficulty. The bridal procession then moved through the city to the ap-

plause of the public; nuts, sweets and small coins were thrown to the onlookers, as symbols of fertility.

The procession was headed by torchbearers carrying blazing hawthorn twigs. On the bridegroom's doorstep the torches were thrown aside and everyone would try to get a piece, because it brought luck. The bride put some oil and a small piece of wool on the lintel of the door. The young men in the procession lifted her up and carried her over the doorstep. Her young women friends went in after her, carrying a symbolic distaff and spindle. The husband offered his wife water and fire, the elements of life, and the guests withdrew as a matron led the bride to the nuptial chamber, where her husband waited to welcome her.

BIRTH

In Rome, as in Greece, the birth of a child was an event which had become surrounded by religious ritual. There is in fact, little information available on the details of the ceremonies and the beliefs relating to them, perhaps because these were acts of private worship performed in the privacy of the home and seldom discussed. The ritual was left in the hands of the women, particularly the older women, and was steeped in popular superstition.

The first duty of the midwife (*obstetrix*), once the infant had arrived in the world, was to bathe it; for this a large basin (*alveus*) was used such as may be seen on bas reliefs. In the imperial household custom demanded that this basin be shaped like a shell. As soon as the baby was washed it was placed at the feet of its father who made clear, by a gesture, whether or not he wished to recognise the child as his own. If he took it up in his arms it was recognised as legitimate and became one of the *familia*; if not, it was put out in the street. Deformed children or monstrous births were killed by drowning.

When the child had been acknowledged he became the object of lavish attentions from the women of the household. Firstly, signs supposed to ward off the evil eye were traced on his forehead with the middle finger moistened with saliva; charms and amulets intended to bring good luck were tied to his body. For the first week (counted as eight days for girls, nine for boys), a period during which the child was regarded as particularly menaced by the powers of evil, offerings were kept in readiness for two divine protectors, Juno and Hercules, deemed helpful above all others. For Juno a couch was prepared in the *atrium* and for Hercules (the slayer of monsters) a table was laid. At the end of this « week » came the *dies lustricus*, the day of purification. On that day a sacrifice was offered and the *Parcae* (the goddesses of Fate) also known as the *Fata Scribunda* (the Fates who write) were specially invoked.

These Fates were supposed to inscribe the future life of the child in the book of Destiny. Later, under the Empire, they were sometimes represented on coffins examining a celestial globe and determining the horoscope of the newborn child. But this belief in the goddesses of Destiny antedates the spread of astrology. It was also on the day of Purification that a name was given to the child and that the locket of gold or leather was tied round his neck to signify that he had been born free. This locket contained charms against the evil eye.

The child was brought up by his mother or a nurse. Tiny babies were bound up very tightly in bandages or swaddling clothes which permitted no freedom of movement. When they were not feeding, they were strapped in cradles placed on the ground and rocked with a foot. Their first steps were aided by a sort of carriage on small wheels which helped them to keep their balance.

A variety of divinities was invoked and each one presided over a fresh stage in the child's development: *Vagitanus*, his first cries; *Ossifragus*, the cutting of his teeth; *Statilina*, his first steps, etc. Likewise, portents were drawn from the actions of the baby: if he laughed right from birth, it meant that he would not live long; but if a little later he laughed at his father and his mother, then a happy destiny was predicted for him.

THE LAST FAREWELL

When a Roman died in his own house it was customary for the corpse to lie in the *atrium* of his house, feet towards the door, dressed in the garments belonging to his rank. During the seven days he lay there, the ceremony of calling aloud his name to summon his soul (*conclamatio*) took place. The women of the family took it in turns to watch round the bier, crying,

A bas-relief votive tablet dedicated to the Nutrices Augustae, *the protecting divinities of wet-nurses and of children, who were especially honoured in cults at Pettau in Yugoslavia. (Museum of Pettau). Below: Youth with a seal hanging round his neck. The gold and leather seal was the symbol of free birth and contained amulets against the evil eye. (Archaeological Museum, Parma).*

The man lying on the couch with a bag in his right hand and a scroll in his left is writing his will. His wife and a slave with a counting table are helping him. In the medallion behind is a figure of the Flavian era. The bas-relief was erroneously believed to show the making of a will by an emperor. (Capitoline Museum, Rome).

Mausoleum at Ghirza in the Fezzan (Tripolitania). This funeral monument is decorated by a frieze in rough local style, depicting hunting scenes.

sobbing, striking their breasts, and totally neglecting their appearance. This ritual of lamentation was a kind of debt of honour to the dead person.

When the day of the funeral arrived, a procession formed to carry the body across the city to a place outside the walls where it would be cremated or buried. The procession was organised by the undertakers (*libitinarii*), a class of low social standing.

Originally funeral ceremonies took place at night, and as a reminder of this torches were still carried in later times when they were held by day, except in the case of very young children. Burials were the occasion for solemn parades; at the head came the musicians, then the torch-bearers and the hired mourners. Traditional dirges, or *naeniae*, were sung during the journey.

But these eulogies were represented principally by tableaux or placards representing the dead man's exploits and victories, as in a triumphal procession. In fact, if it were a nobleman who had died, and if his family had the traditional privilege of *Ius imaginum*, the funeral carriage itself was preceded by actors who portrayed the family's ancestors; they covered their faces with wax masks (which were preserved in the *tablinum* of every noble family) representing the features of each ancestor, whose clothes and insignia they wore. The procession gave the curious impression that the dead had returned to life to welcome the newcomer. At the funeral of very important people the procession passed by the *Comitium*, in front of the *Curia*, and there the nearest relative pronounced the panegyric from the top of the *Rostra*.

At last the procession left the city and made its way towards the funeral pyre, prepared between the tombs on the grass verge of a road leading into the country. The corpse burnt slowly amidst perfumes and offerings of all kinds; the relatives remained in the vicinity till all was consumed. Then they collected the remains, washed them in wine and sealed them in an urn which was placed in a monument bearing an inscription perpetuating the memory and the deeds of the dead man.

For the poorer classes it was a simpler affair, but even then free men took care to provide themselves with a monument, however small, to contain their remains. The necropolis at Isola Sacra, near Ostia, still has many of these modest tombs. Slaves, as a rule, were thrown into a common grave.

Burial places were outside the walls, along the roads leading out of the city. This is the tomb of Cecilia Metella on the Appian Way.

NUPTIAL FEASTS

The relations and the friends had come in from the country for the feast days, abandoning their labours to let the oxen and bulls lie lazily in their stalls, leaving the vines half-weeded, the leafy trees unpruned and the ploughs lying in every corner of the home acres, damp with dew and rusting in their idleness. Even the urgent work of harvesting had been postponed, but it was the end of June, traditionally the most propitious time for nuptials, and there was no question of waiting any longer.

The bride, still almost a child, had taken off her childish garment the night before, the *praetexta*, to don her fine marriage dress and had slept in it.

She had gone to bed early, while the other members of the household were busy adorning the house with crowns of flowers, branches of myrtle and laurel and coloured ribbons. They had laid the banquet table with the most precious gold and silver vessels, taken out for the occasion and shining in the light of the torches. In the *atrium* they had laid out the marriage gifts which the guests had brought with awkward smiles.

At dawn the women had come to prepare her, laughing, full of tenderness, while she, childlike, stood a little frightened and still, and let them do as they pleased. First they plaited her hair with ribbons, parting it in six plaits with an iron spear she had often seen about the house, without knowing what it was, or for what it was used.

Then they tied her girdle with the Hercules knot and covered her head and face with the *flammeum*, the fine orange nuptial veil, crowning her temples with a wreath of sweet-scented marjoram.

Already the voices of the guests could be heard outside: the noisy greetings, the laughter and the shouts, and then when she appeared, timid, trembling and almost weeping, everyone cried out with admiration and congratulations because the dress fitted her perfectly and the face under the flowing veil had the freshness of a rosebud.

Near the bride was her bridesmaid, the *pronuba*: she would accompany her to the altar where the priest was ready for the sacrifice.

Until that moment everyone had been cheerful and carefree, but now, as the priest « read » the auguries in the entrails of the sacrificial victim — and they were good, with promise of many children and a happy old age — as the couple broke the bread and ate a piece each, as the contract was signed before the witnesses and all the other tedious ceremonies were gone through, the atmosphere changed; one guest was overawed, another too much at ease, another too serious. The solemnity of the rite had moved everyone, and the *pronuba* took the hands of the couple and united them amid a general silence.

Then all sat down to the banquet. The young bridegroom admired the delicate way the bride took morsels of food from the dish with her fingers without leaving a trace of it on them. Outbursts of merriment grew among the guests, especially as the meal progressed and the most appetizing thirst-provoking dishes appeared. The bridegroom almost choked on an olive, but nothing else happened.

When the banquet was over, the bridegroom, encouraged by his friends, made as though to seize the bride from the arms of her mother, where she pretended to have taken refuge, while everyone laughed and shouted. And now, instead of a struggle, a nuptial procession developed. Someone gave the bride a distaff and a spindle, the emblems of her new life. Two little boys escorted her and one preceded her, carrying torches of hawthorn. Other torches were lit by friends and girls following the procession and chanting an *epithalamium*, expressly composed for the occasion by a poet friend. The chorus of boys and girls sang alternate verses in a kind of half comic half sentimental dialogue. Every now and again someone cried « *Talassio! Talassio!* » without knowing why, but that was the habit.

There were faces everywhere at windows and doors; some laughed and some threw flowers and cried good wishes, and in return the guests threw showers of nuts which fell on to the ground, where small boys fought to pick them up, rolling in the dust, all sweating and happy. At last the procession reached the bridegroom's house and the girl stopped a moment to decorate the door with woollen strips and place some oil on the lintel. The husband watched her attentively. At a certain moment, seeing she had finished, he asked her: « What is your name? » And she, smiling and blushing, replied, « *Ubi tu Gaius, ego Gaia* ». This, too, was a ritual phrase.

Then those who accompanied her lifted her up and carried her over the doorstep, for it would have been bad luck had she stumbled there.

Immediately afterwards the bridegroom offered her fire and the *pronuba* offered her water as she went to the nuptial couch (*lectus genialis*) which stood directly opposite the entrance. And she whispered the words of the prayer prescribed for a bride to say to the Lares and Penates in her new house.

Then a last cry of « *Imene! Imene!* », and everyone left, with a last few scuffles round the burnt-out torches of hawthorn, especially by the girls. For a small piece of hawthorn twig was propitious for the future.

(source: Catullus, Carmen LXI)

SCHOOLS AND CULTURE

The ancient learning of Rome, the sapientia, *was utilitarian and tended* ad res (*towards the practical*). *It had little in common with the speculative quest for truth typical of Greek learning. Knowledge for the good Roman was the acquisition of experience in the art of sensible living and in wisdom, in the finesses of life rather than the absolutes of science. This was the climate in which the Roman family educated its children until the day when the conquest of the Middle East marked the arrival of Greek teachers, mostly prisoners-of-war, and they opened wider horizons in the teaching of the young. Private schools were opened, the precursors of the imperial state schools, and knowledge of the Greek language became an essential part of a good education. The discovery of a wide new world of the mind quickly attracted the best of Roman youth. But despite these new horizons, traditional Roman culture and respect for the family remained the foundation of education. The cult of ancestors within the family continued to give its daily lesson in civic virtues, and it was within the family that the strictly Roman traditions were handed down.*

The family was the natural setting for the education and teaching of the young in Rome.

The provision of schooling was not considered a duty of the state, and by the time private schools began to open, several centuries had passed in which a rudimentary education and teaching of the children had been dealt with at home. The Romans were by no means less civilized on this account than other peoples of the time. Two centuries prior to the imperial age, Rome had become more and more involved in political and military action in the Near East. The Greeks were perforce absorbed into the Roman community. What happened next was of great interest and importance. The Greeks brought with them into the Roman world a precious contribution — their own civilisation. They took culture to the homes of Roman families who often acquired them as slaves, captured in war. They were appreciated and honoured: they enjoyed ease and freedom. An educational tradition of « the Greek teacher » grew up inside the most powerful families and in the teaching profession itself. The traditional cult of the family peculiar to the Latin

world was not on that account diminished, but wider horizons came into view.

By the time of Augustus, the wealthiest Roman families could already send their children to schools whose teachers commanded payment in accordance with the reputation they had acquired. Horace gratefully records the sacrifices made by his father — only a modest official — to enable his son to go to a good school attended by sons of the best families.

By the end of the first century A.D., at the time of Quintilian, the question of education was in the public domain and the state was gradually coming to assume responsibility for teachers' salaries. Diocletian fixed by edict the remuneration of all teachers according to their grading.

Some of the fundamental aims in traditional Roman education are of basic importance: the sense of family, of the homeland, of religion, of duty, and of justice. The cult of the ancestors, whose altars were inside the home, already provided a daily lesson in civic virtues. The *ludus litterarius*, the cultural striving, might be practised in school, but it was preceded and super-

A teacher with his pupils. Lessons were held under a colonnade almost in the open, in full view of passers-by. The schoolboys brought their writing materials with them in a capsa. *(Museum of Trier).*

seded by education in the family, not according to any academic rules, but always regarded as very important.

CLASSROOMS AND TEACHING AIDS

Before the state was concerned with education, the normal school was a simple, poor place called the *pergula*, a kind of teaching shop set up by the teacher, the private *magister*. At best, lessons took place in the open under a portico, according to a fresco in Herculaneum, which depicts a loggia supported by very elegant columns, with a class of boys sitting on stools without backs and writing on their knees. The scene also shows a boy held up sideways by his companions and being thrashed on his behind, as a punishment. The rod was widely used during education: children were beaten very freely and Latin authors recall their teachers along with the thrashings they received from them. Teachers, as Horace said, were fond of flogging: in fact some believed more in the efficacy of the stick than of the word.

The walls of the school were usually hung with didactic bas-reliefs in marble which represented the chief episodes in the poems of Homer, and were hence called the Iliac tables. Sometimes, especially under the empire, a famous teacher would decorate his walls with maps (*tabulae* or *formae*). The Romans had learnt this from the Greeks: they very roughly drew a few lines to denote such areas of the world as were then known. The most famous was the *Orbis pictus* made under the orders of Agrippa and based on documents which Augustus had collected. This map was on view in the portico of Polla in the Campus Martius. It was probably round. Apart from general maps, there were regional maps showing the chief produce of different areas.

Many maps tried to reproduce the heavens. At that time astrology and astronomy were not separated and the two subjects were often studied simultaneously. A belief in the relationship of stars to human fate was widely accepted.

Sometimes the walls of the *pergulae* were adorned with busts (*imagines*) of poets and writers, blackened by smoke from the lamps used by the pupils in the dark hours.

Apart from the maps and the Iliac tablets, the teacher provided apparatus in the shape of a calculating board, spheres and cubes, which helped teach subjects such as geometry. The children for their part came to school with a bag (*capsa* or *scrinium*) used to carry writing materials and lunch. There were no textbooks, but public inscriptions often provided the necessary reading exercise. Cicero recalls how painfully he learnt to read by using the Twelve Tables as a text.

WAX TABLETS, PENS AND INK

The pupils wrote on tablets called *cerae* or *tabulae ceratae*, such as all the Romans used for notes, letters and memoranda. These were rectangular wood tablets with raised edges, upon which a thin layer of wax was spread. One wrote by indenting the letters on the wax with a little rod of ivory or metal (*stilus*), sharpened at one end and flattened at the other, in order to smooth out the wax again for more writing. Since it was rather dangerous and inconvenient to carry these styluses about, they were kept in a special case, the *graphiarium* or *graphiaria theca*, which pupils, scribes and copyists always carried with them.

Along one side of the *tabulae ceratae* were a few holes through which a small cord was passed to bind two or three tablets together, forming, as it were, a small book with wooden pages covered with wax on both sides; the front and back tablets were waxed only on one side and served as covers.

For writing on parchment or papyrus, black ink was used (*atramentum*) compounded from soot, pitch, the ink of cuttlefish and wine lees, mixed with water. The inkpot (*atramentarium*) was formed of two cylinders joined together. Book titles were written in a special red ink, and there were various kinds of invisible ink which appeared and disappeared according to treatment.

For writing with ink the stylus was replaced by a quill (*penna*) or a small reed (*calamus*) sharpened with a penknife (*scalprum*) or, rarely, by a copper pen.

BOOKS: PAPYRUS AND PARCHMENT

Roman books were nothing like ours, but enjoyed a signal importance in that they were the only means available — apart from the human voice — for spreading ideas and culture. Their basic component was papyrus, originally made by the Egyptians from the pith of a water plant by a process specially developed for this purpose. Its use spread throughout the eastern Mediterranean lands, though the Romans did not start using it till the end of the third century B.C. when they came into direct contact with Egypt and her neighbours.

The elder Pliny describes how papyrus was made into writing material (*charta*). The stem of the plant was peeled off into very thin strips about a yard long, which were then placed side by side to form a sheet. Another series of strips were then placed crosswise on top of the first until a close network of papyrus was obtained. This was then pressed, dried, and beaten

Celestial globe with the signs of the Zodiac. This is the globe supported by Atlas (Farnese) in the National Archaeological Museum in Naples.

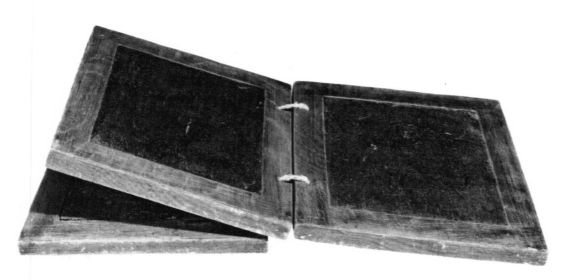

A trio of tablets on which wax was spread and writing was done with a stylus. (Museum of Roman Civilisation, Rome).

with a hammer into a fine sheet of paper, a word directly derived from the Greek *papyrus*. The Romans soon excelled at the art, outdoing the Egyptians, and began to make different grades of paper.

Before Augustus the finest paper was the *charta hieratica*, reserved for sacred books. *Charta Augusta* (called thus in honour of Augustus) was an improved form of this as was *charta Liviana* (in honour of his wife), a wider and whiter paper. There was paper from Egypt too, the *charta amphitheatrica* (made near the amphitheatre in Alexandria), which was rough, but once subjected to further treatment in Rome in the workshop of a certain Fannius it became smooth and was sold as one of the best kinds (*charta Fanniana*). Other types of paper called *charta emporeutica* were very rough and used only for wrapping.

In order to make a book, the papyrus leaves had to be stuck together side by side so as to form a long scroll. This kind of book was quite different from our books in that it had to be rolled up: in fact the long scroll of papyrus was rolled (hence the word *volumen*, from *volvere*, to wind) round a baton of bone or of wood called the *umbilicus*. The end of the book was the first to be stuck to the baton, so that once the parchment was wound up, the beginning of the book would appear as the reader unwound the scroll. Often a small stick was also attached to the scroll, at the beginning. The *umbilici* were always longer than the width of the scroll, and the pieces that stuck out were called the *cornua*. The top and bottom margins of the scroll which could easily fray and become damaged were well shaved and rubbed with pumice stone and vividly coloured.

The book was written in parallel columns on that side of the papyrus on which the filaments ran horizontally to the writer (*recto*). The other side was supposed to remain unused (the *verso*), but often shortage of paper caused it to be used as well. The cost of books in Rome, as everywhere else in the known world at that time, was extremely high owing to the complexities of making the paper, and to the number of people and the time required to make more than one copy.

The papyrus book did not have a binding in the modern sense, and the title of the work, written at the beginning, remained unseen from the outside; frequently, however, it was noted on a piece of parchment attached to the top edge of the scroll.

Papyrus was a delicate material: a little humidity could damage it badly. To preserve it and protect it from worms, it used to be covered with oil of cedar, and kept inside specially-made holders. Many Greek papyri have survived, mainly discovered in Egypt where the soil is exceptionally dry, but we have very few specimens of Roman papyri written in Latin.

From the first century B.C. when parchment came into use, books were made of vellum sheets gathered in wood, or, as here illustrated, in copper covers, instead of scrolls of papyrus. (Museum of the Baths, Rome). Below: Volumina of papyrus, being easily damaged by humidity, were kept in round boxes (capsae). (Museum of Roman Civilisation, Rome).

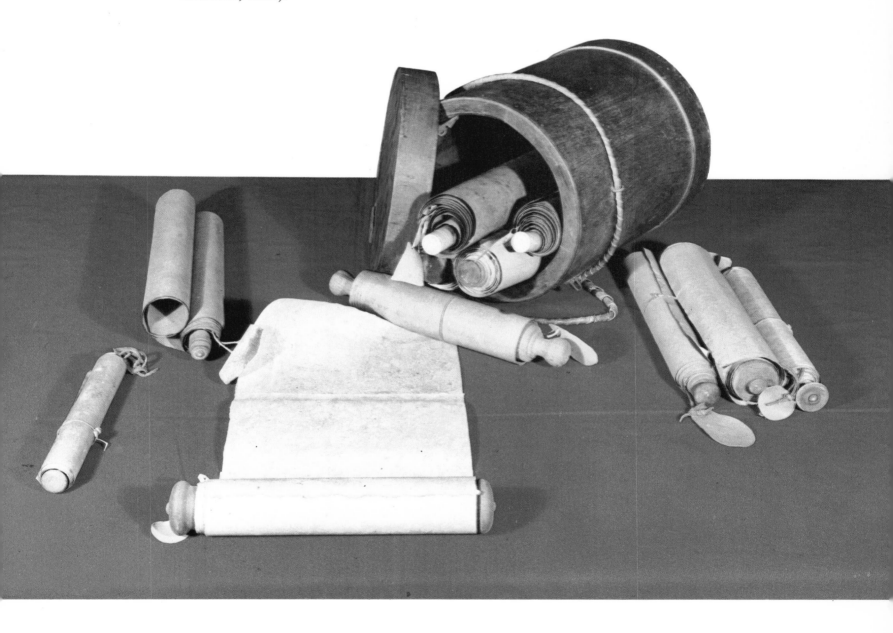

Besides using papyrus, the Romans also wrote on vellum or parchment, the treated skin of cattle, sheep or goats, but its high cost always limited its use. Parchment (*pergamena*, called after the inhabitants of Pergamum, whose learned men invented and perfected its use in the second century B.C.) was at first used in scrolls like the papyrus, but later it was folded in sheets, so as to make a *quaternio* or notebook, and each folded sheet was sewn together and put into a cover, rather like a modern copybook.

This was the kind of book that came into use alongside the papyrus scroll at the end of the Republic and in the early days of the Empire, and eventually replaced it altogether.

PUBLIC READINGS AND LIBRARIES

We who are accustomed to seeing thousands of copies of a book in circulation may be surprised at the Roman way of publicizing a book.

Someone has suggested that the slave-copyists were to ancient literature what the printing press is to modern literature. This may well be, but the book in those days was a real privilege reserved for the rich. Anyone who wanted a library had to find certain slaves, usually Greeks, called *servi litterati*, who were cultivated men and skilled in copying manuscripts. They copied or wrote under dictation, often using abbreviations which came to be known as *Notae tironianae*, after Tiro, the freedman of Cicero who invented them.

At first works were copied at the expense of the private reader, but soon individuals who were known as *librarii* opened shops for the sale of books which they had copied. The title then was extended to those who employed a workshop full of copiers to produce books for them to sell. They were really the publishers of Rome: Titus Pomponius Atticus, the friend and publisher of Cicero, owned a publishing house in Rome famous both on account of the accuracy of his copiers and because of the numbers of books he sold. Cicero congratulated him in a letter on how well he had sold his *Pro Ligario*.

The Romans do not appear to have been acquainted with authors' rights, and only rarely does the author seem to have been paid. Profits were solely for the publisher, and if it would bring in more money they would gladly alter a text.

Books neatly arranged in bookcases (*armaria*) were on sale in the *tabernae* of the booksellers (*bibliopolae*) which were plentiful in the Forum, near the *Curia*, in the *Vicus Sandalarius*, and in the busiest parts of the city generally. Here the educated people met to have lively discussions on the newest publication, or to listen to readings of new works by their authors before copies had been made.

Every author has at some time wanted to read his work to a friend, a master or a powerful patron. The poet Attius, in the second century B.C., had shown his tragedies to the old poet Pacuvius, and Virgil read passages from the Aeneid to Augustus. These were private readings, but public readings soon were started and became enormously popular — indeed were an accepted literary institution. Seneca recounts how Asinius Pollio, poet and orator, was the first to invite people to come and hear his works. Others soon followed suit.

The public would gather in the bookshops or in special halls built in the form of a small theatre, with a pulpit or high chair in the centre for the reader. The emperors favoured the public readings and Au-

Reconstruction of one of the libraries — Greek and Latin — in the Forum of Trajan beside the Ulpian Basilica. (Museum of Roman Civilisation, Rome).

On the page opposite: *A private library reconstructed on the model of the library of Hadrian's Villa at Tivoli. (Museum of Roman Civilisation, Rome).*

Reconstructed model of the Stadium of Domitian. The stadium was built as a centre for games in the Greek style with prizes for foot races, eloquence, boxing, discus throwing and poetry. (Museum of Roman Civilisation, Rome).

gustus even encouraged them. Claudius took an active part in them, once reading his own Roman history which he had been advised to write by Livy, but more frequently coming as a member of the audience to listen to others reading their works. Later the Emperor Hadrian had a special *Athenaeum* built where poets and orators read their works. Under the Empire the habit of public readings was often marked by casual behaviour from the public, not unknown in public lecture halls even today. There is a notable outburst by the younger Pliny to his bookseller friend Sosius: « The public goes to a hall but either stays outside or talks during the whole of the reading; every now and then they ask whether the reader has arrived, whether his preamble is over, or how soon he will end the reading, and only then, slowly and unwillingly, do they go in. Nor do they stay to the end, but leave beforehand, some furtively, others openly and even slamming the door... ».

As the books became available proper libraries began to be made, a privilege originally reserved for the rich.

Under the Empire, if the evidence of Martial and the younger Pliny is valid, private libraries greatly increased. Public libraries which were a key factor in Hellenistic civilisation (one only has to think of that most famous of libraries at Alexandria) came late to Rome: Caesar had wanted them, but the first to establish one, in 39 B.C., was Asinius Pollio, to commemorate his victory over the Parthini. A second public library was founded by Augustus. He divided it into

two parts: one Greek and one Latin. Subsequently many more were established.

The library was a monumental hall with an apse opposite the entrance door, probably used for a statue of Minerva. The hall usually faced east to get the morning sun and to avoid damp. The books were kept in wall cupboards or in bookcases. There were catalogues and librarians.

Sometimes, under the Empire, the ruler, either directly or through subservient senators, ruled that certain works should no longer be available. But almost always such a decision was quite personal and had no real element of censorship. Nevertheless Augustus had a good many soothsaying books burnt, and Caligula had Virgil's and Livy's works thrown into the flames. At the critical height of the ideological struggle between the persecuting emperors and the Christians, their sacred texts were destroyed. Then with the Christian triumph came the banning of classical works.

PHYSICAL EDUCATION

Physical education was considered a vital part of the young Roman's upbringing even if it did not quite reach the competitive level that was a feature of the Greek tradition. Professional athletics, like the professional theatre, were the province of a socially inferior stratum of society.

For the young Roman, physical training in the Campus Martius had a military purpose: throwing the discus, fencing with a wooden sword, racing on foot fully armed, wrestling and riding prepared the young man for war. We know from Plutarch that the elder Cato had all these things taught to his son, and brought him up to bear both heat and cold, and made him box, and swim the rough and icy waters of the Tiber. Horace and Virgil frequently remember the military exercises they did in their youth, and Horace upbraids Lydia for having used her affections to lure the young Sybaris from his sporting activities in the Campus Martius. Formerly he had spent his days in the heat and the dust, riding the fiery fast steeds from Gaul, diving into the waters of the Tiber and excelling everyone in throwing the discus and the javelin.

Most Romans engaged in gymnastics: they afforded physical fitness and were, in any case, a pleasant distraction. The Roman gymnasium was always attached to the thermae and so gave people the opportunity to stretch their muscles either before or after the bath. Thus the Baths of Caracalla had the usual annexes: the *ephebeum*, a great hall dedicated to gymnastic exercises, a *conisterium* where the wrestlers, after being covered with oil, covered each other with dust. It had special seats for the spectators. Both the young and the healthy middle-aged spent a part of their day at gymnastics. In private houses there were tracks and porticoes set aside for physical education, and somewhere there would always be a *sphaeristerium*, an open space for ball games.

In this field the Romans were doubtful about adopting Greek practices. The basic foundation of a Greek physical education was the athletics of the gymnasium and the stadium. The Romans always preferred the spectacle offered in the circus and the amphitheatre to active participation in sports.

With the fall of the Republic and the increasing influence of Greece, the Roman Empire took over education where it had hitherto been a private activity. Augustus founded the *collegia juvenum* for young men. It was a religious foundation, but its main activities were fencing, riding and hunting.

The Romans also seem to have considered the training of the body as inferior to the training of the mind. Plato and the Greek philosophers had lauded the ideal of a mature mind in a body that was beautiful by virtue of its carefully controlled development. A Roman philosopher like Seneca bewails exaggerated exercises, writing to the satirist Lucilius: « What a stupid and ridiculous thing it is for an educated man to exercise his muscles, stiffen his neck, train his thighs; even were he to grow as stout as you like, with big muscles, he would never have the strength or the weight of a lusty bull. »

Seneca's letter does not imply that Roman education should drop the principle of *mens sana in corpore sano*, but noting that every excess is a mistake, it expresses the traditional Roman belief in a wise balance between ability and suitability.

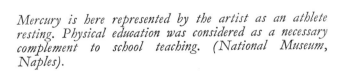

Mercury is here represented by the artist as an athlete resting. Physical education was considered as a necessary complement to school teaching. (National Museum, Naples).

TEACHERS AND PARENTS

The school of the *ludi magister* was under the colonnade. A few benches and an armchair for the teacher, who was a freed man, who for a modest reward had taken on the task, unenviable indeed, of instructing this band of rascals in the art of reading and writing.

People passing near the portico could see and hear the boys, tablets propped on knees, repeating in turn what the teacher said, or writing to dictation. Every now and then someone would get a good thrashing, for this, too, was part of the system the teacher practised between October and the end of June. There were also some unfortunate pupils who frequented the school of the *ludi magister* right through the summer, before going to *grammaticus*, where one could learn Greek, mathematics and geometry and use the *calculator*, or to the higher school, under a master of rhetoric.

Things were probably not so very different under the master of rhetoric. A narrow room or the portico, the same thrashings until one was almost grown-up, and the same sing-song of repetition for six hours. The rhetoric master tried to show the boys how to speak in public, but it all ended in few paying the fees, on the grounds that nothing had been learned. It is always the master's fault if the child has a potato instead of a brain. But if the boy does well, then it is entirely on his own merit.

And the teacher's pay? It was not worth mentioning. Instruction like this, of course, has no price, but there were those who made a price and then haggled over it. The teachers did not like this, but most drove their pupils hard, hoping that their labours served some purpose and that the long night hours which no craftsman would ever have lavished on his apprentices would not be entirely wasted. Those poor sleepy instructors breathed in a great deal of lamp smoke.

But those were the best days, when parents were their children's teachers and brought them up according to the old strict ways! For it is not always easy to find a teacher who is both gifted and aware of the importance of his mission. Some do it just for the money, and pass on to the pupil a hotch-potch of learning or worse. They force the children to learn by heart enormously long passages from the classics, or prepare them for public oratory just to cut a figure. Nothing more.

Others try to increase the meagre pay of a teacher by taking on clerical work as a public writer, and hardly do their teaching duties. They just keep order in the class by holding their cane ever ready, while they are really engaged in writing letters and petitions. The boys are idle and yawn, or chatter in a whisper or gape at the flies.

However, during the public oratory exercises the room is full of relatives, parents, aunts, gathered to see the prowess of the young genius. Tears and applause fill in the sheer emptiness of these exercises which are quite worthless. Here, for example, is a young lad thinking himself a pocket Cicero, who struts on the improvised platform pretending to be Hannibal hesitating after the victory at Cannae as to whether he should march on Rome or not. The sheer awfulness of these speeches! The syntax is all right, the grammar too, but where is the common sense? If Hannibal had been half as hesitant as that, he would never have got near the Alps.

Or take the two boys pretending to argue a case in court, each representing one of the parties, and the case constructed on sheer hypothesis, and argued according to an even more hypothetical Greek law which punishes sacrilege by cutting off hands. The case was this: a city of Hellas has asked Athens to lend them the sculptor Phidias to make them a fine statue of Olympian Jove. Athens is agreeable but naturally insists that the sculptor shall return after the work is done, or failing that, a fine of 100 talents will have to be paid. But what happens is that when the work is finished, Phidias is accused of pocketing some of the gold set aside for making the statue. His hands are cut off because of the sacrilege, and thus maimed he is sent back to Athens. But Athens had lent a sculptor and a man without hands was returned who could not be considered a sculptor, so the fine of 100 talents is insisted upon. But the city in Hellas will not pay for they maintain that Phidias was a sculptor, yes, but was also a man, and the man has been returned to Athens.

So these two boys represent the two cities in dispute and bring out argument on argument in an attempt to win by means of the clever subtleties which the master of rhetoric has taught them. But the case, having no reality, nothing useful or positive for contemporary life except as an exercise in language, serves merely to excite the vanity of the boys and their spellbound relations.

In fact everyone is happy, winking and grinning with contented admiration. The teacher struts round like a peacock; that little fee is well earned. Now he has his revenge for all bitter things he has had to swallow from parents who expect him to know all the rules of speech, and all history and geography and every piece of literature; who try to catch him out when they meet him on a walk or at the baths and ask him suddenly the name of the nurse of Anchises or the name of the mother-in-law of any old Sceptic philosopher.

(source: Juvenal)

MARKET, KITCHEN, AND TABLE

For a long time the Romans were a frugal people — « reared on polenta meal porridge, » wrote the elder Pliny — as befitted farmers and shepherds who had hard lives and had to earn their bread from day to day. But at the height of her greatest glory, the Rome of the nouveaux riches changed her style of living. Eastern influences brought a sense of luxury and relaxation, and cooking was one of the things they most affected. Meals amongst friends became an excuse for exotic banquets. One cannot imagine dishes more complicated or more extravagant than those of this period; chefs had to show their skill in creating fantastic concoctions of incredible virtuosity; each dish would involve some spectacular surprise; the triclinium *was no longer a simple dining-room but a theatre for ballerinas, acrobats and clowns.*

But this pleasure-seeking, lavish Rome, already moving towards her own decline, was counter-balanced by the other Rome, praised by Pliny and Martial, where the table was laid with lettuces, eggs, olives and onions, and lamb seasoned with mint and rue. It was a Rome which drank only in moderation and never abused its palate. The Romans preferred peaceful conversation and the pleasant company of good friends to the tight-rope walking of acrobats.

It was this Rome which heralded the Christian love-feasts, at which, as at the table of the plebs, bread and fish were the main dish, or even the only dish of a communal banquet.

A gastronome as fastidious as Apicius was more or less obliged to offer his fellow citizens a collection of recipes destined to preserve forever the methods of a supreme art made perfect with the passage of time. He was writing at the time of the emperor Tiberius, at the moment when Roman cookery lost the frugal character which had been a matter of pride in former times, especially in those households not forced to economise by lack of means. Amongst the 450 recipes collected by Apicius (every quantity and every ingredient carefully listed) there are some for every taste and every purse.

A rapid glance at Apicius' collection could lead the modern gourmet to believe that there was hardly any difference between the culinary art of olden times and that of today: sausages, meat-olives, chicken, venison, pork and hare, fish... But the character of Roman cookery was provided by its sauces — and therein lies the whole difference. We with our modern tastes would be hard put to it to eat a dish prepared with these sauces, in fact we would probably recoil at the very smell. For the Romans sweetened with honey dishes which we would have salted, and they liked a pungent and at the same time sweetish cuisine in which celery, raisins, vinegar, honey, oil and mint were mixed together. But worse still, this fantastic mixture of flavours was usually seasoned by a strange sauce made of fermented fish called *garum*, which was obtained with great difficulty: a mixture of various fishes were left out in the sun to rot and then were pounded to obtain an extract. This was a basic seasoning used in nearly all dishes: there were different qualities of it, but none was more highly prized than *garum* from Spain.

Rabbit and figs: fresco from Herculaneum.

To appreciate the difference in tastes between Roman cuisine and our own, it is a good idea to read some of the recipes of Apicius. Here is one, for example, for cooking baby marrows (a form of squash): « Boil the marrows and drain off the water, add salt, then put them into a saucepan. Grind some pepper, cumin, coriander seeds, garden mint and asafoetida roots. Add a few drops of vinegar, a carrot, a handful of pine-kernels, crushing the lot together in a mortar. Thin the honey with a little vinegar and mix the oil with some cooked grape-must and stock. Pour the sauce over the marrows, sprinkle with pepper and serve ».

At the rich man's table the flesh of boiled ostrich might be offered accompanied by a very rich sauce, on which Apicius most strongly insisted: « Pepper, mint, roasted cumin seeds, chopped celery, dates or carrots, honey, vinegar, sweet wine, a little stock and oil.

Boil all the ingredients in a saucepan, then thicken with a little flour. Arrange the pieces of ostrich on a dish and sprinkle with pepper. If the seasoning needs strengthening, add a little pounded spelt ».

The Romans used the normal method of roasting a joint: but after it had come out of the oven they basted it liberally with a mixture of salt and honey. Naturally Apicius gives us a whole set of recipes for roasts which are very much more complicated.

Perhaps we might have been able to raise some enthusiasm for a piglet prepared like this: « An ounce of pepper, a pint of wine, a large vinegar glass of best quality oil, one of stock, and a smaller one of vinegar ». But our palates are hardly likely to be tickled by an eel in a sauce in which are mixed pepper, honey, vinegar, oil, stock and cooked must.

The lack of such food-stuffs as rice, potatoes, tomatoes, citrus fruits, liqueurs, coffee, tea and choco-

Silver gilt wine beaker. Hildesheim treasure. (Antiken Sammlung, Berlin).

The favourite fishes on the Roman menu. Mosaic. (National Archaeological Museum, Naples).

Wild ducks. Mosaic from the Museum of Roman Civilisation, Rome).

Fruit and wine. Fresco. (National Archaeological Museum, Naples).

late, which are now in common use, would only increase our discomfort when faced with a Roman meal. Sugar was also unknown, but honey took its place.

THE TABLE OF RICH AND POOR

It is important to remember that at least amongst the rich, cookery had become a real art in which culinary methods were less highly considered than the skill and even the extravagance with which a chef sought to present the dishes to the guests.

Above: *Silver-gilt bowl.* Below: *Large dish decorated in high relief with figure of Minerva. Both belong to the Hildesheim Treasure, Antiques Collection, Berlin.*

Mosaic wild boar hunt found near Santa Bibiana, possibly belonging to the gardens of Licinius. (Antiquarium Communale, Rome).

Eggs and Game. Mural. (National Archaeological Museum, Naples).

Now, as today, the meals of the poor were frugal in the extreme, and the methods of cooking far more simple.

Less fortunate folk had preserved (more through necessity than by virtue) the thrift which had formerly characterised the life of the ancient Romans, when their staple diet was a thick porridge made from meal (*puls* or *pulmentum*). This remained the traditional dish for a long time with baked spelt, dried vegetables (peas, beans, lentils and haricot beans) and greens. Bread did not make an appearance until later, and the elder Pliny states that *puls* (meal porridge) remained the basis of their diet for a long time. But bread, of which the Romans knew three kinds, replaced the

73

meal porridge as soon as it come into common use. For the poor, there was black bread of inferior quality (*panis plebeius*), or sometimes on special occasions a whiter, rather better bread (*panis secundarius*). Only the rich could afford the very fine, white bread (*panis candidus* or *mundus*).

The common people ate meat only rarely, and ate vast helpings of pickled sprats (*menae* or *gerres*), costing little and therefore easily obtainable; fish and other choice sea-foods (turbot, sole, red mullet, crayfish, cuttlefish and squid) were kept for the tables of the rich epicures.

Oysters (*ostrea*) were considered a speciality which Pliny called « the glory of the rich man's table » (*palma mensarum divitium*). They were bred in fishponds like many other delicate fish. The fishponds of the orator Hortensius are still famous: Hortensius loved his moray eels so much that he wept bitterly and remained inconsolable for a long time when one of them died! Fish was not the only favourite on the menu of the rich; there were also birds, bred in large aviaries (*vivaria avium*) where pheasants and peacocks were crammed in anticipation of their fate in a cooking pot.

Kitchen equipment was simple at the beginning, and so it remained in unpretentious households. If some unusual occasion required the services of a professional chef, all that was necessary was to run to the market where large numbers of chefs were standing around ready to offer their services. In one of Plautus's comedies one of these kitchen experts bewails the fact that people prefer those who are unqualified and cheap to a talented chef like himself. « When they come to hire a chef, they never address themselves to those who know their job and who naturally expect to be paid a little more. They always engage those who ask for small wages: that's why I'm always sitting around the market-square... and I can tell you that my dinners are not like those of other chefs who serve half a meadow at table as though they had oxen for guests! They pile herbs upon herbs, and end up by seasoning even the green vegetables with herbs... ».

In rich homes, especially after the conquests of Greece and Asia, chefs hired by the day became a thing of the past. The table held a very important place in the household economy, and a whole army of people was assigned to its service, with chefs, scullery lads and waiters drawn from the slaves of the household.

The number of courses and the choice of dishes became the most important concern of the stewards, and, as we have already mentioned, above all else brilliance and extravagance were expected from the chefs of ancient Rome.

Literature gives us a complete picture of what to expect from a rich man's table. The elder and the younger Pliny, Horace, Petronius, Martial, and Juvenal, to mention only the best known, describe to us in great detail the menus and customs of the best Roman society, both in the capital and in the provinces. To have some idea of the outlandish ostentation of a rich man's banquet, one has only to read the description of Trimalchio's feast given by Petronius in his Satiricon; Martial's numerous epigrams directed at the feasts given by certain rich people; or to remember the official banquet provided by Lentulus, described by Macrobius several centuries later.

WHEN AND HOW DID THEY EAT?

As a rule, the Romans ate three meals a day, of which the *cena* remained the most important. In the earliest times dinner was eaten at midday, with breakfast before it (*jentaculum*) and a light supper in the evening (*vesperna*).

In time habits changed, and the dinner-hour moved to the end of the day, replacing the *vesperna*. In classical times the order of meals was *jentaculum* (breakfast), *prandium* (lunch) and *cena* (dinner).

In actual fact, not everyone kept to the traditional three meals, and many Romans skipped one of the first two. Many got up, drank a glass of water and took nothing else until *prandium*. At all events, even for those who did not stick to the three meal system, *jentaculum* and *prandium* were only light snacks. The first was eaten at about the third or fourth hour, that is, according to the time of the year, between seven and nine o'clock in the morning; children on their way to school bought the equivalent of croissants (*adipata*) which the baker had baked especially early for them. The grown-ups dipped bread in wine or sprinkled it liberally with salt and garlic. They also ate a great deal of bread and cheese, dates, honey, eggs and dried fruits.

Prandium took place at about the sixth or seventh hour (between eleven o'clock and midday), a little

These two illustrations show the reconstruction of a market (above) and a grain store (below). Throughout the Roman world the organisation of food supplies was highly efficient. (Museum of Roman Civilisation, Rome).

Bronze scales identical with those in use today. (National Archaeological Museum, Naples).

earlier for those who had not had any *jentaculum* and who by the middle of the morning were beginning to feel rather hungry. Again it was a quick, light, normally cold meal: vegetables, fish, eggs, mushrooms, fruit. Often they finished up the left-overs from dinner the evening before, and in any case, there was no need for the table to be laid, nor, afterwards, for them to wash their hands. At the end of a tiring working day, *dies solidus* as Horace called it, after a refreshing bath, they had the *cena*, the only meal eaten by the poor. Depending on the choice available and on the occasion, it would consist of one or more courses (*ferculae*), which in turn represented the *prima, secunda, tertia cena* and which followed the *gustatio*, a kind of hors-d'oeuvres made up of foods intended to stimulate the appetite.

When these courses were finished, an offering was made in silence to the god Lares; then the meal moved on to the *secundae mensae* — fruit, cakes and delicacies intended to give a thirst.

At this point during the banquet, the guests, garlanded with flowers, began to propose toasts (*comissatio*). During the meal wine was drunk only in moderation, but afterwards the libations might go on far into the night. They drank wine of every sort and from every source, almost always diluted with hot or cold water. The best vineyards were those on the Vatican hill, and in Marseilles, those of Campania, of which the Falernian was the most famous; from Latium (the Cecubian, the Alban or the Sabine); the exotic wines of Chios and Lesbos; and the Egyptian wine from the Mareota was very highly prized.

There was not a great quantity of table-ware, but though in modest homes it would be of earthenware or at best of bronze, in a well-to-do house it would be of the finest chased silver. They used a flat plate (*patina* or *patella*) and a bowl (*catinus*). Wine was kept in a special goat-skin bottle (*cadus*) from which it was decanted into a large two-handed earthenware jar (*lagoena*) with a narrow neck. The shape of the glasses varied according to their use: the *poculum* without handles, the *cantharus* with two handles, the *scyphus*, quite a large goblet, and the *cyathus* which could also serve as a ladle with which to pour the wine from the wine jar into the *pocula*.

The « dining-room » was at one time in the *atrium*, which could be looked into from the courtyard, as were also the kitchen and the altar to the Lares. Later it was moved to a more secluded place (the *tablinum* or *cenaculum*). In the earliest times, meals were eaten sitting round the hearth but under the influence of the Greek way of life the Romans later began to take their meals lying on a sort of couch (in Greek *kline*), leaning on their left elbow; the room became called the *triclinium*. Women and children continued to eat sitting on stools; then in time women were permitted to take their meals reclining, and with the men.

As the name of the room suggests, there were three couches placed in a horseshoe around a square table with one side free for the slaves who were serving. Each couch could take three guests and generally their number did not exceed nine. If by chance an unexpected guest turned up at the last moment, he had to resign himself to eating upright. The place of honour, called the *locus consularis*, was the place immediately to the left of the middle couch. Later the square table was superseded by a round one and in consequence the couch became semi-circular, with room for eight.

A slave shopping at the poulterer's. Usually men did the shopping. (Torlonia Museum, Rome).

The places of honour were then at the ends of the couches (*cornua*).

The Romans ate straight from the plate, with their fingers, the food being cut up for them by the slaves in attendance. The spoon (*cochlear* or *ligula*) was used only for liquid foods. It was therefore necessary for the guests to wash their hands from time to time during the meal — all the more so since their napkins were often put to quite a different use: into them were put — with or without the permission of the host — those delicacies the guests could not manage to eat. Martial tells us of the good-for-nothing Santra, who hides a quantity of food in his napkin, and who, when that is full, slides some cutlets and a roast turtle-dove under his garments.

Such practices were only possible at the tables of the rich and not even imaginable at the lowly tables of the poor, who certainly had no need of emetics such as were used by the greedy guests of the wealthy, unable to digest the excessive quantity of food which they had swallowed.

PRIVATE AND OFFICIAL BANQUETS

Having already studied the ordinary meals, it is not difficult to grasp the nature of the special banquets given by the well-to-do. They were meetings of gourmets who, once at table, did not rise until late at night, having wined and dined well. The last part of such evenings was enlivened by various entertainments: music, dancing, readings, poetry recitals or even comedies such as the amusing « match » between Sarmentus and Messius performed in honour of Horace and his friends in Cocceius' villa at Caudium, during the poet's journey from Rome to Brindisi.

Sometimes toasts would be repeated several times over, for example, to someone's mistress (as many toasts as there were letters in her name); toasts were often drunk to several women, to the emperor, to the officers commanding the army, to the head of the house. The general atmosphere must have become somewhat heavy by the time the dancers, musicians and acrobats arrived to display their talents.

Allowing for possible exaggeration, what Cicero has to say about the banquets given by Varro for his friends remains relevant: « Some are carried away as though fatally wounded, others who have passed out are left where they fell; it is more like the battlefield at Cannae than a Praetor's banquet ».

Such was the point of degeneracy which had been reached in what had been in primitive times a sacred ceremony, as indeed it still was in some increasingly narrow circles. In both Greek and Roman banquets of classical antiquity the fire used to prepare the food was considered divine and the gods presided over it. The table was a sort of altar, and it was often called the *ara*. Household meals on special occasions proceeded as did the Curial Banquets or those of the various religious bodies, according to hard-and-fast rules, which even determined the length of cooking to be given to the meat, and the state of mind of the recipients. The name formerly given to these sacred banquets was *daps*, but by the end of the Republic, the name *epulum* was more often used.

The whole population took part in certain banquets, for which tables were laid the whole length of the Forum. Some of these were for the priests, others for the Senate, and others again for the members of the special funeral colleges. The general organisation of the banquets and the fixing of their dates were entrusted to priests called *epulones*.

These public functions took place on days of special religious importance (*epulum Jovis, epulum Minervae*, etc.), on the occasion of religious games, at the consecration of a temple or in the course of an elaborate funeral. The most important part of a triumph was the sacrifice, followed by a public banquet.

A modest attire was prescribed for these great occasions. The banqueting rules of the funeral college of Lanuvium — handed down to us on an inscription — recommend good order, discipline and proper attire.

But the sacred nature of these feasts became degraded over the years; their religious significance faded and then disappeared altogether; the public banquets became no more than a means of quelling the turbulent Roman mob from time to time.

HUNGER AMONG THE VERY POOR

The political situation in Rome at the time of Augustus was that of an aristocratic republic which had become a monarchy, whilst its society lived in a state of transition between being a conquering city and a large organised State. It was a society characterised by enormous social differences, where fabulous riches existed side by side with overwhelming poverty. Rome had a proletariat who grew every day more turbulent and menacing, an easy prey for the demagogue and ready for revolt. This mass of unfortunates owed its growth rate less to a high birth rate (since infant mortality was on the increase) than to immigration, which was rising all the time: the immigrants were peasants who either had lost their holdings or were sick of leading a miserable existence, freed slaves and poverty stricken people from every province, attracted by hopes raised by the capital city. An enormous crowd surged into Rome, filled the least salubrious quarters and sought for any means, legal or not, of keeping itself alive. Very few of them succeeded in finding work; so for the most part they lived in idleness, trying to obtain some sort of help from any source to provide for their needs.

So it was that the State was finally obliged to take into its charge the greater part of its poor citizens, having tried ever since the time of the Gracchi to fix by means of « corn » laws, a price for cereals which would make grain available to all. But even fixed grain prices were beyond the means of part of the population, and so in 56 B.C. a law was passed which instituted a regular free distribution of grain, to which in time were added gifts of silver pieces. At times, public banquets were an added and gratefully received source of free food.

Various individuals made themselves the organisers of such banquets when, for political and demagogic reasons, a brief and temporary generosity was judged appropriate. Votes and propaganda were the weapons which the poor kept for their *patroni*, the rich men to whom they had bound themselves as *clientes* in return for provisions and clothing. It was for these poor people that the patron kept his distributions of food (*sportulae*), other items and sometimes even money.

The Romans were not very particular in their choice of meat, and the use of sweet or sour sauces often altered the original flavour. Roasts and stews were based on beef, veal, pork, wild boar, donkey, lamb, venison, dormouse, hare, snail, chicken, duck, goose, peacock, swan, parrot and every variety of game. Cheese was greatly liked and was also used in pastry making.

Both fresh and salt water fish were considered great delicacies and more than a hundred different kinds were eaten. Those enjoying the greatest popularity were sea perch, red mullet, dolphin, mackerel, grayling, moray, tunny, sole and eel. The passion for fish was so great that the habit was formed, and quickly grew, of raising them in hatcheries. Shellfish often appeared at the beginning and the end of a meal.

Lentils, chick-peas, beans, peas, lettuce, cabbage, artichokes, carrots, turnips, onions, marrows, asparagus, cucumber and mushrooms and herbs like mint made up the Roman kitchen garden. Olives were never missing from the table of rich or poor. The most common fruits were apples, pears, cherries, grapes and peaches. Apricots from Armenia were used principally in sauces, and dates were imported from Africa in great quantities.

There was no great variety of beverages in Rome, only milk (goat's for preference) and wine. The wine was thick and full of impurities, and whether it came from the Vatican or Marseilles, from Setia in Latium or Corsica, Chios, Lesbos or Mareota in Egypt, whether it was a Falernian or Cecubian, Alban or Sabine, it was rarely taken neat: cold or tepid water, honey or salt was added, according to the season and host's taste.

THE EXTRAVAGANT BANQUET OF A NOUVEAU RICHE

There were temperate men who were satisfied with barley bread, vegetables, chicken, or fish, olives and nuts, fruit and a morsel of cheese. From time to time they invited their relatives and friends to a modest meal at which pigeons were served in a highly elaborate sauce made of pepper, oil, vinegar, wine, honey, dates and mustard, with mushrooms cooked in honey and tiny pieces of pork with cabbage and lentils.

But there were others who, to parade their riches and dazzle their friends, did not hesitate to display the most ludicrous vulgarity.

A group of slaves received the guests on arrival, accompanied them to the bathhouse, or offered them precious vases containing water for them to wash their hands.

Then the servants accompanied the guests to the *triclinium* and showed them their places at table. Each reclined on a sofa, before a beautifully arranged display of hors-d'oeuvres: the marvels began with a little bronze donkey carrying two panniers, one loaded with black olives and the other with green. The donkey supported silver dishes engraved with the name of the master of the house and with the weight of each dish so that all might know their value and appraise the wealth of their host.

On the dishes were dormice seasoned with honey and poppy seed, smoking hot sausages lay on a silver grill and underneath, to simulate live charcoal, were black prunes spinkled with red pomegranate seeds.

At the beginning of the banquet, and while musicians scraped out a light and lively tune, other slaves entered bearing a great dish with a wooden hen hatching what appeared to be peacock eggs. The master of the house pretended to mistrust their freshness and in so doing discovered that the 'shell' was made of cooked flour and that inside nestled a good fat beccafico rolled up in spiced yolk of egg.

When one of the slaves dropped a silver platter weighing half a hundredweight, the master had it thrown on the rubbish dump. Then the other slaves bustled in to wash the hands of the guests in unwatered (and by no means the worst) wine. The wine which they then placed on the table in a sealed jar of thick glass was Falernian, one hundred years old. And at this point the first important dish of the evening arrived; a round plate with the twelve signs of the Zodiac set in order, and in each one the artist had laid some food proper to the symbol: Pisces, two red mullet; Cancer, a large crab; Taurus, a round of beef, and so on.

When everyone had had a chance to admire and exclaim, at a sign from the master four slaves entered with dancing steps and, lifting the top portion of the set piece, revealed an enormous dish filled with plump fowl, and paunches, each of which contained a winged hare got up by the chef to look like Pegasus. At the corners of the dish four figures of Marsyas poured a pungent sauce from their wine skins over delicate fish which seemed to swim around in the liquid.

The conversation became more and more lively, if not particularly refined, by reason of the type of guest present — almost all freedmen who had grown rich. Then there was another surprise: after the slaves had spread fresh covers on the couches, painted with nets and hunters, and after a pack of boisterous hounds had rushed into the chamber, servants entered bearing a gigantic wild boar stretched out on a dish. From his tusks hung two baskets woven from palm leaves, one full of dates from Caria and the other from Thebes.

Amidst exaggerated cries of wonder from the guests there now entered a sort of bearded huntsman, his legs covered with thonging and wearing a short damask cloak; brandishing a knife he lunged at the side of the boar, and from the gash flew out a flock of thrushes.

The birdcatchers stood ready, their sticks coated with lime, and in an instant they had caught all the birds who were flying wildly round the *triclinium*. The master then ordered that a bird be given to each of the guests. While the birds were cooking the servers approached the baskets suspended from the boar's tusks and distributed to each guest a helping of both kinds of dates.

The banquet was barely half way through: the master still wished to amuse and amaze his guests and so, although by this time they had had enough, they were obliged to join in the game to the very end.

The servants now placed on the table a fairly large pig which the chef pretended not to have gutted for lack of time, and just as the host was about to punish this unforgivable lapse he feigned compliance with his guests' entreaties and ordered the chef to open up the belly of the pig, to disclose sausages and black puddings.

Finally appeared a splendid triumphal centre-piece of sweetmeats and fruits from which a grotesque saffron-yellow fountain spouted upon the guests; and yet, more nauseatingly, fat fowls surrounded by goose eggs and thrushes made of pure wheaten flour filled with raisins and nuts, and quinces bristling with thorns to resemble hedgehogs, and a plump goose garnished with fishes and birds of all kinds that the chef, sculptor that he was, had fashioned from pork meat. And more ostriches and snails...

If some of the guests slid under the table, others, the wiser ones, called their slaves and, in an undertone, ordered their litters and their torches and quietly slipped away.

Upon their departure the master of the house, sad and melancholy from the wine he had drunk, began to speak of death...

(source: The Satyricon of Petronius Arbiter Trimalchio's Feast)

DRESS: FASHION AND TRADITION

For centuries Roman dress remained unaltered, completely formal and lacking trimmings, as befitted a people proudly and firmly aware of owning the world. The toga in its solemnity symbolized the equipoise of the Roman people. One might suppose that this equipoise was often superimposed — a matter of mere outward show. Yet it had roots deep in a tradition which had never been cast aside, and to which the Romans turned time and again in the course of a thousand years, whenever an institution needed defending or the fatherland was in peril.

Frivolities in dress were forbidden by law, being considered a sign of decadence. A citizen who affected a new style with ornaments that were not traditional would lose dignity thereby and might well be labelled effeminate.

The Romans therefore knew the rules, and refinements in dress, if indulged in, would be neither excessive nor dangerous. They were after all a tough people, engaged in matters of greater import than fashion.

The intricacies of fashion were left to women, and they were more fanciful in their hairdressing, their make-up and their jewels than in their clothes. Generally speaking they loved striking trinkets, ankle bracelets, heavy bangles and precious or false stones.

The national dress of the Roman citizen, the *civis Romanus* was the ample, solemn and cumbersome *toga*: but the garment usually worn by free men and slaves alike was the *tunica*, a kind of long shirt of linen or wool made of two rectangles of cloth sewn up the sides and across the shoulders with neck-openings and armholes. It slipped over the head and fastened round the body with a belt so that the wearer could gather it to whatever length he wished. It usually had no sleeves, and the arms were protected only by the fullness of the cloth on the shoulder. Thus the richer the tunic, the more the arms were covered by pleats, softly and elegantly draped. Sometimes this elegance in the pleats was held to be excessive and effeminate, even though Julius Caesar encouraged it to the point of adding a fringe.

Besides the common tunic, there was the *tunica palmata*, so called because it was probably decorated with leaves or flowers. It was worn by generals when celebrating a victory, and by consuls attending a public ceremony.

The people who wore the tunic wherever they went were actually called the *tunicatus populus*. Members of higher classes always put on a toga over the tunic whenever they had to appear in public, or even just leave the house.

The first togas were all made of wool but later they were also made of linen. They were the mark of the citizen of Rome, the symbol of his dignity. Later, under the Empire, when people began to consider the wearing of such a bulky garment too impractical, citizens were expressly ordered not to appear in public without it.

Free youths wore a toga bordered with purple (*toga praetexta*) which was replaced at the age of sixteen by a toga without a border and completely white (*toga pura* or *toga virilis*). The purple-bordered toga had been worn by kings under the monarchy, and later by consuls and citizens who held high positions in Church and State.

The chief characteristics of the toga did not change, but its size and the ways of wearing it did alter slightly down the ages. It was made of one piece of cloth, elliptic in shape, whose width varied according to the fashion of the times. In length it was three times the height of the wearer and it was draped round the figure in such a way as to form many folds and leave only the right arm free.

Quintilian has described in great detail how the toga should be draped so as to give the wearer an appearance of solemnity and dignity, but the description is not really clear, and the chief impression it leaves behind is that the process of draping a toga is highly complicated. For this reason, although the toga was a solemn garment, people began to wear it less and less in the later Empire, confining its use mainly to special occasions, and attempts were made to reduce its bulkiness and impracticability. But the more it was reduced in size the more it was embellished with ornaments and embroideries, until it became so sumptuous that it could be worn only for public ceremonies.

By then the toga had in most cases been reduced to a *pallium*, a kind of broad stole draped round the shoulders, crossed in front and fastened at the waist by a belt. This was a simple, light and practical garment, but because it lacked the elegance and dignity of the toga, some emperors forbade its use by the more important State dignitaries.

CLOAKS

When it was cold the Romans wore over the toga a loose mantle of dark wool (*lacerna*) fastened at the shoulder or under the chin by a brooch and usually equipped with a hood (*cucullus*). Those who wore it must have appeared ridiculous to the emperors, keen as the latter were on their citizens maintaining a dignified appearance, and its use was forbidden at ceremonies, and even in the Forum. In time, the *lacerna* lost its clumsiness and fashion necessarily turned it into a garment of bright rich cloth, embellished with embroidery and fringes.

Another hooded cloak was the *paenula*, especially useful for travellers as it was simple and practical. It was made of a circular piece of cloth with a hole in

The toga, traditional dress of the Roman citizen. (Statue of Cato, Lateran Museum, Rome).

the centre for the head and it fell in thick folds round the body, down to the knees. Sometimes the *paenula* was made of skins and then it was not only warm but also quite waterproof.

Soldiers all wore the *sagum*, hence the phrase *sagum sumere* (to take up the *sagum*) and *sagum ponere* (to lay down the *sagum*) meaning to go to war or to make peace. This cloak allowed the greatest freedom of movement, being square, fastened at two corners on the shoulders or the chest and draped only over the back. An officer's *sagum* was smaller than a soldier's and brightly coloured. Red was reserved for the general and for the lictors who comprised the official escort of the senior magistrates and who accompanied the general into battle. The army commander alone could wear the *paludamentum*; originally the term stood for all military insignia, but under the Empire it came to mean a short red or white, or red and white draped cloak worn by the general in the field or at public parades or ceremonies as an official garment.

Lastly, there was a kind of dressing gown (the *synthesis*) which combined the best features of tunic and toga, and was worn by men when dining in company.

The tunic *was in common use; when travelling a man would shorten it at the waist, with a belt. (Museum of the Thermae, Museum of Roman Civilisation, Rome).*

WOMEN'S DRESS

Except in very ancient times, the wearing of the toga by a woman was a mark of infamy decreed by the State for those guilty of grave misdemeanours. The tunic, however, was an essential part of a woman's wardrobe, though longer than the male version of the garment.

Over the tunic patrician matrons wore a *stola* which the Senate had ordered them to wear to distinguish

The sagum *with a small cloak used by soldiers. It was fastened on the shoulder by a buckle. (Bust of Vespasian, Capitol Museum, Rome).*

them from women of the people and slaves. It was a long, rich garment, gathered at the waist and bordered at the hem by a purple band. Matrons with three or more children could wear a different kind of *stola*, but such documents as we have do not tell us where the difference lay.

For going out the *stola* was covered with the *palla*, a kind of rectangular toga folded round the body, with one end acting as a hood. When attending sacrifices or religious rites, women covered their heads with a square of purple or blue-fringed material, called a *rica*.

HAIRDRESSING

Until 300 B.C. the Romans ignored the refinement of hairdressing, but when the first barbers (*tonsores*) arrived in Rome, short hair for men came into fashion. After a few centuries hair was worn a little longer, new styles were adopted and some men even had their hair curled by the barbers who were now to be found all over the city.

Under the Republic and the early years of the Empire, women did their hair simply: it was gathered at the neck and fastened back with clasps and ribbons in a chignon, or else it was plaited and worn in a coronet on top of the head. Soft curls on the forehead were the only obvious concession to vanity. In the first century A.D. a new, attractive women's fashion appeared with a centre parting from which the hair fell away on either side to frame the face in a few curls. This fashion was soon followed by ever more complicated hair arrangements, some piled so high as to require additional hair pads arranged by slaves skilled

Women's dress for various occasions. (Frescoes in the Vatican Museum in Rome and in the Villa of the Mysteries in Pompeii). The Roman matron wore a stola above her tunic, which was like a man's tunic but longer. Over the stola she wore the palla, a kind of rectangular toga, folded round the body and occasionally over the head.

Men's hair styles in Rome. (Statues from the Louvre Museum in Paris).

in coiffure (*ornatrices*). Some constructions were twice as high as the head, and crowned with diadems, clasps, single flowers or wreaths.

The matrons of the imperial court favoured such coiffures at official ceremonies and if these exaggerated fashions were allowed here it seems likely that others practised them too.

These artificial hair styles declined in the first centuries of the Empire in the face of the simplicity preached by Christianity, and although hairdressing probably did not become as natural in style as that which we find portrayed in catacomb frescoes, yet fashion did not escape the influence of the new era.

At the end of the second century A.D. the face was framed by slightly waving hair gathered in a plait at the neck, or in a plaited coronet on the head.

SHOES

Probably one could say in any age: « Tell me what shoes you wear and I will tell you who you are ». Footwear is always an important part of dress. In ancient Rome footwear was so varied that a mere glance at it would reveal what rank a person had and even what work he did.

At home, men and women wore sandals (*soleae*) consisting of a simple sole fastened with a few thongs of leather tied round the ankle. It was not considered suitable for a man to go out in sandals, so men put on a kind of boot (*calceus*) reaching to the calf, with two holes at the side through which leather thongs were passed and tied round the leg. These *calcei* could not be worn by slaves. Some were of red leather (*calcei mullei, calcei senatorii*), and if they belonged to important State officials from a noble family they had a silver or ivory half-moon at the top. Others wore plain black boots.

When visiting or dining out it was customary to take sandals along or to have a slave bring them, as it would have been impolite to wear inside a house shoes worn in the street.

Women, too, wore boots like the men's, but made of thinner, softer, leather, brightly coloured and decorated with precious stones and pearls.

Women's hair styles also followed the fashion, passing from a noble simplicity to a complicated headdress. (Museum of Roman Civilisation, Rome).

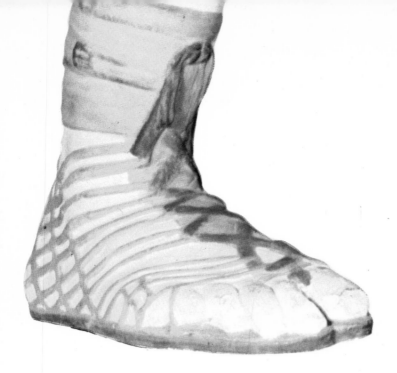

A sandal and a calceus senatorius. *(Models from the Museum of Roman Civilisation, Rome).*

Soldiers wore special shoes called *caligae* with heavily nailed soles, the uppers being made of leather thongs which left the toes free but bound the ankles and the foot in web of leather.

When Germanicus commanded the Roman army on the Rhine, he had his son with him in the camp so as to bring him up in close touch with military life. He dressed the boy as a soldier and even had a small pair of *caligae* made for him, and the old soldiers nicknamed him Caligula.

Actors wore different kinds of shoes according to the parts they played. Comics wore a kind of slipper, the *socci*, and tragedians wore *cothurni*, though the latter were not confined to the stage. One kind was used in hunting, in the form of a half-boot; another had the usual very high wooden sole with uppers of leather or stuff matching the colour of the toga. The sole of the *cothurni* followed the outline of the foot only approximately so that it could be worn equally on right or left — hence the word *cothurnus* to denote a man who easily puts up with political changes.

The country slaves and the poor wore wooden shoes (*sculponae*), or they wrapped their feet, especially in winter, in uncured leather or strips of wool.

TRINKETS AND JEWELLERY

The women of Rome liked jewellery for the value it had rather than for the beauty of its workmanship. Their lack of taste in this matter is revealed in the most famous surviving pieces of Roman jewellery. Where excavations have yielded treasures showing skilled craftsmanship, these are usually of Greek, Eastern or Etruscan origin. What mattered to the matrons of Rome was the weight, the size and the quantity of jewellery, at least up to the time when Greek influence began to spread. One solid gold bracelet found in an excavation weighed a whole pound.

Ornamental brooches and clasps have been found in abundance, but the embossing, like the engraving, is somewhat coarse. Roman ladies knew little of the art of wearing a single ornament of exceptional beauty and workmanship. They put on all they had, even to the extent of wearing several pairs of earrings. These must have been rather heavy for it was fashionable to set pearls, precious stones and glass in the gold; even if the last had little value, it looked striking and added to the showiness which was a feature of the ladies of Rome.

Necklaces, earrings and medallions. Roman jewellery rich in gold and silver, rarely reached the perfection and refinement achieved in other crafts such as the manufacture of drinking vessels. Roman ladies valued their bracelets more for their weight than their beauty. (Vatican Museum, Rome).

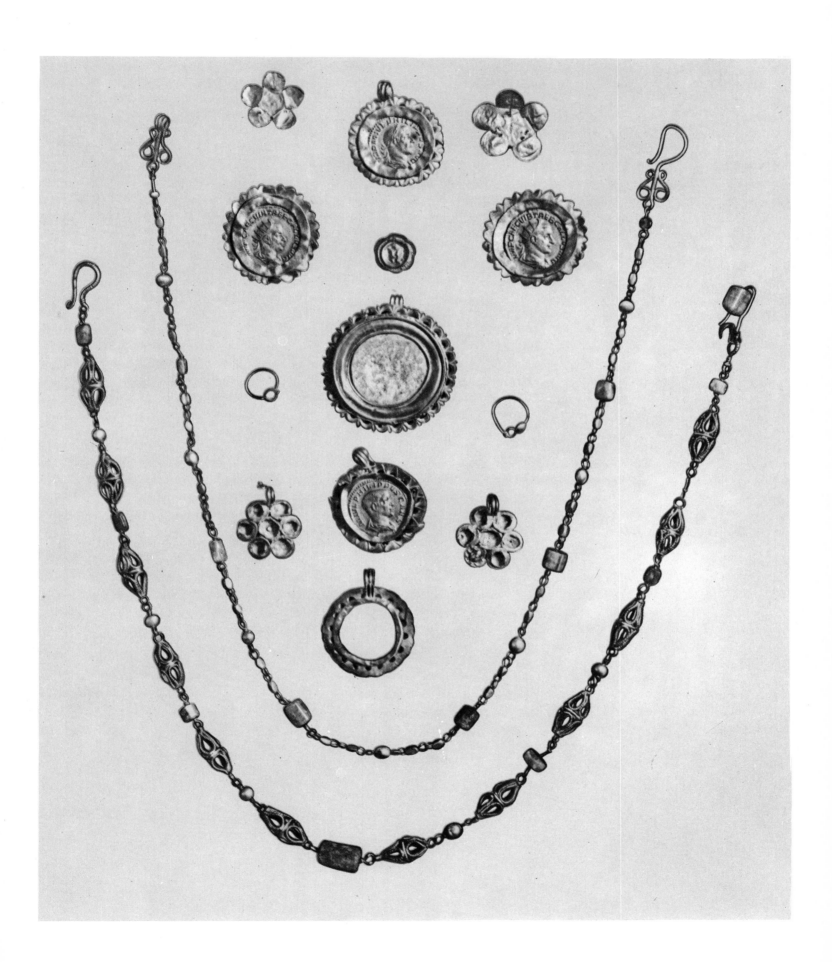

WHEN A MATRON DRESSES...

Matron Cestia is in a bad temper this morning. Her women slaves exchange troubled looks as they dress her. The hairdresser especially is unlucky today; twice she has had to begin Cestia's complicated hair-do all over again, and her mistress eyes her with displeasure.

Cestia's complaints had started earlier when the slaves were putting the make-up boxes on the table, and one clumsy slave was so intimidated by her mistress's cross looks that she upset the box of horn powder used to whiten the teeth. So Cestia had to forego cleaning her teeth, and simply rinsed her mouth with water and sweetened her breath with a perfumed sweet.

After this incident she then followed every movement of her women with a critical eye, ready to rebuke the smallest lapse, and to insult the assistant who was plucking her eyebrows if she felt the slightest pain and everyone knows that this is never a painless operation.

The make-up women could do nothing right; the white which they used on her face and arms was either too thick or too thin and the same went for the ochre they used to brighten the pallor of her cheeks and her lips. As for the black eye shadow it should be a mere suggestion, according to Cestia, just enough to enhance the beauty and brightness of the eye, without being too noticeable.

Cestia does not like people knowing how much she makes up; her husband knows, yet does not know; at any rate just now, while she is being made up, he is not allowed into the room. A slave on duty at the curtained doorway will, if necessary, remind him of her desire for privacy.

The precaution is not needed for he, too, is busy preparing to go out. Cer-tainly his morning toilet is far less complicated — a quick wash for his hands, face and head to wake him up, a swift gargle and he is ready. Later he will go to the barber to be shaved and have his hair arranged, and in the afternoon he will go to the baths to do some gymnastics to keep him in trim, and to have his daily bath.

As soon as the hairdresser has finished, Cestia puts on her *stola* which falls in elegant pleats over her tunic, right down to her feet. She is still wearing her pale coloured, soft leather slippers. The slaves fasten a girdle with a gold buckle round her waist; there are so many laid out in the cupboard that they have trouble in finding the right one.

Cestia might like the girdle, but not the buckle; if she liked the buckle then the gold sandals she liked so much would not match properly.

Two serving-maids come forward, one carrying a mirror finely chiselled by a Greek artist. Horrors! The matron raises an eyebrow, a sure sign of trouble. The hairdresser is called back; perhaps she is in for a beating...

No. It was only a wisp of powder left at the side of the mouth. Hurry now, Cestia wants to go out. The litter has already been ordered.

The servants bring more ornaments. Their mistress wants to visit the wife of Caius Sestus and display her riches, but without ostentation. Golden necklaces are examined at length; Cestia tries on one after another, stretching her neck and turning her head this way and that, undecided. Just when she seems to have made up her mind, she hesitates again. Today the mistress seems really too exacting for words. Finally she chooses the heaviest necklace of all.

Today she wears three rings, the onyx one, the aquamarine and the sparkling one with three oriental pearls. Then she considers the question of bracelets, while the terrified hairdresser binds madam's hair in a scarf interwoven with gold and dotted with gems. With great care, lest Cestia's fine skin be pricked, a few gold hairpins are pushed in to hold on the scarf.

Now for the earrings. No — these are too vulgar; they are suitable at the most for a cattle dealer's wife, and are cast aside, back into the jewel box.

Fortunately no one now remembers the infamous Oppian Law which Cato tried to enforce immediately after the defeat at Cannae. All the women of Rome rose up against it, asking, « What have bracelets and brooches to do with patriotism ? » How they objected to any limits placed upon their luxuries! It was far worse than Hannibal at the gates. It quite put the war in the shade.

So Cestia can wear her anklets of gold, but in that case it would be better to change into the soft, red Moroccan leather shoes, otherwise the gold will not show up properly. But now the girdle and its buckle no longer match. Everything must be revised, and the wife of Caius Sestus will just have to wait.

When Cestia is finally ready she is wearing a tidy portion of the family gold and precious stones. She has put on the *palla* with which she will cover her head for a moment before getting into the litter. She has chosen a tiny purse, a useless little fan and a small sunshade. The sun is not shining; in fact it will soon be raining.

It is of no consequence. Fashion wills it so.

(source: Various Authors)

AT THE THERMAE:
BATHS AND RECREATION FOR ALL

No modern establishment can compare with that entirely Roman institution: the thermae. *They usually offered both hot and cold baths, swimming pools, a gymnasium, gardens, museums and libraries. The Roman went there to relax his mind and refresh his body. He walked in the gardens, talked with friends and passed the hours until supper time. It was a moment of peace after the day's work, business in the Forum or discussions in the Senate.*

This need for rest and cleanliness in Roman life was so real that Agrippa made entry to the thermae *free so that even the most penniless person might have access. The emperors built ever grander* thermae *with the finest amenities. Going to the baths became a general habit; every day millions of gallons of water flowed out of the reservoirs of the* frigidarium *into those of the* tepidarium *and the* calidarium. *The Romans spent their free afternoons there, bathing and playing games, unless they went to see the extraordinary circus shows which were frequently put on. The thermae were for leisure, and this they provided in its most convenient form, lending substance to the motto* mens sana in corpore sano *which has little currency today.*

The Romans were not really at home in the sea. They never went on the beaches and their athletes were never as keen on swimming as modern athletes. They liked fresh water for their baths, since these were taken for cleanliness. Best of all they liked the running water of rivers, lakes, deep pools and icy streams. In any case a high sense of modesty kept them, at least at one period of their history, from undressing in public, and therefore from building seaside bathing places for general use.

We know that a father was forbidden to bathe with his son, his father-in-law or his son-in-law in the austere days of the Republic, and the presence of women in male baths was then considered improper.

Under the early emperors right up to Trajan there was no formal prohibition of mixed bathing, but a certain amount of scandalous behaviour resulted in Hadrian's decree separating the sexes in the baths. In Hadrian's own villa at Tivoli there were two separate establishments, one large for the men, and one smaller,

more elegant and ornamental in its architecture, for the women. The emperor Heliogabalus early in the third century A.D. abolished the division, but it was immediately re-imposed by Alexander Severus who succeeded him. A mosaic in the great Roman villa at Piazza Armerina, a work of the fourth century A.D., depicts ten young women at exercises in the gymnasium, dressed in a two-piece costume very like the present day « bikini ». This shows that the use of a bathing costume, however limited in covering, had been introduced in gymnasia and baths, at least in the late Empire.

All the baths at Pompeii, which are the only baths of the Republican and Augustan Age that we know in detail, have two groups of halls each with their separate entrance. Nevertheless women who frequented the public baths were not numerous and were considered rather free and easy: matrons and girls usually washed at home as best they could with the inadequate means available there.

Bold structure of Trajan's aqueduct at Segovia, which has forty-three double arches at the end of its course.

THE BATH

The art of the bath came in fairly late, after the Romans had come under the influence of Greek refinement. In the earliest times it was customary to wash all over once a week; on other days face, arms, legs and whatever part of the body was dirty received summary attention. There was no special room in the house for washing. A dark little room near the kitchen was used for the sake of being near hot water, and it contained a sunken wooden barrel with a stopper at the bottom. The room was called a *lavatrina* and was often used as a lavatory, hence the word, the use of which has survived even after the separation of bath from water closet. When Seneca visited the villa where Scipio Africanus, the conqueror of Hannibal, had lived near Literno, he described his bathroom as « bare, narrow and dark, lit by means of a grating and not a window, a place which in our day would not have served a slave ».

Cato the Elder tells us in his *De re rustica*, that in his youth during the last decades of the second century B.C., baths were not taken daily. The habit only came with growing experience of the Greek world at the beginning of the following century. Then two or three washing rooms appeared in houses, still near the kitchen, fitted with baths and basins (*labra*) made of stone and later of marble. Such rooms have been found in Pompeii in aristocratic houses belonging to the second Samnite period. The House of the Faun has one such room, the House of the Labyrinth has three, albeit rather primitive. In the House of Diomedes there is a series of well-equipped rooms, with a swimming pool and a gymnasium attached. The so-called House of Livia on the Palatine has two rooms equipped with bathing facilities.

The baths of Caracalla and the districts between the Aventine, the Palatine and the Coelian Hills, traversed by the Appian Way. (Reconstruction in the Museum of Roman Civilisation, Rome).

Once the bathroom was accepted it was known as *balneum* or *balineum*. In the plural, *balnea* or *balinea* usually meant public baths, whereas the *thermae* were the vast establishments of imperial days, built by the city authorities or the emperors with a particular aim in mind. *Lavacrum* in common parlance signified fountain.

Apart from the difficulty of finding sufficient space for a bathroom in most houses, there was the problem of water. The oldest aqueducts ran under the street, and only rooms on or near the ground floor could use them. People on higher floors (the *insulae* of Rome could be three and more floors high) and people in all districts on the hills had to get their water from the public fountains, so that the supply was always short. « High » aqueducts (the Claudian and the New Aniene, built by Caligula and Claudius, and by Augustus at the same time as the Marcian fountain) at last produced enough water to supply those who lived on the hills of Rome.

In the grand suburban houses which had more space and water available than in the city itself, baths acquired greater importance and have often been found alongside swimming pools and gymnasia. In those days heating was still simple in form. It consisted mainly of braziers (*foculi*). According to Pliny and Valerius Maximus a certain Sergius Orata invented a way of heating floors at the beginning of the first century B.C., with an underground system. He apparently built a middle floor above the foundations, supported on little pillars or thick terracotta tubes about two feet high (*suspensurae caldariorum*). A fairly large opening out into an external corridor allowed brushwood to be inserted into the cavity (*hypocaustum*) and ignited; in this way the whole floor was heated. Later the system was developed with *tegulae mammatae*,

Bathroom with cavity for heating by suspensurae caldariorum. *(Reconstruction in the Museum of Roman Civilisation, Rome).*

tiles which had small feet to keep them separate, or with rectangular tubes (*alveoli*, *cuniculi*) which made the fire draw better and also heated the walls with hot air. Some of these were decorated with mosaics or marble and fixed in place with bronze nails.

PUBLIC BATHS

The first public baths were built by private enterprise. They have been found in ground floors of *tabernae* or rented premises and consisted of a few rooms, with primitive equipment. Sometimes they were attached to taverns and to houses of ill repute. Baths here were taken in common, both hot and cold, the bather passing from one to the other. Sufferers from rheumatism and those recovering from broken limbs could have massages. The price of a bath was a *sestertius*, equal to about seven pence (or eight cents) now. With all the extras it could cost two *denarii* (eight *sestertii*) according to Diocletian's list of prices. Rich owners of the *balinea* often presented their friends with free season tickets.

In the survey of the XIVth Region of Rome, made under Constantine between A.D. 334 and 357, 856 baths are listed. Martial describes some of them; many even in the first century of the Empire were rather

Double water wheel from the Stabian Baths at Pompeii: movement was obtained by pressurized water. (Museum of Roman Civilisation, Rome).

The baths were a complex set of services, gradually considered indispensable by the Romans: baths, libraries, gymnasia, surrounded by gardens and colonnades for walks. They were supplied by great aqueducts which collected the water from distant springs and brought it to every part of the city. (Reconstruction from the Museum of Roman Civilisation, Rome).

dirty. Martial describes in his Epigrams how Selius, who hangs about the baths waiting for an invitation to a free meal, visits all the baths, the Gardens of Europa, the *Saepta Julia*, the Isaeus, the Portico of Pompey, « nor did he despise the baths of Fortunatus or of Faustus, nor the dark tavern of Gryllus nor Lupus's draughty hole. He washes and washes in the public baths but still finds no one to invite him. And finally soaked to the bone he returns once more to the fine box tree gardens of Europa, in case some late comer might yet invite him. » The poem reveals some of the characteristics of some of the baths which were refuges for the idle and the swindlers, and sometimes, indeed, hiding places for assassins and thieves.

The great marble slab with a plan of Rome at the time of Septimius Severus (ruled A.D. 193-211) shows several baths in private houses: they had a vaulted room, the *calidarium*, and a circular room, the *frigidarium*, with smaller rooms for massage and single baths attached, running along little courtyards.

THE STABIAN THERMAE

The Stabian Thermae at Pompeii, the most ancient public baths extant, show a studied arrangement of the various rooms, all designed for communal bathing.

Entry was through a gymnasium with a colonnade on three sides, and on the fourth side a swimming pool supplied with running water. The men's baths were on the right, with a waiting room and a dressing-room (*apodyterium*) with a bench and high wall cupboards for hanging up clothes. The ceiling is still finely decorated with stucco, a later addition. The bather went from the dressing-room to the *frigidarium*, a circular room with a skylight, or into the *tepidarium* which had a constant and moderate temperature, so as to avoid too brusque a change for those coming out of the hot bath (*calidarium*) and hot basins (*alveus* or *calda lavatio*).

All the rooms were insulated with *tegulae mammatae* (hollow tiles).

The Stabian Thermae demonstrate the complete principles of the bath according to medical rules: first one passed into a strongly heated room so as to sweat abundantly and expel ill humours. After drying one took a hot water bath, with more sweating. Then into the *tepidarium*, a room of moderate temperature, where one strolled about, and finally a dip into cold water to give a shock to the body. The process ended with massage and rubbing in of oils and perfumes by which time the body was fully restored and blood vessels and muscles had recovered their tone and elasticity.

95

After the bath, the client would spend some time in the gymnasium, where he could choose between exercises, wrestling and ball games.

The women's bath had the same purposes, though not quite so strenuous. It stood on the opposite side of the gymnasium, and had a separate entrance. The great metal stoves which heated the water were three in number, and were described by Vitruvius as « *calidarium*, *tepidarium* and *frigidarium*, so disposed that the quantity of warm water passing from the *tepidarium* into the *calidarium* shall equal the quantity of cold water entering the *tepidarium* from the *frigidarium* and the vaulted rooms with the basins shall be heated by the common stove ».

THE FORUM BATHS AT POMPEII

The Forum baths like the Stabian baths were built by the city's magistrates with public money in the first days of the settlement, after 80 B.C. Each could accommodate twenty to thirty persons at a time, a small number when one recalls that the population of Pompeii at the time of the eruption in A.D. 79 was supposedly about 20,000.

There was a third and larger central thermae, still unfinished in A.D. 79 but notable in that windows opening on to large courtyards and gardens allowed far more air and light to enter them. Moreover it had spacious adjoining halls typical of the great baths in Rome; meeting rooms, rest rooms, libraries and restaurants.

On the subject of improvements, Seneca wrote approvingly: « At first the baths were small dark places, for our ancestors thought warmth and darkness must go together... but now our baths are flooded with sunshine pouring through big windows from early morning to late at night. Bathing alone is not enough, one has to lie in the sun and see the countryside and the sea through the windows at the same time ».

We do not really know whether this development originated in Pompeii or whether it was modelled on oriental arrangements. Excavations of cities which enjoyed contacts with Pompeii, like Alexandria, Pergamum, Delos and Athens, have so far revealed nothing resembling these baths. Probably something of the kind existed in the Campus Martius in Rome, but on a limited scale owing to the lack of space.

In any case it was not until the age of Augustus that Rome acquired a thermal establishment worthy of the capital, planned expressly as public baths and maintained by the city magistrates. Agrippa, aided by rich subscribers, built the first public baths in the Campus Martius.

THE BATHS OF AGRIPPA, THE *STAGNUM*

It is significant that the official name of the baths of Agrippa, as given by Dio Cassius, is *laconicum* and only much later, after association with similar buildings, was called *lavacrum* or *thermae*. According to Vitruvius the *laconicum* was a room built so as to gather the maximum amount of heat rather like an oven for vapour or tub baths, and for a violent contrast to the cold bath, this form of treatment being prescribed for certain illnesses. Vitruvius in fact associates it with the sweating chambers and gives the following instructions for building it: « Next to the *tepidarium* are the *laconicum* and the sweating room, both as wide as they are high, at least to the rim of the cupola of the roof; see that the opening in the cupola is in the centre whence the copper shield should hang by means of chains which can be drawn up or lowered so as to regulate the temperature of the room ».

A fountain dedicated to the nymphs — or Nymphaeum *— surrounded by covered colonnades and chapels. This is a reconstruction of the so-called Temple of Diana at Nîmes. (Museum of Roman Civilisation, Rome).*

Agrippa built not only the baths but also a swimming pool called the *Stagnum*, so enormous that Tigellinus, the notorious and much hated prefect of Nero's day, kept a sort of dining float on it, which was towed around by a boat. Between this lake and the baths, Agrippa laid out walks lined by shrubs of laurel and box so that the Romans could talk and discuss their business in the shade. Ovid says in letters from his place of exile on the Black Sea that he is homesick for the warm afternoon hours spent with his friends in the pretty gardens of the Campus Martius near the Stagnum and the Euripus. Strabo tells us of a carved lion, the work of Lysippus, which was an ornament on one of the paths among the trees laid out by Agrippa. The Euripus was the open channel which carried the overflow of the lake to the Tiber. Along its banks were benches where poets and philosophers sat and talked and recited verses.

THE ROMANS AND THE BATHS

As we saw in the quotation from Seneca, the baths gradually changed their character. The bath itself lost its importance compared with all the other amenities available, especially the treatments offered for so many diseases. In particular, there were special vapour baths (*sudatoria*) followed by massage with oil (*oleoteria* and *consisteria*) for wrestlers, and rooms (*districtaria*) where they would lie down after their bouts so that slaves would remove the oil and sand they used to make it more difficult for opponents to get a hold. Then the wrestlers went on to the *calidaria* or the *frigidaria*, as they chose.

Those too old or otherwise disinclined to take part in the games would walk in the shady paths (*xysti*) or sit near *nymphaei* or fountains, enjoying the fresh air, even in the winter.

Present-day view of the calidarium *in the Forum at Pompeii.*

Reconstruction of the Nymphaeum of the Licinian Gardens, called the Temple of Minerva Medica. (Museum of Roman Civilisation, Rome).

The Romans really liked cold better than heat. As children they were accustomed to sleep in winter in unheated rooms where a loose curtain acted as a door, so that they became hardened to outdoor life and resistant to lung diseases. In Pompey's day, Asclepiades, the doctor, prescribed cold baths to cure many ills, and according to Suetonius Musa restored some strength to the failing Augustus by making him bathe in the lake at Gabii. From the same source we learn that Augustus slept with his bedroom door open. If it was very hot he would sleep in the peristyle near a fountain, or near anything which made the air move.

Apparently he also often oiled his body, and after a sweat in the steam heat of a vapour bath, he would cover himself with tepid water, or water just warmed by the sun.

Charmis, a doctor who lived under Nero and came from Marseilles, also used cold-water cures. Followers of this cult were called *psychrolutes*, and frequently they would perform orgiastic dances ending with a final plunge into an icy swimming bath. The so-called Nymphaeum of Diana, discovered in 1923 in the Via Livenza in Rome, was perhaps the seat of one of these mystical cults. Even when it had no religious significance, the cold bath was frequently preferred to a hot one. To prove this there are many large swimming pools attached to Roman villas. Seneca used to swim in the Tiber even in winter, or in a pool in his garden (a *baptisterium*) which was heated only by the sun.

Clearly the Romans were very fond of fresh, cool places. *Nymphaea* or semi-underground grottoes with running water and cool breezes have been found in great numbers. No Roman villa was without its *nymphaeum* or its semi-portico with narrow, transverse pas-

View of the pool sacred to the nymphs in the « canopus » of Hadrian's Villa at Tivoli.

sages to cool the air. Special rules existed as to how often one should walk these semi-underground passages in order to achieve a good digestion after luncheon or dinner, with alternating walks in the upper gardens.

A feeling of acute discomfort fills us today when we enter some of those old houses of Pompeii, in which the *atrium* on to which all the rooms open out was a small dark and humid courtyard and all the rooms were on pavement level without heating and with the window frames filled only by straw mats stirring in the wind. Yet the middle-classes of Pompeii lived in them for centuries and so did the Romans, for conditions were fairly similar for the average citizen in all cities of the peninsula at least until the first century A.D.

When Rome was to be rebuilt in Nero's reign after the fearful fire of A.D. 64 Tacitus wrote: « All these dispositions (free-standing *insulae*, wider streets with colonnades and pavements, limitations to the height of houses etc.) doubtless enhanced the city. But there were those who held that the old architecture had been more conducive to health, in that the narrowness of the streets and the greater height of the buildings had kept out the heat of the sun ». The old Roman's comment is significant. Certainly it stands in direct contradiction to modern ideas on hygiene.

THE BATHS OF NERO

Nero's thermae in the Campus Martius, slightly to the north of Agrippa's, had a new feature, which may be due to Nero himself, or may come from Alexander Severus who rebuilt them completely in A.D. 227, renaming them after himself, *Thermae Alexandrinae*.

The new feature consisted in dividing the baths into two exactly even halves, like two pages of an open book, with the same arrangement of rooms round the central and main *frigidarium*, *tepidarium* and *calidarium*. This axial symmetry was henceforth to be the architectural pattern not only in Rome but for Roman baths elsewhere.

Next to his baths, Nero had built a Gymnasium for the practice of athletics, but very shortly afterwards it was destroyed in the great fire. It seems very probable that it stood where Diocletian later built his great stadium — where the Piazza Navona is now.

The baths of Titus (on the side of the Esquiline, towards the Colosseum) must have been comparatively small, though richly decorated. They were built on the old pattern with little rooms, few fittings and space for small numbers only.

The plan of the Roman baths was altered again with the building of the baths on the Oppian Hill in the reign of Domitian. Trajan completed the structure and the baths bore his name. Once more, there was a cross axis of the three main rooms and the rest of the smaller rooms were duplicated on either side.

For the Romans of this period, the baths had a new role to play, combining a system of intellectual benefits alongside the physical ones, so that the combination of the useful with the finer pleasures allowed the afternoon to be spent agreeably.

We have seen how Agrippa provided his baths with extra rooms for treatment and massage. Domitian went further. He added two libraries to his, one Greek and one Latin, with adjoining refreshment and meeting rooms. To give non-bathing visitors to this area greater peace, he concentrated the baths in a central building, surrounded by ornamental gardens full of statues and fountains (*gestationes, circini, ambulationes, nymphaea, musaea*) and only on the outskirts of the grounds did he place the intellectual centre we have described.

The two great rectangles of the baths had always had one wall in common. Caracalla, in his baths in the Via Nova, separated the two halves completely. He increased the recreation rooms and decorated them much more luxuriously.

The imperial baths had now reached their zenith: they offered the population communal and private baths, and a whole afternoon of relaxation; they began to draw the people away from the somewhat sordid places on the outskirts of the city which they had hitherto liked to visit. The baths were open from an hour after midday till sunset.

The baths of Diocletian on the Viminal Hill and those built by Constantine on the Quirinal merely perfected the existing type of baths.

THE BATHS OF CARACALLA

These are the most completely equipped baths which we know of. The entire basement of the building was intersected by a covered carriage way, down which two carts could pass each other, carrying wood for the ovens and clean and dirty linen. Personnel could use them of course, and they communicated with the ground floor and other floors by means of trap doors and staircases.

There were entry and exit corridors under the circular chambers, some with doors. Servants' staircases were carved into the walls and slaves could go from the cellars to the top floor without being seen. Beneath the *calidarium* there were vast chambers for the storage of wood. Near the baths there were big store cupboards for bathtowels and accessories. A complicated web of channels and pipes was cunningly arranged in pavements and walls to carry water to the reservoirs and to the various hot and cold baths.

About 1,600 persons are reckoned to have been easily accommodated at the same time in the baths of Caracalla or Diocletian — rather less in Trajan's baths. Probably, therefore, an average of 5,000 visited each bath every day and probably about 10,000 servants were required to cope with such large numbers. One can imagine what vast crowds milled round these establishments. Each was practically a self-contained little city, richly decorated with many-coloured marble columns, friezes, statues everywhere in niches, mosaic pavements sending shimmering reflections on to the walls in the sunlight, everywhere baths hewn out of solid marble brought from the furthest ends of the Empire, gardens full of flower beds, walks lined with statues and fountains and shaded by trees, and eating places and libraries, resting places and gymnasia.

On very special occasions the baths would stay open late into the night and then they were illuminated by great bronze lamps.

BATHS IN THE PROVINCES

From the second century A.D. all the important provincial centres vied with each other to build baths like the *thermae* in Rome. Among the most luxurious were the ones in North Africa: Leptis Magna at the time of Septimius Severus; Timgad, where the richest of many establishments was known as the Southern Baths; Cyrene and Lambesi. In Gallia Belgica the sumptuous thermae at Trier (or Trèves) reached their point of perfection in the fourth century A.D. There were other famous ones at Ephesus in Lydia, called the baths of Antoninus Pius.

Climate obviously determined the character of the buildings in the provinces: in Africa the gymnasia and the swimming pools were often out in the open and there were no *laconica*, while the *tepidaria* went unheated. In the colder climate of Gaul hot baths were in the majority, and all the halls were covered and heated.

As well as ordinary baths some cities, which had a predominance of iodine and sulphur in their waters, or iron in the sand or hot mud, had special baths which made use of these minerals for curative purposes.

The most famous of such regions, round Baiae and Pozzuoli on the Bay of Naples, abounded in hot sulphur springs. Hence the large establishments there, once wrongly believed to be temples to Mercury, Diana, Apollo and others, where the arthritic and the rheumatic went for treatment. Sand baths were especially favoured; if there was a shortage, the sand would even be brought from distant places and heated up artificially. In Hadrian's villa at Tivoli there was a special sand bath (*heliocaminus*): a circular hall with wide arcades open to the west, with steps leading down to the bath, so that the appropriate quantity of sand could be maintained. The sand was heated from below as in the *calidarium*; and surrounding rooms, also heated, were devoted to supplementary treatment.

Clearly, similar halls existed in all the chief *thermae* to complete the treatment which the Romans believed essential to good health and cleanliness.

The Nymphaeum *of the so-called House of the Great Fountain in Pompeii.*

EVERYONE TO THE BATHS

Much commotion at the baths. Lucky the man who can take a cold bath at home, in a leisurely fashion. But for anyone who has only a pail in a little windowless closet behind the kitchen, who likes company and takes pleasure in watching people and listening to homely back-chat, the baths are ideal.

After a day at the office, in a shop or a workshop, this recreation is indispensable; one comes away refreshed, even if the head aches from the cries of the sellers of soft drinks, sausages, nuts and buns, and the shouts of greeting floating through the dense steam from the farthest corner of the hall.

Add the wail of the restaurant boys selling their snacks, and the picture is complete.

Lucky too the man who can frequent the rather less popular baths and take a peaceful turn in the *calidarium* with all the new comforts, free from the dread of not finding his clothes afterwards. The masseurs there know their job and are no charlatans, and the slaves are so well trained that you find exactly what you want silently and appropriately at the right place. Organisation is what makes everything work in a large establishment, and organisation is not lacking.

Hundreds of slaves bring the logs and brushwood to feed the fires which heat the water and the air ducts to maintain the rooms at the right temperature. Others look after the flow of water, making sure that it is always at the right level in the *frigidarium*, the *tepidarium* and the *calidarium*, so that no one is stranded half way in a hot or luke-warm bath. Others flit by this way and that, mere shadows in the vaporous steam, laden with towels, or carrying little amphorae full of oils for the massage, or pushing small cartloads of sand for the sand baths, or wiping up discreetly where someone coming out of the palestra has muddied the floor with its precious mosaics.

Here, too, rooms are better kept and lighter. The swimming pool is pleasant after the games or the exercises in the gymnasium and it is refreshing to dive straight into it.

If you like silence and solitude, then do not go to the baths: you can hear the noise from a hundred yards away.

Those who are trying to get their figures back by weight-lifting pant and groan like a pair of bellows thanks to the fat on them and the effort they are making. The slaps of the masseurs on the greased shoulders of their patients and the pummelling they give them resound from another hall.

Shrieks, cheers and applause float out from the area where a ball game is in progress. Someone is shouting out the score, others are arguing or roaring with laughter. You can barely hear the ball bouncing for the amount of noise going on.

One of the bathers and a slave notice a shady character hurrying away with a whole bundle of clothes over his arm. They raise the alarm, people rush in from everywhere cursing and making a tremendous racket: fists and voices are raised. The man is caught and the affair might have ended rather nastily if someone, a bath attendant probably, had not managed to hide him until the police arrived.

Peace is restored at last, but suddenly there is the voice of someone talking and apparently with no one answering. Perhaps he likes the sound of his own voice or is just talking to himself, interrupted only by the occasional splash of a body diving into the swimming pool. What a fantastic noise! It is someone teaching himself to dive, and trying over and over again but falling flat every time.

All these are the true sounds of the bath. It is the piercing shrieks of the itinerant vendors, and the sing-song of the barbers offering their services which really do disturb. If they should happen to fall silent, then come the cries of those at the barbers' having hairs pulled out: at first they grin and bear it, then they howl and grumble, but it seems they end by slitting the barbers' throats.

But without all this, what fun would there be in going to the baths? A bit of confusion does no harm: it is just too bad for those who have chosen a flat near by, for no one can do without this refreshment every afternoon, winter and summer. In the oppressive heat of summer when you sweat, and clothes begin to stick to you, a few dives into the *frigidarium* refresh the body for the rest of the day and the whole of the night. In winter, chilled to the marrow by the cold and wet, one feels re-born in the *calidarium*. The blood starts to circulate with renewed vigour; even the anaemic get roses in their cheeks, and when they come out of the baths no frost is too icy to face. When you get home and sip that good glass of sapid hot wine mulled with spices and honey in front of the glowing fire that awaits you, you think it is all due to the baths and you bless whoever invented them for the benefit of the Romans. Truly a sign of civilisation, even more than the conquests of Augustus.

(source: Seneca, Letters)

COUNTRY LIFE

More than any other society, the Romans preserved in their spirit and customs traces of a profound and deeply-rooted attachment to the soil. The rustic element in Roman civilisation permeated the language, the law, the religion and, during the great centuries of the Republic, even the structural organisation of the State. Conquering both by inclination and by necessity, the Romans' first demand was for land where they could establish as colonists the veterans of their successful campaigns; and the greatest part of such land, the ager publicus, *they held to be State property.*

Inevitably the smallholders of the early centuries disappeared as the power of Rome increased and as the phases of her expansion brought social and economic upheavals in their primitive society.

The small properties gave way to the big latifundia, *concentrated in the hands of the old patrician aristocracy. Here lay one of the principal causes of decline, for the countryfolk moved away from the land to become town dwellers and formed the* plebs, *while the fields were worked by foreign slaves. But Rome, jealous of her traditions, preserved a certain nostalgia for her rustic origins, and she considered the* Bucolics *and the* Georgics *as the ideal expression of the Roman genius in terms of the humanities.*

In 37 B.C. Varro wrote: « You who have travelled through so many different countries, have you found land better farmed than in Italy? For my part, I do not think there is any to be seen. One must remember, besides, that Italy offers greater facilities for cultivation than Asia, first of all because she forms part of Europe and secondly because she enjoys a more temperate climate. Is there a useful plant that does not grow in Italy and does not yield the best fruit? What grain can be compared with that of Campania? What wine with that of Falernia? What oil with that of Venafrum? Is not Italy so covered with trees as to appear one enormous orchard? Are the vineyards of Phrygia more prolific than those which Homer describes as 'rich in wine'? Argos, which the same poet calls 'wheat-growing land', is it richer in wheat? Where else other than in certain regions of Italy can one obtain ten or fifteen barrels of wine from a single acre? Is not Cato justified in writing, in his book *Origines* that the *Ager Gallicus* is called *Romanus* because it has been distributed to Roman colonists from this side of Rimini

and because each acre produces as much as ten barrels of wine? It would appear that the inhabitants of Italy, in devoting themselves to farming, asked themselves two questions: firstly, whether the soil would yield a crop which would compensate for both the time and the trouble involved, and secondly, whether the area might be healthy or otherwise ».

Thus wrote Varro at the beginning of the reign of Augustus, as an introduction to his famous work about life in the country. He praised Italy as a land of fertility, and as one which, as though by divine providence, produced everything bigger and better than any other. In fact, even when their social development had advanced, and when urban life and city preoccupations seemed to have smothered and depreciated the simple rural life, the Romans still thought of themselves as, and liked to be called, « a peasant people ».

A people close to the land who, although they appreciated their good fortune in having the richest soil of any, were also proud that, through hard, well-planned and persevering work, they had succeeded in persuading this same earth to yield up fruits to them which she would not have produced so abundantly for others less inclined to work hard at the improvement of the land.

Virgil in the *Georgics* praises the fertility of the fields and the « contented flocks » of the Italian landscape. He nevertheless points out the contrast between the easy restful life of those in Arcadia, who gather the fruits which the earth offers so generously to them, and the Italian farmers for whom the hard daily struggle is both the means and the price of happiness.

There is no doubt that when the Italian peoples settled on their peninsula they had been cattle-breeders and farmers for a long time. Even if some places were swampy and malarial, the fertile soil of Latium encouraged the hardworking and energetic nature of her new inhabitants. By inter-marriage and settlement they imposed their characteristics on the indigenous neolithic population. There is no point in trying to decide whether it was arable farming or stockbreeding which came first with the ancient Latins who settled on the left bank of the Tiber, the site of early Rome, particularly as the legends woven round the origins and first years of the Urbs refer to both of these activities. The ancient name Palatine and the feast of the Palilia are connected unquestionably with Pales, god of shepherds, but the cult of Consus, god of the fields, whose altar is at the foot of the Palatine and in whose honour the Consualia games were celebrated, is no less ancient.

In time, however, tilling took precedence over grazing; the development of farming in Latium probably owed a great deal to Etruscan influence, just as the Italians of the South and of Sicily learnt much from the Greeks and the Carthaginians.

THE SMALLHOLDING

Modern experts, in trying to reconstruct the different periods of Latin agriculture, are generally agreed that there were three successive stages; during the first (which corresponded roughly with the Kings and the first two periods of the Republic) Latium must have been divided into smallholdings, where cereals were the principal crop and where any stock-raising was probably carried out on common pastureland. In the course of the second stage, from the third to the first centuries B.C., following the Roman expansion in the Mediterranean, medium and large properties appeared. Variety in crops increased, vines and olives taking precedence over cereals which were by then being supplied cheaply from the markets of Sicily, Sardinia, Africa and Asia Minor. The third period (the last years of the Republic and the first decades of the Empire, about 100 B.C. to A.D. 100) was distinguished by the breeding of cattle and by « villa husbandry » to which farming was specially geared (growing of fruits and vegetables, and poultry-farming). During the last three terms of the Republic, only in Northern Italy and a small part of Central Italy were small-holdings to be found.

Some details from « The Twelve Tables » seem to substantiate the existence of this combined system of smallholdings and communal property during the earliest days. This codification of laws refers to country property by the name *hortus* (literally « enclosed land ») which later came to mean a garden, whereas the garden was originally called *heredium*. The country property, the *hortus*, amounted to a small plot of two *jugera* (about one and a quarter acres) for each member of the family, who had the right to fence it in. The rest of the land was for common use, sometimes divided up again temporarily, and it was usually intended for grazing. With the increase in crop growing at the expense of cattle raising, the area of common land gradually diminished before disappearing altogether. It had no place in the growth of cultivation and improvement of the soil, which tended to occupy the peasant to the exclusion of all else.

The humble farmers of Latium worked very hard and lived very frugally. In the time of Augustus, Ovid portrayed their life in a famous idyll in his *Metamor-*

phoses. He writes of an old Latin peasant and his wife living alone in their hut in Phrygia, obtaining from the surrounding patch of ground the bare necessities for a frugal though contented existence; undoubtedly in the idyll of Philemon and Baucis the poet is calling to mind, in a stylised way, the hospitality which a poor peasant of Latium could offer a distinguished visitor who arrived unexpectedly.

Ovid's account of the food offered does not mention bread, the excellent wheat bread (*triticum*) which was much used by the Roman peasants once it had replaced the spelt, either roasted or ground down into flour (*spelta*), which was eaten in the early days. Spelt and barley, used to feed the horses, were grown by the Latins until the middle of the fifth century B.C., when they began to cultivate wheat. With the spelt flour, cooked with salt water, they made a sort of porridge (*puls*) which was accompanied by *pulmentarium*, usually dairy produce and vegetables such as beans, onions and radishes. Even after they knew wheaten bread the country Romans continued to prefer their porridge. Very little meat was eaten in the country: beef was kept for religious festivals; on ordinary days a little pork or lamb might be eaten, fish almost never.

THE LARGE ESTATE

For many years the austerity of life in the town equalled the sobriety and economy of the rural way of living. In the days of the Tarquins, the Decemvirs and Camillus, and at the time of the Pyrrhic wars from

Symbols of Roman civilisation: a plough and a lance; the legionary conquered the land then abandoned his weapons for farming tools. The plough with its wooden ploughshare is one of the most ancient pieces of machinery reconstructed in the Museum of Roman Civilisation, Rome.

the fifth century down to the first half of the third century B.C. both the Roman peasants and the *plebs* in the towns preserved their attachment to the ancient national deities and their respect for the rites prescribed by their ancestral religion. In the family, rigid discipline, austere habits and the severe laws laid down by the Decemvirs were all observed. Throughout Latium and even in Rome the standard of living was very modest; the plainness of the house, the simple furniture and clothes, and the small number of slaves kept, contrasted strongly with the luxurious life led in the Italian, Etruscan and Campanian cities where the houses were filled to overflowing with beautiful furniture, priceless tableware and exquisite pottery. There gold and silver coins circulated freely, and the hard work of an army of slaves increased the already substantial capital of their patrons.

But then came the long and bitter struggle with Carthage. The twenty-four years of the first Punic war in Sicily (264-241 B.C.) changed Roman society and the population of Latium and Central Italy more fundamentally than had the thirty-nine years of the campaigns in Campania and Apulia against the Sam-

A groma: *an instrument which was used to determine the exact lie of roads and boundaries when the land was being divided out. The figure of the legionary shows him starting his work of colonization after leaving the army. (Museum of Roman Civilisation, Rome).*

nites (between 343 and 304 B.C.). It can be fairly said that during these twenty-four campaigns against the Carthaginians, there was not one Roman citizen of military age who had not spent three or four years, and often more, in the Sicilian camps and garrisons.

Returning from Syracuse and other Greek or Graeco-Phoenician cities, the Roman and Italian soldiers brought back to their homes, their villages and even to Rome itself a whole new knowledge of words, ideas and customs, different from anything they had known before. The ancient civilisation of Rome was completely transformed by their influence.

The blow which was dealt to Italian farming by this long war was particularly severe. Casualties caused great gaps in the ranks of the country farmers, but worst of all it meant long absences from the land, and this in turn ruined crops and long-term agricultural projects; the young recruits, who had enjoyed their stay in the cities and the easy gains to be had from pillaging and looting, were reluctant to return to the hard and often unrewarding work in the fields.

But more grave yet were the economic and social consequences resulting from the wars of conquest and the Roman expansion throughout the whole of the Mediterranean basin at the end of the third century B.C. Love of money came before all else; trading became an obsession for the Romans, who threw themselves into commerce in the footsteps of the Greeks, the Sicilians, Etruscans and Campanians. So it was that, by the middle of the second century B.C., the merchant class had grown in size and had acquired considerable importance. Another new group of people growing daily in wealth and power were those who had to value businesses and farms for the purposes of state taxation.

The former senatorial oligarchy, the real *nobilitas*, had so far succeeded in keeping themselves apart from the new rich, and a law passed in 218 B.C restraining Senators from investing their capital in commerce, even if promulgated with a different result in mind, had the effect of perpetuating the situation. However, the Senators had other opportunities for self-enrichment, either through looting, or else whilst governing the provinces; being unable to use their wealth in commercial enterprises, they found a ready-made investment in land. Consequently, the senatorial nobility

A plaustrum, *a heavy farm cart. Reconstructed by the Museum of Roman Civilisation, Rome.*

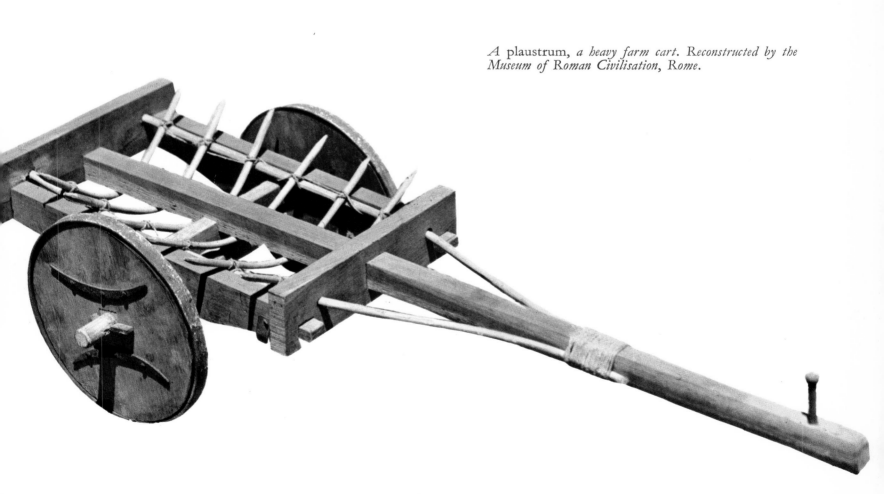

was gradually transformed into the class of landed proprietors. The most important of these large estates, called *latifundia*, were mainly to be found in those regions of Italy, such as the south and Sicily, which had suffered the greatest devastation and taken the hardest knocks during the war against Hannibal. In these parts the small landowners, lacking the means to put their property in order, had been obliged to sell at a ridiculously low price. This was how the *latifundia* came into being and developed to the detriment of the small and medium-sized property.

There were, it is true, some smallholders who had enough funds at their disposal to keep their land sufficiently productive to be an economic proposition. And besides, centurions and even ordinary soldiers returning to their land after the wars received a certain gratuity. But then something else came along to threaten the existence of the small or medium estate, the use of slave labour. During the years which followed the second Punic war (218-201 B.C.) the number of slaves arriving from the battlefields and from the oriental markets grew out of all proportion; it is enough to remember that in Sicily alone, the number

of slaves who took part in the slaves' war of 135 B.C. was estimated at 200,000. Slaves, who in ancient times were considered indispensable to the well-to-do, who did all the menial duties, or who worked as farmhands for the free peasant, now became a marketable commodity; they were bought by the hundreds and thousands and sent to the *latifundia*, condemned to working on the land in conditions of extreme hardship, and sometimes under cruel supervision. Bought for almost nothing and fed on scraps, the slaves represented a labour-force of such cheapness that competition by free labour was quite uneconomical. This was yet another reason to convince the owner of the small and even the medium-sized property that he should sell his land — its value dropped daily and he would be better served by investing the little money he made on the sale in a more lucrative enterprise.

These then were the various reasons which, by the middle of the second century B.C., had caused the gradual disappearance of the smallholding in Italy. Apart from this decline in small and medium-sized properties, the growth of the *latifundia* was further promoted by the continual and often arbitrary appro-

The four seasons, from a huge mosaic in the Villa Dar Buc Ammera (Zleiten) Museum, Tripoli.

priations by the aristocratic families of the *ager publicus*, the often extensive regions which had been confiscated from conquered communities and had not yet been included in the allocation of land to colonists.

As the size of the *ager publicus* grew it was decided by the State to allocate parts of it to private individuals (not only Roman citizens but also Latin and Italian allies) who were granted the right to enjoy the life interest from these properties, whilst the freehold remained in the hands of the State. In 133 B.C. it was arranged that these holders of public land should pay an annual tax (*vectigal*) as a tangible proof of ownership. Unfortunately this system, which should have benefited the smaller country landowners, became instead one of the dominating factors in the development of the *latifundia*, since the greatest share of the *ager publicus* fell into the hands of the wealthiest estate-owners.

At the beginning of the Empire there were in being enormous inherited estates such as those of Agrippa in Sicily, or Seneca's property, famous for the beauty of its vineyards. But the reader who attempts to weigh the harm done by the spread of the *latifundia* should not be influenced overmuch by the famous phrase of Pliny's,

« *latifundia perdidere Italiam!* ». « The *latifundia* ruined Italy! ». Certainly, the *latifundia* did much harm to Italy, but if their effects were far-reaching in the social, moral, political and military fields, from an economic point of view, agriculture, now based on well-founded enterprises and large capitals, made amazing advances. Different methods were tried and new crops introduced from conquered territories began to be grown; afforestation increased, crops which were no longer a paying proposition were replaced by vineyards, olive-groves and orchards. By the end of the Republic, Italy had attained the height of expertise in farming and was called the garden of the world.

Later a slow process of desertion and decadence began. Many different reasons contributed to it: the falling birth-rate, bureaucratic excesses, heavy taxation, depreciation of the currency. However, even during the first decades of the Empire, here and there the medium-sized property continued to flourish alongside the large estate, protected by sensible laws and helped by the encouragement given to public works such as roads and bridges, making possible easier communications and an abiding peace.

The Villa at Boscoreale near Pompeii. A typical country building of the first century A.D. *Reconstruction in relief from Museum of Roman Civilisation, Rome.*

THE *VILLA* AND THE *FAMILIA RUSTICA*

To Cato, farming represented the noblest and most useful of all occupations. It was free from the risks and accidents to which commerce was prone; farming produced healthy men and valiant soldiers; farming furnished an honest and sure reward unlikely to arouse envy. In short, work in the fields allowed a man to increase the value of his inheritance and represented a school of patriotism and good-living.

Cato (234-149 B.C.) was writing at a time when agriculture, in the form of actual farming, was at its zenith; the smallholding had had its day almost every-where, and the medium-sized property, which was the most common, was not yet seriously menaced by the *latifundia*, which were just beginning to appear. The owner of an estate directed and supervised as much as possible himself. When political or military duties necessitated his absence from his lands, he could leave them in the hands of his bailiff or *villicus*, a trusted and experienced slave who was able to give orders to the *familia rustica*. This chosen group of labourers, both bond and freedmen, consisted partly of farm workers (*mercenarii* or *operarii*) and partly of neighbour-ing small-holders who needed to make some extra money.

Farming did not remain the only occupation for the medium-sized property owner, and if he was more interested in politics than in the administration of his estate, or preferred an easier method of gain, he could always have recourse to tenant farming, or sometimes share-cropping. In this case the farmer or share-cropper (*colonus* or *partiarius*) was of course a free worker who through his own means, or by those furnished by his landlord, cultivated the land and gathered the fruits from it.

What would the average area of these estates have been? According to Cato about a hundred acres, a reasonable figure if the farm was to be self-supporting. But if it were a little or even a lot bigger it was far better, if for instance its vineyards and olive-groves alone covered the hundred acres; the important thing to remember was that the owner must « always sell and never buy ». Everything needed in the home also had to be produced on the estate; tools, wooden and straw containers, waggons, harness, clothes for the *familia*; the men were responsible for crushing the olives to make oil, grinding the corn and kneading the bread, while the women had the task of spinning the wool provided by the sheep and weaving it during the winter. Other tasks which were the province of the men were growing vegetables, of which the surplus would be sold in the market, the upkeep of the meadows which provided all the cattle-fodder needed, and maintaining the woods, from which timber would be taken for making ploughs and farming implements, and which also furnished firewood, part for the owner's use and the rest made into charcoal to be sold in the market.

The *familia rustica* under the management of the *villicus* and the *villica* (the bailiff and his wife) was usually made up of a book-keeper (*actor*), when the bailiff did not deal with the financial administration himself, and a certain number of overseers (*magistri officiorum, magistri operum*), who were in charge of the

slaves and the freed workers (*operae*) working in the fields. There were also other slaves whose duty it was to attend to food and clothing for the workers; there were barbers (*tonsores*), and, in the large concerns, even doctors. While it may have been true that the life of slaves who worked in the country was far harder than that of those working in the town (*familia urbana*), and that the discipline which they had to endure was more strict, nevertheless, under enlightened ownership they could be fortunate in having plenty of food and good living conditions — in certain villas there were even baths for the slaves. Furthermore, it was in the patron's interest to keep his slaves in good moral and physical shape so that they could maintain a good output. Occasionally in the cases of slaves who proved unamenable to discipline, and indulged in petty theft

A detail from the Villa at Boscoreale. Beyond the wine and oil jars is the drinking trough and a porch which enabled work to continue even when it rained. Reconstruction in relief, from the Museum of Roman Civilisation, Rome.

The country villa at Boscoreale combined under one roof the home of the owner and that of the familia rustica which was on the ground floor. It was a building 130 feet long by 65 feet wide. Three quarters of its area was used for the preparation of wine and oil. (Museum of Roman Civilisation, Rome).

and unprovoked assault or tried to escape, they were punished by being made to work during the day with their feet fettered, and by being chained in a cell during the night.

Cato tells us the rations which were allowed for these workers: four measures of wheat a month during the winter (approximately two pounds a day), about four and a half measures a month during the summer when there was more work to be done in the fields and the days were longer; only three measures (three pecks) all the year round for those who were not doing hard physical work (the book-keeper, the overseers, the shepherds and the bailiff's wife). The slaves themselves had to grind their grain or make their own porridge; as for the chained-up slaves, they were given bread, not grain: « four *librae* a day (about three pounds) and five when they began to work in the vineyard; this ration remains in force until the beginning of the fig season (about the middle of August), then it goes back to four *librae*. As an accompaniment to the bread, you will keep ready windfall or old olives, from which you would not expect to get much oil; you will give pickling brine and vinegar to eat them with. As for oil, give each one a gallon a month, and a bushel of salt per head per year will be enough ».

The rules for drink were as follows: during the three months following the wine-harvest, second-quality wine for all in unlimited quantities; from the beginning of December, half a pint per day per worker, a pint from the month of March, and a pint and a half during the summer; special rations were laid down for the feasts of *Saturnalia* and *Compitalia*.

As for clothes, Cato says: « You will give a three and a half foot tunic and a cloak to each man every second year; when you hand out a cloak or a tunic you must take back the worn garment to be made into waistcoats (quilted and stuffed with rags); once every two years you will need to give them new boots ».

When the master was in residence, the *villica* concerned herself with his food, which was prepared to a much higher standard than that of her usual cooking, though in the country simple food was quite acceptable. Cato gives us this recipe for the preparation of the *libum*, a cake to be offered to the gods on feast days, and then to be eaten by the worshippers after the ceremony: — « Carefully pound one and a half pounds of cheese in a mortar, add three-quarters of a pound of coarse flour, and, if you want to have a lighter cake, six ounces of pure wheaten flour; add one egg and knead this paste for a long time; shape it into a loaf

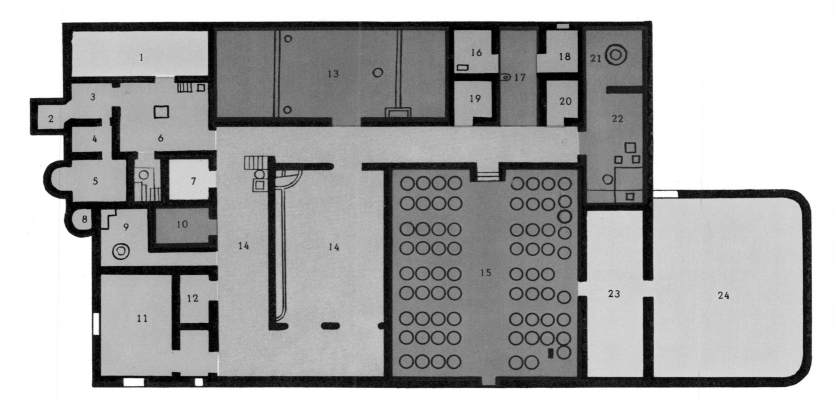

Plan of the Boscoreale Villa: 1. *Cowshed;* 2, 3, 4, 5. *Bathrooms and Lavatories;* 6. *Kitchen;* 7. *Tool Store;* 8. *Oven;* 9. *Room for bread making with millstone;* 10. *Bedroom;* 11. *Dining-room;* 12. *Bedroom;* 13. *Room for pressing grapes, with places for the press, receptacles and storage tank;* 14. *Courtyard with storage tank;* 15. *Wine jars;* 16. *Press;* 17. *Hand mill;* 18, 19, 20. *Bedrooms;* 21. *Press;* 22. *Oil-crusher;* 23. *Hay loft;* 24. *Threshing floor.*

and place it on some leaves and cook it in a slow oven ».
Placenta was also a cheese cake sweetened with honey.
Amongst other popular cakes were rolls (*globi*) and
cheese rings made with spelt flour and sometimes
stuffed with poppy seeds.

THE COUNTRY HOUSE

Archaeological excavation has provided us with
more information than literary documents on the
subject of what the Roman country houses were like.
These proved to be of several kinds: the farmer's hut,
a single room in which the whole family lived, with
a hearth and an altar to the Penates, and a tank in the
courtyard to catch rainwater; the house proper, the
farmhouse as we should call it, with a few extra rooms
or small cells against the wall surrounding the courtyard,
used either as a lodging for the slaves or as sheds for
the cattle; and the *villa rustica* of high quality, in which
the original single room had been transformed into
the *tablinum* or living-room, while the remainder of

the house was considerably enlarged by the addition
of a number of rooms both for household use and for
stores, and the courtyard had the addition of a walled
garden on the side opposite the *tablinum*.

This was the kind of rural house which had evolved
by the end of the first century B.C. and of which there
are several examples to be found in the excavations at
Pompeii. The best known and best preserved is that
at Boscoreale, near Pompeii, unearthed at the end of
the nineteenth century.

The villa has two courtyards (*cortes*), one inside,
the other outside: the pool (*piscina*) in the interior
courtyard was used for watering the cattle, the one
outside for various farming purposes (the soaking of
hides, or cattle-fodder, etc.). Around the inside courtyard
were stone huts for the slaves and for the beasts; in
front, the sleeping quarters; behind, the dining-room
and the kitchen separated by rooms used as bathrooms
and lavatories; backing on to the kitchen there was a
cowshed. It is important to remember that in the farmhouse the kitchen was not, as in a town house, a room
solely set aside for the preparation of food, it was

also a meeting place and a workroom. Besides the stalls for the oxen (*bubilia*) and stables for the horses (*equilia*), the henhouse was also placed near the kitchen, if possible, as it was thought that the smoke was good for the birds.

On the side of the courtyard facing the entrance, a doorway opened on to a passage connecting the rooms already mentioned with those on the righthand side of the courtyard; these were all for the storing and care of farm implements and machinery. Opposite this door was the wine-pressing room; to the right along the same passageway, the great cellar (*cella vinaria*), with all the equipment for storing the wine in special earthenware jars, and for the fermentation of the must. Further on in the same direction, was the barn (*nubilarium*, so called because the grain was placed there temporarily in case of storms); this room opened on to the threshing floor, placed outside the farm buildings proper but enclosed by walls. Opposite the cellar and the grain-store there were various other places for grinding grain, crushing olives, and then other sleeping quarters for the farm-workers.

In all, the area of the villa was a rectangle 130 feet long by 65 feet wide; of this space three-quarters was set aside for workshops and stores, and a quarter for living-rooms and service quarters.

The layout of the villa at Boscoreale also reveals the existence of a staircase which led from the kitchen to an upper floor of which nothing is left, but where, one may suppose, the owner's quarters were situated. Clearly the rich landed gentry lived for at least part of the time in their spacious farmhouses, where the best rooms were kept for them.

THE SUBURBAN VILLA

Among the rich Romans, the custom soon sprang up of building country houses as spacious as they were sumptuous, with all the conveniences which they had hitherto expected only in the town, decorated with precious marble and art treasures and well furnished with books. So it was that the « country seat », *villa suburbana*, came into being, sometimes built on the estate but quite separate from the *villa rustica* and

Grain mill: it was worked by two men. (Museum of Roman Civilisation, Rome).

often a considerable way from it. There the owners lived the same life as they would in the town, not bothering at all about the business of farming which they had left in the hands of the *villicus*. This was the more common when the country house was some distance from the farm, as in fashionable holiday centres such as the banks of the Tiber, the countryside of the Romagna, Ostia, Tivoli, Baiae, and various places in Campania. Every person of importance in Caesar's time owned a villa of this sort; Cicero had nine; the villas of the orator Hortensius, Seneca and Pliny the Younger were famous, as were the splendid imperial villas, such as Hadrian's.

But there was nothing rustic about these villas; in reality they were more like luxurious palaces, set in splendid gardens and parks of positively oriental magnificence. Certainly the taste and style for these gardens came from the East; it was after his victorious return in 63 B.C. from the war against Mithridates that Lucullus established the first great park surrounding his palace, on the spot occupied today by the lawns and avenues of the Pincio (*Horti Luculliani*).

Cato's agricultural handbook is just as rich a source of information on the farmer's equipment. Here is the text of Chapter X: « A field of 250 acres planted with olives, needs a bailiff, his wife, five workers, three labourers, a labourer's mate, a donkey-boy and a shepherd; in all thirteen people. Also, three yokes of oxen, three pack-donkeys with baskets for carrying manure, another donkey for turning the millstone, five ewes, three sets of implements for oil-making, a good-sized cauldron with lid, three iron hooks, three earthenware jars for water, two pots, a small lidded cauldron, two earthenware jars for oil, a pail for water, a pitcher, a tub, a preserving pan, a frying-pan, a bowl; then, three large waggons, six ploughs with their ploughshares, three yokes with their straps, and six sets of harness for the oxen, a harrow, three handcarts for manure and six baskets for the same purpose; three donkey pack-saddles; as for iron tools, eight forks, eight hoes, four shovels, five pick-axes, two four-pronged rakes, three large scythes and six sickles, five billhooks for pruning, three axes, three iron bars, two pairs of tongs, a scraper and two pokers; a hundred jars for oil, two buckets, ten jars for the inferior wine, ten for the marc (the refuse from the pressed grapes), ten for good wine, ten for wheat, a trough for the cattle-fodder and so forth ». The list continues for several chapters. With such a supply of tools, and with plenty of storage space the farmer need not have been daunted by the wide range of tasks which the changing seasons provided.

Foremost amongst these tasks, according to an expert such as Cato, were tilling and fertilizing the land. Tilling was done several times over, according to the needs of the piece of ground in question. At the same time the clods of earth were broken down, a process known as *pastinatio* from the name of the tool *pastinum*, a two-pronged hook or mattock used to set the seeds or plants and to break up the soil.

When the ground was prepared and the seed was sown, the next stage was the removal of the weeds which grew up among the young plants; for this job a tool was used which naturally enough was called a weeding-hoe (*sarculum*).

Then the moment for reaping the benefit of this hard work arrived. First came the wheat harvest (*messio*) at the beginning of the summer, then the

Above: *farm implements:* Below: *a* mola asinaria, *i.e., a grain mill worked by a donkey. (Museum of Roman Civilisation, Rome).*

116

threshing (*tritura*) carried out on the threshing-floor (*area*) carefully built and ready since the middle of June. The grain was then sifted with a *ventilabrum*, or winnowed with a *vannus*; then it was stored in the granaries (*horrea* or *granaria*).

For all these jobs the Romans had a variety of tools of various shapes and applications; there were simple ploughs and ploughs with earthboards (*aurita*), hoes with two sharp edges (*bidentes*), axes (*dolabrae*), scythes of various kinds for pruning (*putatoriae*), for harvesting (*messoriae*), for mowing (*fenariae*), hoes (*ligones*), small hooks for cutting the vine (*lupi*), dibbers for pushing the plants into the ground (*acus*), billhooks for clearing brushwood (*runcones*), axes and pickaxes of all kinds. A writer of the fourth century A.D., Palladius Rutilius Emilianus, describes a two-wheeled farm machine, with a set of prongs underneath it which was drawn by a pair of oxen and used for harvesting in Gaul, where there were a great many level plains. This was a piece of agricultural machinery which some modern authors consider to have been the first real harvester. For threshing, the *tribulum* was used, a wooden plank in which iron or flint spikes were embedded. Mounted on wheels and drawn by oxen, it passed back and forwards over the wheat spread out on the threshing floor.

Olives were processed by first crushing them in an oil-press (*trapetum*); the oil was extracted by means of another press (*prelum*), which was also used for grapes.

Pompeii, oven and mill of the bakery.

Until the last years of the Republic, the country's main crop was not wheat, but spelt and barley, but from 400 B.C. onwards bread began to be made of wheat. From early times the Latin farmers had used the fallow land system: a field which one year grew wheat was left idle the next. Much later the Romans, who probably used Carthaginian rather than Greek methods, practised the method of three-yearly rotation. The land grew wheat for two years running, and was left fallow the third year. But during that third year the farmer sowed such vegetables as beans or fodder-plants, whose manuring qualities were well known, and these were often turned over, or ploughed in. Taking into account the rather poor nature of the Roman soil, the necessarily light treatment which was possible with such a rudimentary plough, and the lack of proper manure, it is estimated that the Romans could hardly have obtained more than one and a half quarters of wheat per acre.

The small landowners of Latium really excelled in the production of cereals and vegetables; without a proper system of barter they had to obtain all the food needed from their own ground; however, they did not ignore the « princely » crops, and of these the most important were the vine and the olive tree. There is no doubt that the use of wine in Latium goes back to the earliest days. It is clear that the Indo-Europeans found vines on their arrival on the two Mediterranean peninsulas, as is proved by the very name wine which stems from a Graeco-Latin root of Mediterranean origin. It is clear that vines have been grown in the region of Rome from the very earliest times since the use of wine was known there, but it was drunk only within very strict limits, since this beverage was considered one of the sacrificial liquids, together with milk, blood and water. The feast of the *Vinalia* belongs to the earliest Roman culture, it was the duty of the *flamen dialis* (the priest in charge of the worship of Jupiter) to dedicate and inaugurate the wine harvest. A law attributed to Numa, the second King of Rome, about 715-673 B.C., forbade the offering to the gods of a libation produced from an unpruned vine. Women were forbidden to drink wine under pain of death, and some historians think that this prohibition was due to the fact that wine was thought to be akin to blood and that a woman drinking it would be

introducing a foreign blood into her body and therefore would have committed adultery. For a long time the Romans regarded wine as a purely sacrificial drink.

Viticulture spread rapidly, and the greatest care was lavished upon it, starting with the choice of suitable terrain. In the *Georgics*, Virgil recommends hillsides, though according to Columella vineyards on the plains could produce abundant wine, whatever the soil was like.

As for the olive, the early writers agree that it was not grown in Italy before the time of Tarquin the Elder (616-579 B.C.). However correct this information may be, and possibly it is a trifle too precise to be strictly accurate, it is certain that olive-culture was introduced into Italy only fairly late and that it was brought there by way of the cities of Greece.

The first fruit tree mentioned in the old legends is the fig tree; one story tells how Aruntus, a rich Etruscan merchant from Chiusi, sought to avenge an insult from one of his fellow citizens, the proud Lauchme, by crossing the Alps and tempting the Gauls to invade Italy. He showed them some items of the peninsula's produce, which were unknown in their country, and of which he carried an abundant supply; these were wine, oil and figs. This legend goes right back to the fifth century B.C.

As examples of trees grown especially for their wood, and used in the making and maintenance of implements, Virgil mentions willows, which he says should be planted along water-courses, alders which like swampy ground, flowering ashes which grow best on rocky mountains, and myrtles which are most suited to the sea-shore.

The flourishing agriculture of the first century B.C. began to suffer more and more competition from the eastern provinces and particularly from Gaul and Africa, where certain crops, originally natives of Italy, had been introduced and had given results exceeding all expectations. During the Julio-Claudian and Flavian dynasties (A.D. 14-96), wine from Gaul and olive oil from Africa were forcing home products into second place, a situation reminiscent of earlier times when the farmers of Latium had been forced to give up growing cereals in the face of competition from the South and Sicily.

The Italian farmers answered by accepting this defeat and changing their crops in order to adapt them to the demands of a market growing ever richer and more exacting. Fruit trees now absorbed the agriculturalist's attention and capital. The pear, the apple and the pomegranate were known in Italy before the Punic wars, but on the other hand citrus fruits (with the exception of the lemon itself) were unknown in the ancient world. The cherry was introduced by Lucullus, returning from Anatolia and his war against Mithridates in about 74 B.C. Fruit of every kind and of the highest quality began to make its appearance on the banqueting tables of the rich Romans, and Varro and Virgil never tired of encouraging the farmers in their endeavours, for trade in fruit guaranteed a healthy profit, and on the Via Sacra constituted a commodity which was paid for in gold.

This tendency to substitute luxury goods for the ordinary crop, forced on farmers by competition from top-quality produce coming in from the provinces, also made itself felt in the realm of stockbreeding.

Here, Varro counsels the raising of luxury fowl and game, geese and hens, pheasants and peacocks, cranes, marmots, wild boars and other kinds of wild animals. The income obtained from fish-farming must not be forgotten, a speciality of the fish-ponds of villas which were built beside the sea.

One might well ask who was responsible for the introduction and development in the western provinces of the Empire of those very crops which had been the prerogative of Greek and Italian growers. The answer is: the Italians themselves, and in particular those Roman senators who were forbidden to enter trade and who were forced on that account to invest their capital in practical farming. Once they had availed themselves of the most fertile ground in Italy itself, they passed on to buying land and property in the provinces, and soon found themselves in possession of enormous estates in Sicily, Africa, Gaul and even Greece and Asia. From these estates came the flood of merchandise (cereals, wines and oil) which banished home produce from the markets of the peninsula.

Born as countryfolk in the little villages of Latium, the Romans remained countryfolk right up to the decline of their Empire.

Above: *oil-press*. Below: *wine-press reconstructed from the remains found in the Villa of the Mysteries in Pompeii. (Museum of Roman Civilisation, Rome).*

THE ROMAN FARMER AT WORK

In spring when the snow began to melt on the mountain tops and the first soft breezes thawed the earth, the farmer yoked his oxen to the plough, safe in the knowledge that this field, fallow for two winters and two summers, would fill his granary anew with grain.

Before ploughing a new field, he looked first at the influence of the wind and the climate on the ground; he studied its aspect and he considered what crops he had previously grown there. Each piece of land is disposed by its very nature towards one particular crop: cereals, vines, wood or pastureland.

The soil was turned over during the first months of the year, and left to bake in the summer sunshine. The least rich ground was set aside for pastureland, and this was worked only lightly, but he made certain that these pastures were well away from his wheatfields lest the grass should take away the nourishment from the grain, and the sandy soil absorb the all-too-rare moisture.

When the stars changed, he sowed the seed, from which he had earlier removed the tares, lupins and other incidental seeds he wanted to avoid. The farmer knew that flax, oats and poppies impoverished the soil, and therefore he rotated the crops, and between whiles enriched the earth with plenty of manure or a sprinkling of ashes. At the end of the summer the stubble crackled and smoked in fields not long since golden with ripe crops. In this way, thought the farmer, the earth re-charged itself with unseen energy, or else the fire destroyed the impurities by steaming off the excess moisture; or perhaps the heat opened tiny channels through which the nutritive sap could rise to the new shoots. Or on the other hand perhaps in hardening the earth, the fire closed certain fissures and thus protected the plants from the rain, sun and wind.

Sometimes the farmer broke up the clods of earth with a rake and then spread willow hurdles on the ground in the hope that heaven would grant them mild winters and wet summers.

Other farmers made furrows in the ground after sowing, and collected water in them to irrigate their fields in case of drought. Others thinned the wheat by nipping off the extra shoots whilst they were still in bud so as to avoid stalks so fragile that they bowed down under the weight of the ears.

Others drained their fields of stagnant water, especially when a nearby river had overflowed its banks.

But none of this hard work could guarantee the harvest. The farmer had to protect his crops from wild geese, sparrows, cranes and weeds. In spite of all his care, mildew attacked the stalks, thistles sprouted on every side and with them a whole wild forest of brambles, burdocks, and wild oats. He had to rake over the ground and scare away the birds by banging drums and shaking sheets of copper. He had to avoid too much shade and then pray for rain...

During his leisure hours the farmer had to attend to his tools, his massive oak plough, the slow and heavy waggons, the flails, the rakes, the sledges, the willow baskets, the arbutus hurdles for flattening the clods of earth and protecting the seeds, the sieves... To make a new plough, he chose a fine elm from the wood for the back part of the plough where it formed the ploughshare and the beam; this had to be taken from the tree near the root so as to have the maximum strength. The ploughshare was fitted in the middle of the double mold-board. The beam was made of a thin lime tree and the stilt of beech. To ensure that the wood was well seasoned the farmer hung the various parts of the plough in the smoke in front of the hearth, and if the heat cracked them, it was because the wood was not good enough.

The threshing floor also claimed his attention. He started by turning it over and lining it with fresh clay to stop the grass growing on it, to avoid cracks in the floor during the summer, and to prevent the rats, moles and toads from digging their holes right through it. Finally he flattened it with a great roller.

And lastly the bees. These providers of honey also needed regular and prompt attention, especially when a swarm was imminent (and a hundred signs warned the observant farmer of this event). Especial care was needed to stop the black cloud of the swarm from going too far from the hive and getting lost. The farmer would spread some crushed balm at the foot of a tree and, by clashing cymbals, attract the fugitives to it. Once he had recaptured them he had to encourage them by providing a comfortable hive, made of bark or of a trellis of rushes, coated with clay on the outside, so that the honey should not freeze in the winter or run out in the summer.

When the rain kept him indoors, the farmer had a thousand and one small jobs to do; sharpen the blunted blade of the ploughshare, fashion wooden bowls, brand the cattle, count the heaps of grain, sharpen stakes and forks, prepare willow ties for the vines, make plaited baskets and grind the wheat.

And when the spring came at last, the farmer watched the blossoming of the almond tree and drew his portents from it; if the flowers were more numerous than the leaves, the wheat would be plentiful and the threshing yield much grain; if the contrary held good, then the harvest would be poor, and produce little but straw.

The best thing of all was to know the star of Arcturus and the time of the Goat and of the Serpent, like people coming home across a stormy sea.

(source: Virgil, Georgics)

CRAFTS AND INDUSTRY

The Roman world was a complete whole, both politically and commercially, without barriers or protective tariffs. Merchandise of every kind travelled along the great roads which linked the capital to the most distant province, or in the ships which carried freight along the sailing routes from Roman ports. From the East came precious silks, from Greece crafts of great skill, fine marbles, spices, metals and grain.

The unified political organisation of the Empire protected the merchants of Asia, Spain and Gaul in their enterprises, just as it assured the entrepreneurs in every Roman province and the craftsmen of the Urbs of their supply of raw materials.

Separate economies did not exist: there was just « the economy ». Had not Cicero said: « The credit of the Roman money market is intimately bound up with the prosperity of Asia. If there were a major disaster in Asia, our financial market would be gravely compromised! ».

The rigid structure of Roman industry depended mainly on specialised slave labour. Such an organisation prevented the formation of a strong class of free workers, but right down the centuries the citizen-artisan had limitations neither to his enterprise nor to his markets.

As Rome grew and asserted its influence over the Italian peoples, it enjoyed an increasing civil power and finally created the Roman Empire. The economy of Rome, at one time wholly rural, began to modify itself in keeping with the general commercial and industrial developments.

It is important to remember that in this context the word « industrial » has no connection with modern industrial organisation, in which the machine reigns and man has an ever more marginal role. Ancient industry was quite different both in its development and its system of production. It was man's kingdom, even when that man was a slave, for it gave him the opportunity of expressing his own capabilities, and each article carried the imprint of his skill. Hence in the ancient world it is almost impossible to draw the line between industry and crafts, because even when industry was well organised with a technical background, and a proper division of labour, it was still based on the work of skilled craftsmen. If a dividing line must be drawn, then strictly speaking, craftsmen did their own work in their own workshops, possibly with the assistance of apprentices. Industry deployed greater numbers. In the first centuries of the Republic Roman life was based on agriculture with each member of the family attending to his own farming tasks. After the victorious campaign over Carthage and the countries to the East (after 100 B.C.) members of the senatorial class and the *equites* (the « knights » or second rank of the nobility) became landed proprietors and the State itself became richer. Slaves and money kept flowing into the hands of the Roman citizen, both in the provinces and in the capital. A network of commercial works joined one end of the Roman world to the other, and industrial activity grew.

Industrial life in Rome cannot be separated from that in the rest of Italy, if only because in the earliest days Rome was certainly inferior in this field to some of the Etruscan and Greek centres in the peninsula, and also because Rome having conquered Italy con-

Silver drinking horn decorated with horizontal gold bands and bas-reliefs. (Part of the Hildesheim Treasure, Berlin Museum).

Large urn exquisitely decorated, belonging to the Hildesheim Treasure, Berlin Museum.

tributed to Italian production by becoming the chief market for Italian goods.

The whole of Latium had been an agricultural area at first, but the influence of surrounding settlements, especially Etruscan and Greek settlements in the south of the peninsula, and the arrival of their artisans in the capital encouraged the imitation and practice of certain of their crafts. However, even after it had become a metropolis, Rome never obstructed or suppressed any local industry. The ever-growing population of the capital absorbed everything that was produced and very soon it was essential to import more.

ROMAN CRAFTSMEN

By far the most highly developed industry in Rome was the building industry. This was due to the continual expansion of the city and the constant demand for public buildings, palaces, baths, temples, basilicas and gardens. Gradually large organised building enterprises sprang up, employing thousands of slaves and free men.

Alongside the architects (*architecti*), masons (*structores*) and carpenters (*fabri tignarii*) who fostered the building traditions handed down from generation to generation, from skilled worker (*magistri*) to apprentice, many allied industries also flourished, all dependent on the main building industry. All had their corporations, from the masterbuilders and the demolition contractors (*subrutores*) to the various woodworking, iron-working and hydraulic undertakings.

Other sectors of production developed with the expansion of the Urbs: the entire food industry grew amazingly: the small fruit shops and grain stores, the vegetable traders, the larger wine and fish enterprises.

The luxurious living of rich Romans and the vast overall increase in population likewise gave impetus to the clothing trade. Workshops of *lintarii* produced linen cloth which the *vestiarii* and the *sagarii* (makers

This little silver jug decorated with gold plane leaves also belongs to the treasure unearthed at Hildesheim. (Berlin Museum).

of garments and cloaks) then made up. Specialised shoemakers appeared (*sutores* and *caligarii* for men, *fabri solearii* for women's shoes).

Rome's great speciality was the manufacture of de luxe goods bought by the rich middle class and the court. The capital attracted all the expert craftsmen, mainly Greek in origin, who produced goblets and jewels of exquisite workmanship and of precious metals. Mirror makers (*specularii*), ring-makers (*anularii*), workers in ivory (*eborarii*), and goldsmiths (*aurifices*) made of Rome the capital of luxuries.

ITALIC CRAFTS

The whole peninsula was rich in industry: southern Italy had a highly developed ceramic industry whose products have been found in many different places. The local kilns and potteries of Sicily, Apulia, Lucania and Campania flooded the markets. Taranto became a sort of clearing house for these pots. The chief ceramic centres in Campania were Cales, Capua and Pozzuoli.

Arezzo's ceramics had an enormous market, spreading from central Italy to the outer imperial provinces. The Aretine industry organised what amounted to mass production, for it used moulds and turn-tables.

Blacksmith's shop.
Fragment of a stele *in the Archaeological Museum at Aquileia.*

Glass was made at Pozzuoli and in Aquileia: the clear and green glass found at Pompeii is famous: probably it was made with sand from the Volturno River which Pliny recommended for the glass industry. Besides glass, amber (*sucinum*) imported from Germany was worked in Aquileia. From it were made little boxes, flasks and mirrors, as well as those little amber balls Roman matrons used to carry about just to smell their delicate fragrance, and feel their smoothness.

Metal, bronze and silver vases from Capua have been found as far away as the Black Sea, as have the small terracotta lamps which were made in Modena. Campania, like Etruria, was one of the richest Italian provinces; it had prosperous wine and oil produce and the oil was essential for the perfumery industry. In the north, Aquileia became famous not only for the production we have mentioned, but for vases,

The fuller's shop did both dyeing and washing. Here cloth and garments were dyed, washed, ironed and renovated by various processes. In the scenes here depicted, from the Fuller's House in Pompeii, where they are painted on a column, one can see the various stages: top left, a worker is busy on a piece of cloth, while another arrives with a pail and a curious frame; below, the washhouse. Since there was no soap, the Roman used to put the clothes in a tub filled with water and some scouring mixture and then tread on them. Top right, a clothes press. Below, examination of the dyed and washed materials. (National Archaeological Museum, Naples).

ironmongery and jewellery. The island of Elba and the adjoining mainland formed the main mining centre for the iron industry from Etruscan times onward; Ostia, Genoa and Ravenna were major ship-building centres.

INDUSTRY IN THE PROVINCES

The peace and unity brought by Rome favoured commercial relations in the provinces and led to the development of local industry.

In the eastern Mediterranean, the province of Egypt was of the greatest importance because of the large production in Alexandria of papyrus, ivory objects, glass finely worked on a turn-table, silver, scent and fine linen cloth, which were exported all over the known world.

In the East, Syria was famous for blown glass, linen and metal work. Dyed wool used for carpets and cloth made a flourishing industry in Asia Minor with exports going as far as Russia and India.

Gaul, like Italy, developed its industries and soon outpaced the latter; it was so well provided with metals, forests and river communications that it quickly came into the first rank of western provinces and captured most of Italy's markets. Various objects became familiar in the imperial markets — high relief terracottas (*vasa sigillata*), glass manufactured on the Rhine, woollen cloth for everyday use, shoes, soap, kitchen utensils and bronze pins.

SLAVES AND INDUSTRY

Work in the small workshops and especially in the larger quasi-factories was largely carried out by slaves. Roman nobles looked on manual labour as unworthy

Examples of Roman glass: square cinerary urns. (Museum of Roman Civilisation, Rome).

of free men; even retail trading was considered unsuitable. Cicero wrote that the work of those who are paid by the day is indecorous and vulgar because it is the body and not the mind which is thereby paid for its employment: for him all craftsmen performed menial work. No occupation was more worthy than the owning of land; none, according to him, gave greater pleasure or was more suitable to the free man.

In the last centuries of the Republic, industry was entirely based on slave labour; under the Empire, however, free men gradually began to replace slaves. The massive arrival of slaves after Rome's conquests and capture of prisoners undoubtedly encouraged industry. It was already standard practice to employ slaves in agricultural enterprises, and their labour constituted the very basis of a well-run farm. They worked largely on the *latifundia* under the management of *magistri operum* and the ultimate direction of a trusted bailiff of the big landed proprietor. In these extensive properties slave labourers, slave shepherds, slave game- and fishing-attendants, slave gardeners and so on, were engaged, often in their thousands.

Quite as numerous, though often in smaller units, were the slaves engaged as manual labourers in urban industries. There was no automation, and each slave was allotted work according to his capacity. Often a slave would reach such a high degree of specialisation in his work that he would become irreplaceable. Yet by the terms of his engagement he could not hope for any improvement in position. These slaves were divided into groups: *classes* and *decuriae* under a master technician who formed a workshop, a kind of self-contained work unit, which the Greeks called *ergasteria*. Owners of these workshops were often freed men.

Under the Empire new corporations (*collegia*) replaced the old *collegia opificum*, the nine bodies of free artisans said to have been formed by King Numa. Slaves and freed men belonged to the new *collegia* under state control. The state had nationalised various undertakings, notably the mint in which the *monetarii* slaves worked, most of the arms enterprises and the mines.

It is true to say that all the mines still in active operation (except the coal mines, for coal was not used in the ancient world) were familiar to the Romans. Work in the mines, where slaves and criminals condemned to this type of labour worked side by side, was terribly hard. It went on day and night without interruption, thanks to relays of men working in shifts by the dim light of lamps in suffocating heat and under military guard, in dangerous and narrow passages, often on hands and knees, or crawling along on their stomachs. A brand mark made with a red-hot iron forever marked any man who tried to escape.

Since in Roman law a slave was not a man but a thing — *res* — he could become the subject of financial speculation. Thus one might buy up a group of slaves skilled in one type of work, maintain them and then hire them out to the highest bidder. Titus Pomponius Atticus, the friend and publisher of Cicero, was

Various craft and agricultural tools. (Museum of Roman Civilisation, Rome).

famed for this kind of operation. Crassus, the financier who was *triumvir* in 60 B.C., owned 500 building slaves with whom he built houses which he then sold at a high price.

The relationship between slave and master, even in industry, was not invariably ruled by profiteering. Frequently slaves were amicably treated, became friends and even confidants. Through their devoted labours many gained the affection of their masters, and that achieved, their liberty was not far away.

THE ARTISANS

The corporations of free artisans, the *collegia opificum*, to which belonged carpenters, flute makers, jewellers, dyers, leather workers, tanners, coppersmiths and potters, were of great antiquity. Besides these eight there was a ninth which at first gathered in all the remaining workers but later split up into single *collegia*. Many of these are recorded in inscriptions. They met in *curiae* and *scholae* and enjoyed special privileges.

There were also the *collegia tenuiorum* which slaves could join with the master's permission, and which, among other things, aimed at gathering funds for their special religious observances and for the funeral rites of members.

The corporations bound the artisan so tightly that he could not change his trade and his sons had to follow it also. Sometimes the daughters were allowed to marry only another member of the *collegium*.

Foreign artisans were always dangerous competitors for these corporations, especially when as freed men they would open independent workshops, or most of all when they went around touting for orders and commissions in rich people's homes, which was always immensely remunerative.

The evidence of the workshops and shops of Pompeii, of the bas-reliefs on tombstones and of surviving tools enlightens us on procedures in the various trades.

Several sarcophagi show the smithy. Usually the craftsman is shown standing or seated, hammering a piece of iron on the anvil, and holding it with tongs. Often two or three figures stand around, probably apprentices or boys. In one such bas-relief a boy is blowing the fire with a pair of bellows, whilst holding a shield to protect himself from the heat.

All around the work goes on with the forging and the finishing of articles. On the walls hang articles just completed and instruments of the trade.

The art of the potter was practised everywhere, and many workshops have been found. Jars were shaped on a potter's turntable; the very big ones had their feet, necks and handles added later. They were glazed and put in ovens which had two compartments, one below for heating and one above for baking, with perforated tiles between.

One bas-relief shows a foundry, where several boys attend to the furnace over which a crucible hangs, whilst others polish a bronze with a scraper under the eyes of the master and the artist who made the statue.

Rome's love of luxury gave rise to a whole sector of craftsmen skilled in working objects in gold, silver, ivory and other precious raw materials; they ranged from modellers (*figuratores*), turners (*tritores*), chisellers (*caelatores*) and gilders (*inauratores*) down to the craftsmen who were really true artists able to create bas-reliefs in silver leaf and fix them on to vases (*crustarii*). Nor should one forget the *aurifices* and the *eborarii* who

Above, *gold chain in the Museum of Villa Giulia, Rome.* Below, *other jewellery made by Roman craftsmen.*

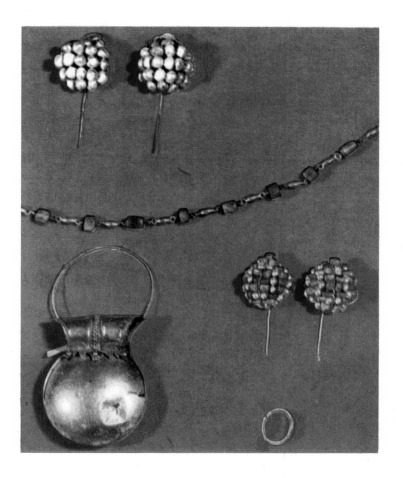

128

knew how to work gold and ivory as skilfully as craftsmen in another field knew how to embroider cloth (*plumarii*) or weave silk (*sericarii*).

A real art, considering the age and the means available, was that of the dyers (*tinctores, infectores*), who were specially skilled in the use of purple, which they produced in a great variety of shades by diluting it with water and urine. Closely associated with them were the fullers (*fullones*), who washed the cloth by stamping on it with their feet in water, and then stretched it out by a variety of processes.

Many other examples could be given of these hard-working Roman citizens who daily performed their humble tasks as an honest way of earning their living.

SMALL HOME INDUSTRIES

Modern industry has taken over modern homes in that there is hardly any object, activity or domestic service for which we do not immediately have some industrial product. Not so in ancient Rome where everything had to be done at home by means instantly to hand. Poor families did without many of the useful objects which specialised craftsmen and the bigger industries could supply to those who could afford them. The poor provided their essential instruments as best they could and never enjoyed the advantages which small industry could provide for the rich. The latter indeed made their slaves do many of the things which today are taken over by the state and by public services or by extra-domestic industries and automation.

Reference has been made earlier to home teaching which for a long time was entrusted either to the father of the family or to a literate slave: similarly each house had to provide for its own letter deliveries, and for this, the rich had certain slaves called *tabellarii* and *cursores*. Lighting was another home-provided service and special slaves (*servi praelucentes*) attended to this.

In rich families specialised slaves such as hairdressers (*ornatores*), barbers (*tonsores*), cooks (*coci*), pastrymen (*libarii*) and sweet makers (*dulciarii*) made the household practically self-contained. In country villas the domestic slaves would do the leather work and even bake bricks. The simpler clothes were mostly woven and sewn in the home. In Rome as in Greece, the chief occupation of a woman was spinning and weaving, so that she, too, contributed to home industry in her fashion.

A product of Italic craftsmanship. Silver mirror found in Pompeii. (National Archaeological Museum, Naples).

A heavy gold earring from the Museum of Villa Giulia in Rome.

129

CRAFTSMEN AT WORK

The small workshops of the artisans sprang up among the old shops and taverns. The heavy air of the Suburra, the slum area of Rome, came on the wings of the wind to the very threshold of the coppersmith, the tanner, the slippermaker, even to the superior establishments of the *pavimentarii*, the mosaicists and the *vitrarii*, all eager to serve the great houses and therefore somewhat haughty about the cobbler who served the modest folk in the suburbs.

The wind also carried the cry of the wine vendor travelling from street to street with a cart precariously balancing a load of *amphorae*. At his passing all the small shopkeepers, the bean-seller, the fishmonger, the pastry shopkeeper, the baker, the greengrocer and the pharmacist, came to the door, and taking advantage of a quiet moment typical of the early afternoon, stayed to comment on the day's events, or leant out of the workshops to watch and gossip.

Apprentices bent low over their work, but as soon as the master's back was turned they too began to gossip and idle the time away, watching the passers-by.

From the coppersmith's old shop you could hear hammering on pitchers, pans and pots, like the sound of the priests' cymbals during the ceremonies in honour of the Great Mother Rhea. This unmelodious but exciting noise went on almost throughout the day, filling the whole of the road with a kind of festive atmosphere so that the movements of passers-by took on a rhythm, almost like that of a dance.

A little further on in the glass workshop, the master craftsman was arranging in panels the thick glass and mica which were to decorate a new house on the Esquiline. The red eye of the ovens glowed in the rear of the shop where a lad, half-naked and glistening with sweat, worked the bellows.

From dawn to dusk, while the sun lasted, the foundations of those old houses trembled and echoed with the throb of wooden machines and the hammering of men. The potter made his wheel turn and his hands, grey with clay, made a pitcher come to life, made it swell and, as by a miracle, take shape. But sometimes, at the critical moment, he would leave everything with a curse to pursue a boy who had dropped a precious Arezzo vase, all decorated with silver leaf — a model which might have sold well to some rich client.

What a racket in the carpenter's shop! Now that they are building behind the temple of Fortune he has won the tender for supplying beams, stairs and doors for four, five or six luxury villas. His boys have trouble managing the planks high up there. Hammering and the monotonous rasping sound of the saw are irritating to the ears.

Odd people, these artisans. They speak their own language and are so used to the trade that if they had to leave it, they would die of despair. This man's father was a bed-maker, so was his father's father and his grandfather's grandfather, in the same way that the wife of the dyer on the corner there is the daughter of a dyer who used to have a shop close by here.

From time immemorial they have practised these trades and belonged to the eight guilds of Numa Pompilius: carpenters, goldsmiths, dyers, flute-makers, cobblers, tanners, coppersmiths and potters. Gradually many more trades have appeared. The needs of the Romans have grown to a quite exaggerated degree, along with their wealth.

Two hundred years ago, whoever would have dreamt of covering his floors with tiles or mosaic, and his ceiling and walls with stucco? And who could have imagined mica in windows? In the autumn, when the first windy rains came to the city, up went the shutters and goodnight until the spring. The lamp was on full-time duty.

The fine work they do with glass today must be seen to be believed. Near the Forum in the house of a very rich man who has building interests in Gaul, there's a pavement just been put down consisting of hundreds of embedded pieces of glass, marble, onyx and gold.

The goldsmiths have chosen the quietest streets, and most of them are Greeks. There you hear them hammering, magically making the most incredibly beautiful and costly things. Anyone who wants such beauty must pay for it. Rome is famous for its goldsmiths. The Greeks have brought the work to a fine art and make marvellous chalices and jewels. They engrave the metal with fish which seem to swim when you fill the cup with water, or birds which seem alive, or flowers lacking only the scent.

In the Argiletum district next to the cobblers, shops are the bookshops. All day long slaves copy verses of the poets and pages of the historians and the philosophers on to thin vellum and great sheets of papyrus. This is a very special craft.

Members of the intelligentsia stroll around these shops, artists who will be remembered down the centuries and miserable poetasters who spend their last penny to get poems copied which no one will ever read. The gossips gather there too, people who say they work but actually do nothing but talk.

Are barbers craftsmen? They do nothing but destroy beards and heads of hair, but they know very well how indispensable they are. No one here shaves himself, or dresses his own hair. And anyway, who is better equipped than a barber for spreading the latest news, the gossip and the tastiest titbits?

(sources: Martial, Juvenal and others)

LAWYERS AND LAW COURTS

The foundations of the Roman legal system lay not so much in documents as in habits and customs inherited from the elders and in the deeply rooted customs of the citizens; it was therefore unchanging in its main principles. However, whenever the custodians of tradition perceived that the old formulae could be adapted to new purposes by altering specialised out-dated details they did so, and the legal system easily took on its new adaptations. The laws and edicts of the magistrates acted as bulwarks against injustices which might arise in the light of a continually developing social conscience. But the basic rules were not affected. Archaic phrases were used to express various concepts — authority over persons and things, obligations to be fulfilled, transfers of inherited wealth. These gave birth to the basic legal categories, which soon incorporated new institutions born of the economic expansion, the granting of universal citizenship and the changes in state religion. These categories are still to be found among most civilized peoples and form the kernel of that part of the law which preserves the classic title « the Civil Code ». The vocation for law which historians consider an especially Roman trait seems to express itself in those aphorisms which make a two-fold demand: that for certainty and that which places law above all arbitrary considerations, including those of the legislator.

JUSTICE AND THE STATE

This chapter is devoted to the administration of the law by the State, or, as the Romans would have said, by the State as controlled by its officers. There will, therefore, be no consideration of the private vendetta which, in earliest times and probably even before the foundation of Rome, was the sole sanction for crimes against property or persons — even the most ferocious ones. Nor will there be any discussion of *patria potestas*, the exercise of a father's justice which, in law, was absolute both over persons called free (wife, sons and daughters, sons' wives) and over slaves. It was a power which was never abolished in pure law but which gradually found limitations in ever stricter social habits and was finally codified by the censors in the infliction of the degrading *nota* against the erring father in the citizen's lists. The domestic or home tribunals belong to this development. They are mentioned in literature. They consisted of the adult male members of the family (not only sons « in thrall » but nearest male relations such as brothers and cousins) called by the head of the family to assist him in assessing the guilt and fixing the penalty.

THE JUDGES

There is no point in reviving the old controversy about which was the first lawsuit; it is better to deal with civil procedures which served to establish some sort of certainty, at least a formal one, in questions of property or private legal rights. How long did the custom survive which authorized private retribution? Did the beginnings of collective action find expression later on in religious colleges, perhaps those pontifical ones which for a long time held a monopoly in preserving the solemn forms of legal acts? Or was that action expressed in the person of the king in the ancient monarchies? And finally when did justice by arbitration gain honourable recognition, justice which was once accomplished by the free initiative of the contending parties and later was controlled by the leading men of the State? Certainly in the historical period from the fifth or fourth centuries B.C. to the end of the third century A.D. the first part of the procedure — i.e., that which decided definitively what was to be judged and the task of the judge in the specific instance — took place before a magistrate. The second part, in which the evidence was weighed and the controversy decided, took place in front of a judge. But these two very Latin words — magistrate and judge — must not be confused with their modern counterparts. The elected or yearly leaders in Rome — the consuls — were called magistrates in the Republic, whatever their function, and the very word praetor which originally meant commander, always implied a certain rank among the leaders of the State. Praetors might have jurisdiction (city praetors, travelling praetors); they might also be generals commanding an army or governors of a province. The judge was a citizen whose name was agreed to by the disputants; if they failed to agree, he would be chosen by lot and even then might still be rejected by one or other party — but not time and again, as this would reveal the contestant's clear intention of avoiding the trial altogether. A well-known jurist might be chosen, as happened in the case of Aquilius Gallus who judged the case of Caius Nevius and Publius Quintius (defended by Cicero), but the judge might just as well be an ordinary person or a man with good qualifications in another field.

THE *FORMULAE*

So the parties would present themselves at the praetor's tribunal. Here, at least until the mid-second century B.C., plaintiff and defendant would have to say certain set phrases, fixed by the pontifices of the day who were well versed in current law, or later, by legal specialists. In these formalities the legal position of each party was quite clearly set out. Then the parties were bidden to remember well what they had heard, and the judge was chosen. Meanwhile he informed himself of the first phase of the procedure and then listened to witnesses, read the relevant documents, heard the lawyers and finally pronounced sentence. So the case ended, and there was no appeal. If, however, there was also a question of compensation for the victor, the latter was entitled to try and get it; he

First-century Lictor. The lictor personified the authority of the magistrate with his imperium. *Like the magistrate, he wore the toga in town and the sagum in military campaigns. Reconstruction based on the Benevento Arch, in the Museum of Roman Civilisation, Rome.*

A hypothetical reconstruction of the laws of the Twelve Tables, according to the generally accepted view which places the rules of legal procedure in the first three tables, family law in the fourth, laws of heritage in the fifth, property laws in the sixth and seventh, penal laws in the eighth, ninth, tenth and eleventh, leaving the twelfth for some complementary regulations and public law. Details are the subject of much discussion, and the arrangement in the Fontes Juris Romani Antejustiniani *is somewhat different. (Museum of Roman Civilisation, Rome).*

Statue of a Magistrate. It stood int he Forum Novum *at Thubursicum (now Khamissa) in Numidia in Africa. (Museum of Guelma).*

could, in cases of debt, take possession of the person of the debtor, and failing payment by the debtor or by another for him, he could kill the debtor or sell him as a slave in a foreign territory. However, this taking possession had to be performed before a magistrate, and here a third party might appear to free the debtor at his own risk.

In the second century B.C. there was apparently a slight reform. Instead of repeating the solemn phrases in front of a magistrate, the parties could agree on one of the *formulae* which the praetor displayed publicly near the tribunal. The phrases were brief, of great technical perfection, drafted in the form of two hypothetical paragraphs: for example, if it was true that the defendant owed the plaintiff the supposed sum, then he should be condemned to pay it; if it was not true, then he should be acquitted. There were *formulae* which differed slightly in grammar but the heart of the matter in the Roman lawsuit lay in the clear alternative we have given. Hence it is clear that in that age the discussion before the praetor was not concerned with whether or not the case was well founded, but only whether that *formula* was suitable to that case, or whether the insertion of a circumstance made known by the defendant, and at a later date would, if recognized as true by the praetor, invalidate the whole case. The praetor could make use of considerable powers, but only if the defendant refused to use the *formula* suited to the case, or subsequently refused all the judges proposed to him, and thereby showed « wicked intent » of avoiding trial.

The judge, compelled as he was to proceed according to the *formula* communicated to him, did not always have an easy task. The allegation inserted in the *formula* might be reduced to a fact to be ascertained or excluded on the basis of witnesses and documents, but might also prove exceedingly complex. The judge might have to decide whether Titus was or was not the owner of a piece of land; whether Caius should or should not have to give Maevius a certain sum of money. In order to find the answer to such questions he had to be conversant with private law, or get assistance, as he often did, from competent assessors.

This is not the place to expound how, thanks to this simple task by which the praetor put into *formulae* the solemn dialogues of the previous epoch, many other reforms took place and multiplied social relations

Temple of Minerva and Forum of Assisi, reconstructed by the architect Ugo Tarchi. In the centre was a monument dedicated to Castor and Pollux, and a throne with seats. (Museum of Roman Civilisation, Rome).

Reconstruction of a bisellium *or curial seat, based on archaeological finds. It was reserved for magistrates carrying the* imperium *and the elders of the curia. (Museum of Roman Civilisation, Rome).*

protected under the law. Nor is this the place to examine the various techniques devised to reach authoritative decisions about situations which could not in themselves be considered as having any juridical connection. One can but note, for example, the protection given to certain accepted situations such as being in possession — saving an eventual lawsuit concerning the right to property; or the new procedure for the distraining of property, a kind of bankruptcy proceeding, which virtually ended the ancient and inhuman execution of the sentence on the person of the debtor.

TRIALS

In criminal cases, the first phases of the historical development of procedure are very uncertain. Some think that the city may have made an early attempt to control private vendettas by instituting a trial similar to the private trial in which it was decided whether or not there was a case for exposing the allegedly guilty party to the vendetta in question. There were undoubted rules about crimes against the city and parricide, and such cases were tried by city magistrates. At one point laws were made giving the people organized in a meeting the power to judge certain crimes. Many points are obscure, and it is not easy to find out at what point the sitting magistrate began to surround himself with a nominated council or how specially binding such joint judgments were.

In the period which will probably most interest the reader, the end of the Republic and the beginning of the Empire, the ordinary criminal trial was called a *quaestio*. This name was given to the trial whenever a case was heard under well-defined laws made for a well-defined series of illegal acts. For such cases a list of jurors was drawn up each year depending mainly on the prevalent party at the time, and chosen from the higher ranks of citizens, senators or equites, or both. The list was displayed, and from it the jurors for a case would be chosen initially by the prosecutor. He chose double the number necessary, leaving it to the accused to reduce the number to the required number. Subsequently the choice was by lots, always for double the number, leaving the accused and the prosecuting party to reject names in turn. A praetor presided over these proceedings. At the trial there were two speeches by the defence and prosecution lawyers and replies to them. Witnesses and documents were produced even when the lawyers' speeches were in progress. Then the jurors voted for sentencing or acquitting, and if they voted in favour of a sentence, the penalty was fixed by law. This penalty might be pecuniary (as it was in the crime of extortion from provincials, called *pecuniae repetundae*) or it might involve prohibition from standing for the post of magistrate (which happened in the case of election offences, the *ambitus*). Often the verdict was, at least nominally, death. There was a provision that the criminal could avoid death by choosing exile. If the accused announced his intention of going into exile before the sentence was pronounced, the magistrate could forbid it, and if he went nevertheless, any return on his part would mean certain death, if he were discovered.

There were other types of trials, such as that held by a commander in time of war against deserters and rebels, and this carried the death penalty. In similar civil trials an accused might be pronounced an enemy of the people and likewise be sentenced to death, and there were trials by the tribunes of the plebs in the presence of the council of the plebs which could inflict serious sentences on ex-magistrates.

Then under the Empire there was the *extraordinaria cognitio* or special legal investigation in both private and criminal trials which gradually swept away all the forms described above. It returned the handling of the trial to the magistrate or rather the emperor and his officials from the moment of citation or denunciation up to the sentencing. So the private judge was removed from all criminal cases and the prosecutor was replaced by the informer.

THE PUBLIC AT TRIALS

Few occasions rouse so much passion among the public as a criminal trial, and in our day newspapers double their circulation during an important trial, and give more and more space to it as the days go by. The court is packed every morning and most conversations are about the evidence and the probable verdict. Having far less variety in their spare time than we have, and no cinema or thriller novels, the Romans made attendance at trials one of their chief pastimes. This was easy since magistrates and judges sat almost in the open, with little shelter from sun and rain, and in front of great open squares where there was room for thousands of people. Curiosity was increased by a taste for legal forms and the correct application of the law which, as the writings of the Roman jurists tell us, was a particular feature of the Roman mind. And there were frequent opportunities for watching the dirty linen of the great being washed in public, not only in cases concerning the obvious misdemeanours of the governing class, but also in cases of quite humble persons when the lawyers might suggest that protection or complicity in high places was involved. Occasionally too they could see their personal enemy or political adversary exposed as a laughing stock

A magistrate speaks to the people. This is a statue of Aulus Metilius called « the haranguer ». This particular type of toga (the tebenna*) belongs to the second century* B.C. *(Archaeological Museum, Florence).*

by manoeuvring him into court on some ridiculous pretext.

The Roman orators habitually attacked their adversaries in politics as in law with incontinent ferocity, exaggerating what there might be to say against them to libellous extremes. The lawyers for the defence did the same in every kind of case, attacking the prosecution in such general terms as to be specifically meaningless and attributing depraved and malicious motives to the most innocent of actions. Cicero, defending the comic actor Q. Roscius Gallus, accused by Fannius Chereus of murdering his father, stooped to describing Fannius' habit of shaving his head as « a visible sign of dishonesty — he even shaves his eyebrows so one cannot even say he has an honest hair on his head », and compared him to one of the infamous masks used in Latin comedies. Personal convictions were not respected. One intellectual activity which Cicero was always praising to the skies was the science of law *juris prudentia*, and the one jurist he venerated was his friend Servius Sulpicius Rufus. Then in A.D. 63 Licinius Murena, a general of undoubted but not excessive ability, was accused of electoral bribery and defended by Cicero: his accuser was none other than the same Servius Sulpicius Rufus, and Cicero (still fresh from his eloquent attack on Catiline only a few months before) confronted him with the statement that when the public meeting had to choose between a general and a jurist, they rightly chose the general, for jurists spent their time bickering in a profession which he (Cicero) had never relished, but which one could master with three days' study. Whatever else this plea produced, it corresponded completely to popular opinion, and it did not lead to any quarrel between the two old fighters — indeed within four years Cicero supported Servius Sulpicius for the candidacy of Consul, and a few years later when Cicero's daughter died, Servius sent the famous orator a *Consolatio*, a moving fragment of which has come down to us, in fine Latin prose.

LAWYERS AND JURISTS

Political men liked the pursuit of the law best among professions. It promised very wide recognition of their gifts of oratory, and then it provided opportunities for contact with influential people, for even if the person whose interests you advocated was not himself important, he might well have important patrons. You could, of course, make more enemies than friends, but in the last years of the Republic when personal relations, relatives and secret agreements counted for more than political parties, the art of politics consisted mainly in knowing how to choose supporters and opponents. Then there was the reward, not in the modern form of lawyers' fees, these having been abolished by an ancient law which upheld the idea that pleas for the defence should be free and without charge, but by gifts, provisions in wills, legacies such as the great wealth of Rome's governing classes could provide on a large scale. Cicero is an invaluable source of information, because he is the only Roman lawyer whose activities are known to us year by year and day by day throughout his life from his *Letters*: he, for instance, could afford to travel to Brindisi or to Reggio from Rome, and spend each night in one of his own villas, always sure of finding it perfectly fitted out and ready, amply provided with food and servants. All of which explains how difficult it must have been for a Roman lawyer to choose his client on the grounds that his case was a good one, or to examine the circumstances clearly or to rigidly observe the meaning of the law.

This is the very point where a distinction was drawn in Rome between the lawyer (*patronus*, *orator*) and the jurist. The very name of jurist could enhance a political career with all that it implied of knowledge of the law, and a disinterested willingness to hold this at the service of all citizens. This interpreter of the law worked in the privacy of his home, and received visits from all kinds of people asking for his opinion on legal matters, with no audience except perhaps a young man studying to acquire a like competence, and of course without any suggestion of remuneration. The jurist certainly had occasional satisfactions: he might, for instance, be called to judge a case of major import; he could be called by a newly elected praetor of the city to help in preparing the legal edict for a given year, including perhaps certain procedural reforms which would then also bear his name; or he might gather with the aid of colleagues a list of the more important judgments passed in the year; or he might produce a work in which the fruit of his own knowledge and experience would serve to define private law, or great sectors of it, and thereby contribute to the development of legislation, which in so many aspects was dependent on such an *interpretatio*.

In this way the tradition of vigilance over the juridical forms of social life, vested until the second century B.C. solely in the colleges of pontifices, was perpetuated by the still sacerdotal attitude of the lay jurists who succeeded them. It was not an activity dear to the social and political climbers, the *homines novi* (« new men »), ambitious for quick popularity and quick returns, but rather the pursuit of members of noble families like the Mucii Scaevolae, who had produced at least one consul before giving four jurists to Rome, or families from the equestrian order with no particular ambition to cross the barrier dividing that class from the nobility.

The jurists had a great spirit of independence, so much so that Augustus decided that the giving of judgments should be subject to their authorization. Under the Empire the jurists preserved this position of authority, even if they were to become advisers of the princes rather than of the people. Henceforth a jurist's career was more often to be in the higher ranks of the imperial bureaucracy than in the magistracies that had survived from the Republic.

It is easy to see how the practical separation between the activities of the jurist and the lawyer (apart from certain features we have described) conformed to the fundamental and indeed eternal demands of the law. The law demands the maximum available certainty, but in human affairs certainty is an approximate term and absolute certainty an unattainable ideal; the law can only realize itself in the daily struggle, always affirming and always being violated, through conflicts of interest and value judgments of human conduct where it is not always possible to draw a precise line of demarcation between right and wrong, or innocence and guilt. The forensic struggle, when vigorously pursued, not infrequently reveals the hidden blemishes of the law itself and urges those who are responsible for it to seek a greater clarity, or it may reveal the gap between the existing law and those other laws which social progress hopes to attain and on which the evolution of justice greatly depends. Everyone knows how one of the effects of a loss of freedom is the limitation, the debasement and the secrecy of battles fought in the law courts, and how certainty or its counterfeit is increased, while law itself loses any progressive force and ceases to find an echo in the public conscience.

But to return to Rome: it must not be forgotten that the forensic speeches which have come down to us all belong to the period of the greatest political controversy, and the orators certainly did not select for publication those speeches which coincided most with the instruction of the jurists, but those which enhanced their reputation as a clever orator or, in a word, their political ambitions. In these pleas the frontier between the probable and the indisputable is rather artificial; imperfection in, or absence of, law is often used to advantage and beyond the dictates of impartiality, and yet the laws as laid down by the elders are never shamelessly overthrown. Anyone who cared to make a methodical comparison in this matter with, for example, the Athenian orators would become aware of the genuinely juridical vocation of the Roman people.

Minerva, goddess of Wisdom. (National Museum, Naples).

THE FAMOUS TRIAL OF CORNELIUS SCIPIO

That day the Forum was filled to overflowing. The accused, due to appear before the judgment seat of the Roman people, was none other than one of the heroic idols of that warlike people, the famous Cornelius Scipio, surnamed Africanus after the great victory over Hannibal at Zama (October 19th, 202 B.C.) which ended in a decisive conquest.

The accusation brought by the two tribunes of Cato's party properly concerned another Scipio, Lucius, brother of Africanus and like him a most famous general.

They wanted him to account for 500 talents which King Antiochus had paid after the Roman victory, but which had never been deposited in the State treasury.

Lucius Scipio would have to prove publicly that the sum was war booty and that he therefore had a right to spend it, provided he had not privately appropriated it. If, however, the tribunes could show that the 500 talents were a war indemnity paid by Antiochus to the Romans, then Lucius would be guilty of nothing less than embezzlement from the State.

But the man who was really on trial was Africanus, who had long been Cato's bugbear and had been accused by him along with his relatives and friends of having corrupted the uprightness of Rome by introducing the soft ways of Greece, where through the labours of those very Scipios, Rome was now pursuing a policy of expansion. Cato, himself a descendant of landed proprietors, wanted Rome's well-being to come from agriculture and good husbandry such as he himself practised, and not from conquest and commercial speculation.

Agriculture, he thought, would revive that genuine simplicity of manners which was rapidly disappearing, mainly through the evil influence of the new ideas brought to Rome by the Greek philosophers. Cato had procured their banishment but they were begging for permission to return, and their patrons, including the Scipios, were pleading for them.

Moreover, everyone knew that the army which had fought in Syria although under the command of Lucius was really led to victory by Scipio Africanus. In fact he had collaborated closely with his brother, counselling and guiding him. By an adroit political manoeuvre he had re-established peace with the Itoni, assured the alliance of Philip V of Macedon on land, and of Rhodes at sea, and finally had brought about the battle of Magnesia, which had been decisive. Officially Lucius was given the credit and had celebrated the triumph, receiving the name of Asiaticus, but no one denied, least of all Lucius, that the master-mind of the whole undertaking had been Africanus.

So it was Africanus who presented himself in front of the solemn tribunal, composed of the entire Senate. He had brought the records of his administration. With a slightly histrionic gesture he tore them all up in front of the people. A confused murmur was heard in the crowd but none of the tribunes dared to object, especially after Africanus, with angry voice, reminded the people that he had enriched the public funds by more than 200 million sesterces (about six million pounds sterling).

« And now the tribunes disgracefully ask what I have done with the other four », he ended, shouting indignantly and lifting his hand to the sky as though to call it to witness such an ignominious request.

The theatrical gesture of Africanus could not of course solve anything. A little while after, another tribune, Marcus Naevius, again cited Lucius before the tribunal of the Roman people, and again it was his brother Cornelius who came forward.

It was the day before the anniversary of the battle of Zama. Scipio so arranged things that the verdicts would be given on the following day, after witnesses had been heard, so he merely reminded the Romans of the services he had rendered the fatherland, without defending himself.

On the following day, the anniversary of Zama, the people all gathered in the Forum. The great square, the steps, the colonnades, the porticoes of the temples and the Curia were crowded with people, the veterans of the Punic wars well to the fore and ready to start a riot if their idol should fall a prey to the law. Suddenly the crowd broke loose; unending clapping, and a great craning of necks everywhere greeted the arrival of the Scipios; they advanced slowly, occasionally responding with a brief smile and a sign to the cheers which went up all over the Forum.

Africanus was followed by a large crowd of friends, partisans and faithful clients.

In a great silence his voice thundered out with an anger shot with menace: « I remember », he said, looking round imperiously, « I remember that today is the anniversary of the day on which, in a great battle in Africa, I defeated Hannibal, the first enemy of your Empire, O Romans! I won peace for you and a wonderful triumph. Let us not be ungrateful to the gods! Let us leave this rogue here and go to give thanks to the great and good Jupiter! »

So saying, Scipio moved towards the Capitol, followed by all the Roman people.

The tribune and his secretaries remained there alone.

(sources: Livy, Gellius, Cicero)

MEDICINE: HALF SCIENCE, HALF MAGIC

Ancient devotion to magic and sacred medical rites did not stop the spread to Rome of the cult of Aesculapius, the Greek God of healing, followed by the establishment of Greek doctors and surgeons who brought with them a solid and positive scientific tradition. These doctors were slaves or freed men, trained in diagnostic and therapeutic arts, or just skilled, even if empirical, concoctors of herb medicines. The first to entrust their health to them, despite the suspicion and hostility of those who preferred the older habits, were equites *and senators. New medical colleges grew up in Rome and under Augustus enjoyed great privileges, and free medical services were being provided for the poorer citizens. The armies had their own hospitals and surgeons, and some of the most famous masters of the science, such as Asclepiades and Galen, had practices in Rome.*
But almost everywhere the old methods survived. A real distinction between science, magic and empirical medicine was never really achieved. As well as the primitive scientia herbarum — *the use of herbs for curative purposes — there existed in practice alongside the indiscriminate prescription of potions and unguents of very doubtful nature, which were sold to the public by a host of charlatans, trading on the credulity of rich and poor alike.*

When a frightful plague broke out in Rome in 293 B.C., the Senate ordered a consultation of the Sybilline books, according to the usual procedure in moments of great peril to the city. These books were a collection of oracular pronouncements and different precepts which originally had been imported from Cumae. Their use in a city where the cult of Apollo as a doctor had already been in existence for three centuries soon led to the introduction of the cult of Aesculapius, the Greek god of healing, who was in any case considered as the son of Apollo. The Roman cult was organised on the model of the sanctuary at Epidaurus, in the Argolid, the most famous Aesculapian sanctuary.

Early in 291 B.C. the new temple of Aesculapius on the Tiber island was dedicated to the god with due solemnity. The new cult with its emphasis on white magic did not immediately produce any change in Roman medicine, which relied on both religio-magical and empirical methods, as did all medicine in the ancient world, with the exception of the Greek schools. Aesculapius was simply added to the long list of those divinities who, in the religious concepts of the Romans, presided over certain moments of human life and protected it from the insidiousness of nature in certain well-defined spheres, as in the cases of the goddesses Quartana, Scabies or Mephitis. Aesculapius was generally considered more efficient and more authoritative. Indirectly the new religion did have an influence on the course of Roman medicine. Some members of the Roman aristocracy had strong prejudices against Greek culture generally and in particular against a medical science imported from Greece and Magna Graecia (the Greek cities of southern Italy) and hated its radical newness, but the effect of this hostility was diminished when the public took to adoration of the Greek god. Marcus Porcius Cato (234-149 B.C.), that strict observer of ancient traditions, actually forbade his son to consult Greek doctors, in no uncertain terms, as recorded by the elder Pliny, in his *Natural History:* « And take

141

this as the saying of a prophet. Once this people spread their doctrine they will corrupt everything; even more so if they send their doctors. They have sworn to each other to kill all barbarians with their medicine ». To combat Greek science Cato collected all the precepts of popular medicine and combined them with magical practices, and botanical and surgical data. However, as the cult of Aesculapius spread, the entry of Greek doctors into Rome became easier and more frequent.

The first surgeon to be recorded in Pliny's *Natural History* is Archagathos, a Spartan who arrived in 219 B.C. At first he won the admiration of the Romans for the skill and assurance of his operations. Then the novelty and the extensiveness of his work caused dismay among those accustomed to the rudimentary native surgery, and Archagathos ended by being called « the butcher ».

For a very long time the practice of the art of medicine according to Greek doctrine was more or less limited to foreigners. After all, as Pliny commented, with some exaggeration, the Romans had managed without medicine for six centuries. Many came from Magna Graecia where important schools had grown up like the one of Pythagorean inspiration at Croton, famed for the doctor Alcmaeon, and that of Elea or Velia. As Roman conquests increased, doctors arrived from Greece itself and from the hellenized Orient. Their social position and their medical knowledge varied greatly. Alongside the doctors of the aristocracy, great men such as Asclepiades and Galen and men thoroughly trained in the most famous Greek schools, there were slaves skilled in diagnosis and therapy. But the appellation of « doctor » (*medicus*), which in popular parlance included users of magic, was commonly extended to nurses, and to those who made up empirical concoctions of drugs, oils and ointments. Slaves who had learnt medicine were, of course, more highly paid, but they could only practise their art if their master was a doctor. They were very often enfranchised, judging by the great number of freed doctors with Greek surnames.

Doctors had professional associations, *collegia*, with their own premises, the *scholae medicorum*, which were not in fact schools proper. The doctors themselves taught privately and used their pupils as assistants.

From the time of Vespasian (A.D. 70-79) public instruction with State-paid professors of medicine was available and this practice increased under Alexander

Aesculapius. (Vatican Museum, Rome).

Severus (A.D. 222-235). Probably the imperial « university schools » provided courses in medicine as well as rhetoric, philosophy and law. Private clinics were sometimes attached to the dispensaries (*tabernae medicae*) where doctors examined their patients and performed operations.

The first Roman hospital opened in the Temple of Aesculapius on the island in the Tiber. It had to be surrounded by water for religious reasons. The choice of the locality isolated by the river from the densely inhabited surroundings seems particularly sensible. From the map of ancient Rome at the Porta S. Silvestro, Rome.

A doctor's remuneration was influenced by the popularity and reputation he enjoyed, and also by his social status and that of his patients. In the age of Plautus, the ordinary fee was a sestertius, a little more than a gram of silver. In imperial times the emperor's private doctor had a salary of three hundred thousand sesterces, and fees were generally high; even the famous Galen charged a fee that was considered worth noting when he operated on a consul's wife and received 400 *aurei* ($3,360 or £1,200). Pliny gives a number of examples of the cupidity of famous doctors.

DOCTORS' PRIVILEGES

Generally speaking, doctors enjoyed a privileged position in Rome. Even when Greek philosophers and rhetoricians were twice expelled from the city (in 173 and 161 B.C.) as dangerous to the welfare of the State, Greek doctors were not included in the ban. Caesar conferred Roman citizenship upon those foreigners who practised medicine in Rome. Hadrian exempted doctors along with professors of rhetoric and philosophy from a series of onerous public functions (imperial liturgies) on the ground that they were already rendering services to the State. The most celebrated doctors and the heads of the *collegia* received the title of *archiatrus*, a title first borne by Nero's doctor, Archidamus. From the time of the emperor Severus, this title was given to doctors in attendance on the emperor, *archiatri palatini*. Some of these were called to high office and made governors of provinces. The *archiatri populares* were State doctors who looked after people in districts of the Urbs and in cities. They were paid by the State or the municipality, as in the ancient Greek *poleis*, and were expected in particular to look after the poor.

These doctors enjoyed much prestige and were exempted from paying taxes, but their number was limited. An edict at the end of the reign of Antoninus Pius (A.D. 161) allowed a limit of five to minor cities and not more than ten to provincial capitals.

Pliny records that very few Roman citizens entered the medical profession, and Celsus mentions the existence of Jewish doctors. In theory as in practice, it was Greeks and eastern people of Greek culture who led the field in medicine, and Pliny the Elder, in his introductory pages to Book XXIX of his *Natural History*, cannot avoid a slightly malicious comment on Greek doctors, voicing the hostility to their theories which was prevalent among the old Roman aristocracy. « Of all the Greek arts, medicine is the only one which still lacks the dignity (*gravitas*) of Rome », he notes. His reasoning is as crude and superficial as Cato's, but in fact as the cultural situation had altered, and as Pliny was an informed if superficial writer, his use of invective and appeals to tradition instead of proper doctrinal polemic shows that some feeling of inferiority still existed.

The theories and practice of some doctors might well have appeared designed firstly to impress the common man. For instance there was a doctor called Carmides who came to Rome from Marseilles, and in no time he amassed a fortune and considerable fame by his indifference to all the traditional therapy, his sole form of treatment being an ice cold bath even in the dead of winter. Nevertheless many a Greek doctor reached a position of considerable authority.

ASCLEPIADES AND GALEN

Asclepiades, a native of Prusa in Bithynia, a friend of Crassus, of Antony and perhaps of Cicero, was a much sought after doctor and had great influence as a teacher. He was over 80 when he died in 40 B.C. Like his contemporary Lucretius, he was a follower of Democritus and Epicurus and ignored the Hippocratic doctrine that illness was simply a manifestation of disharmony in the four fundamental humours of the human organism, and that therapy consisted of a reestablishment of equilibrium (the *vis medicatrix naturae*). Like Lucretius, he applied the theories of atomic physics to medicine. He maintained that health was determined by the regular movement of atoms in the human body; illness by irregularities in that movement, and that far from letting nature do its work — an attitude which Asclepiades derided as a « meditation of death » — the doctor must intervene with his cures, even gymnastic ones, « *cito, tuto, iucunde* » (quickly, safely and merrily). The story goes that one day Asclepiades suddenly met a funeral procession and immediately saw that the corpse was only in a coma, from which he promptly revived him — such was this doctor's reputation.

Above: *an oculist at work. Panel of bas-relief on the tomb of the Sosius family in the church of S. Vittore, Ravenna.* Bottom, left: *a votive plaque commemorating deafness cured. (Museum of Roman Civilisation, Rome).* Bottom, right: *pharmacist's shop. In the centre, a protecting divinity, possibly Meditrina. Now in the Epinal Museum.*

The two chief representatives of the so-called methodical school are associated with Asclepiades: Temison of Laodicea who lived in Rome under Augustus, and Soranus of Ephesus who, under the reigns of Trajan and Hadrian, tried to modify the anti-Hippocratic exaggerations of the school. By far the most influential Greek doctor in Rome and the most famous down the centuries was Galen of Pergamum (c. A.D. 130-200). After studying in Greece and Alexandria and exercising his profession in his own country he came to Rome first for a period from 162 to 166, and returned in 169 at the invitation of Marcus Aurelius and his colleague Lucius Verus, and stayed on as the physician of Commodus until his death. He was a student of philosophy and followed the doctrines of Hippocrates and Plato, but with independent judgment.

His works are based on original observation and deal with anatomy and physiology, pathology, pharmacological and surgical therapy: he also wrote several commentaries on Hippocrates and works on philosophy, especially logic. His writings were to become something of an encyclopaedia of medical science, held in great awe throughout the Middle Ages, even as far afield as Islam. They possessed a profound religious feeling. He was monotheistically inclined, and his austere attitude to life resulted in some unusual expressions of sympathy for the Christian ethic.

GAIUS STERTINIUS XENOPHON

In the first century B.C. another Greek doctor had received praise in high places and high fees. He was not in the same class as Asclepiades or Galen either in medical theory or in personal probity. Gaius Stertinius Xenophon was born on the island of Cos, sacred to the memory of Aesculapius and home of Hippocrates. He belonged to a family which claimed descent from the family of Aesculapius and had already produced several illustrious doctors, among them another Xenophon and Philenus in the third century B.C., founders of the so-called « empirical school ». Once in Rome Stertinius Xenophon received Roman citizenship by virtue of Caesar's decree and became so successful that when the emperor Claudius chose him as his doctor, Xenophon could boast that his own annual income already exceeded by 100,000 sesterces the salary of 500,000 sesterces which Claudius offered him.

Xenophon accompanied Claudius to Britain in A.D. 43 and received honours and offices from the emperor, whose intervention he obtained several times in favour of his Greek countrymen and of his family. One of his brothers, also a doctor, was summoned to serve at court and received the same salary as Xenophon. In his *Natural History* Pliny records the great wealth of the brothers from Cos; they built lavishly in Naples, doubtless attracted there by the thermal baths, and yet left to their heirs a fortune which few people at that time could have matched. When Claudius died, Xenophon returned to Cos. Many inscriptions there both in the city and in the temple to Aesculapius reveal the authority he held at home and the honours his fellow-citizens conferred upon him. However, one grave accusation clings to him, made by his contemporaries and by Tacitus in his *Annals*. Agrippina, he says, seeing that the poison she had put in the food of Claudius was not having the desired effect, « had recourse to Xenophon, whose complicity she had already assured. Whilst pretending to assist the emperor's efforts to vomit, he is believed to have inserted a pen filled with a rapid poison into Claudius's throat, knowing full well that the gravest crimes are initiated at risk and achieved with profit ». This crime amounted to sacrilege on the part of one who had taken the solemn oath traditionally ascribed to Hippocrates and in any case reflecting the ethics of the Hippocratic school, and was therefore bound to exercise his art « in purity and holiness, » and with the sole intent of benefiting the sick. The oath also contained the explicit declaration: « Even if asked, I shall not give any fatal drug, nor will I connive with my advice in giving it ».

The western part of the Empire also had doctors and medical writers of renown, although they were less numerous and original than the Greek and the Easterners of Greek origin. The best known was Aulus Cornelius Celsus, who composed an encyclopaedia in the reign of Tiberius based on a good knowledge of Greek doctrine. The eight books of the second half, devoted to medicine, have survived. It is especially important for its accurate descriptions of bold surgical operations. Other Latin medical writing is of less value: there is a collection of medical prescriptions composed by Scribonius Largus, a doctor attached to Claudius; in the fourth century a book by Marcellus Empiricus of Bordeaux « On medicaments », and in

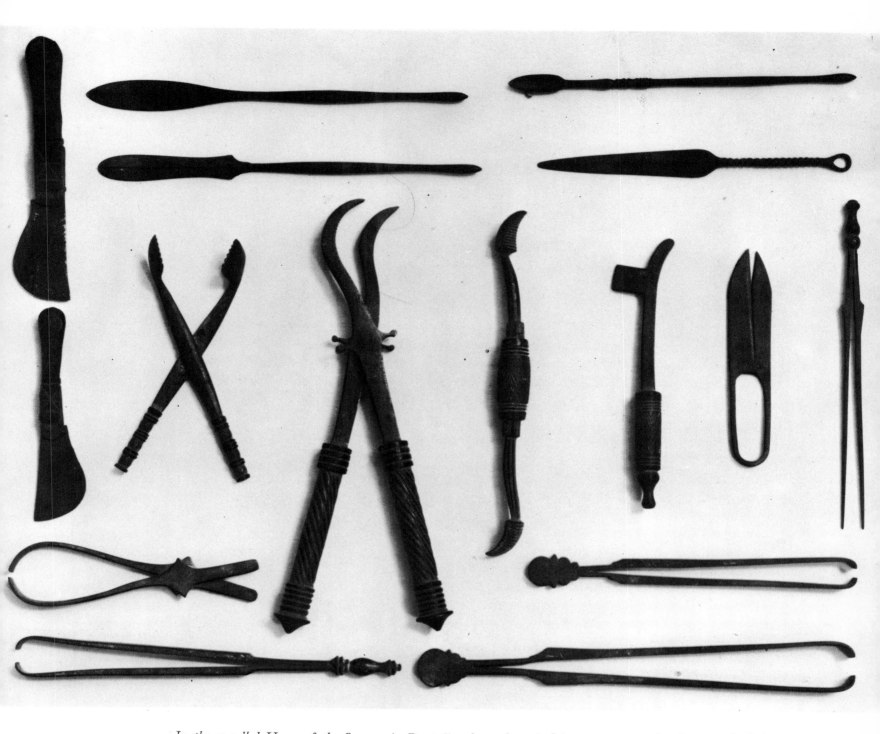

In the so-called House of the Surgeon in Pompeii a box of surgical instruments was found, some of which are reproduced above. The technical skill of the Greek surgeons which had spread to Rome was, for the age, relatively developed and enterprising. (Museum of Roman Civilisation, Rome).

the fifth century, the work of Celius Aurelianus, a Numidian, on acute and chronic illnesses which is more or less a re-write of Soranus. Therapy in optics was largely empirical and depended on the variety of the eye-salves in use, of which we have evidence in the very many surviving opticians' seals with names and descriptions of the medicaments. Nearly all these have been found in the western provinces.

Naturally army and navy medical services were fairly highly organised in the Roman world. There were medical assistants attached to the army at least from the time of the Punic wars, though a regular military medical service probably dates only from imperial times. In the City of Rome the four urban cohorts, the nine cohorts of praetorian guards and the seven cohorts of *vigiles* all had four doctors attached to each

Scale model of the military hospital at Castel Vetera (Xanten) in Germany. The hospital had 180 beds and was equipped with particularly good sanitary arrangements. The exposure and siting of the buildings would have satisfied modern hospital architects. (Museum of Roman Civilisation, Rome).

of the cohorts. There were doctors attached to the legions, the auxiliary corps and the ships of the fleet (*medici legionum, medici ordinarii*) although we do not know how many. They had the rank of junior officers and enjoyed several privileges. Surgery of course took a high place in military medicine, and apart from what Celsus wrote, we have evidence of how far the art had progressed from more than 200 surgical instruments discovered at Pompeii. Medical arrangements for the army encouraged the development of hospitals, the *valetudinaria*. A land-surveyor called Iginus who lived under Trajan left descriptions of military hospitals, remains of which have also been found at Carnuntum, the main garrison town on the Danubian

frontier line (*limes*) and at Novaesium on the Rhine *limes*: these became models for civilian hospitals in the provincial cities, and then for the hospitals of the Middle Ages.

EMPIRICAL AND MAGICAL MEDICINE

Progress in scientific medicine did not entirely discredit popular experimental medicine or magical practices in medicine. Indeed the syncretic fusing of various religions in the imperial era encouraged the practices afresh, and some cases of charlatanism and recurring displays of hostility and mockery towards scientific medicine and its practitioners are recorded in Pliny and on some epitaphs. Pliny mentions one epitaph which tells how the deceased was a victim of the great number of doctors consulted and of their multiple opinions and another in which in bitter sorrow « the most innocent mind » is recalled « which the doctors desiccated and killed ». Certain rural communities held very tenaciously to ancient rites and prescriptions. This gave rise to a superstitious traditionalism, rather than a specific distrust of a science of foreign origin and mainly practised by foreigners.

Of course, even in the parts of the Empire most linked to Greek culture, the quick and notable development of medical science did not dispel faith in the healing power of the gods, and first among them, Aesculapius, nor did the new science much diminish meditation in sanctuaries and the expectation of communications with the god in dreams. Records have survived of healings by divine intervention of Aesculapius in Epidaurus, and in Lebana in Crete, and cases were quoted by medical writers such as Galen and Oribasus in the Aesculapium at Pergamum. A Greek inscription of the second century A.D. in Rome describes a series of miraculous cures in the temple of Aesculapius, where the faithful used to spend the whole night, as they did in Greek sanctuaries: « To Gaius, the blind man, the god commanded (in his dream) to go to the foot of the divine image and prostrate himself, then to move from the right to the left, place five fingers on the pedestal, lift the hand and place it on his eyes. He regained good vision and the people present rejoiced... To Lucius suffering from phlebitis and long since despaired of, the god commanded that he take ashes from the triple altar, mix them with wine and place them upon his thighs. He recovered and gave public thanks to the god, the people rejoicing with him. To Julian, who was spitting blood and for whom there was no longer any hope, the god commanded that he take pine seeds from the triple altar and chew them with honey for three days. He was cured and came to give thanks to the god in front of

Part of a milestone dedicated to Sempronio Hilarius, a doctor of medicine. (Concordiese Museum at Portogruaro).

the people. To Valerius Aper, a blind soldier, the god commanded that he take the blood of a white cock and with honey make a salve to spread on his eyes for three days. He got his vision back and came to thank the god publicly ». The special forms of medicine-magic were intimately bound up with religious practices and were elaborated within the framework of a theological system; they are not to be confused with more popular superstitions and remedies arising out of a long tradition of observation and experience. There is no continuity between this kind of magic used by the ancients and the much later custom of using amulets and charms inscribed with prayers, spells, symbols, and of repetition of incomprehensible *formulae*.

The connection between magic and certain popular conceptions of medicine in the Roman world can be seen in the triple meaning of the terms *medicamen* and *medicamentum*. Like the Greek word *pharmakon* they can all mean a harmful poisonous element, a healthy remedy and a magic incantation. Magic ideas and rites infiltrate medicine again in late antiquity, just when pagan theosophy develops, and traditional religions are in a state of crisis. Magical *formulae* appear — the most famous is the *abracadabra* formula, quoted in the *Liber medicinalis* and probably composed by the poet Serenus Sammonicus in the third century A.D.

GOOD MEDICINE FOR ALL

The whole house is in a state; the master Sulpicius Rufus has an abscess. One side of his face is quite normal, and looks as it always does, but the other is completely swollen and looks like a different man's. As he paces up and down the room like a lion in a cage, roaring with pain, everyone is busy preparing concoctions and poultices. But the old slave Licia, who is held to be a witch, is in favour of *laserpicium*.

The *laserpicium* is a medicinal plant of many virtues, recognized even by the State which has frequently imported large quantities of it. Caesar himself ordered 1,500 pounds of it before the *coup d'état*.

« But what has *laserpicium* got to do with my toothache? » cries Sulpicius jumping about the room and pressing his cheek with his hand, « Isn't it some sort of digestive thing you use in the kitchen? »

Old Licia knows better. With the juices of the root called *laser* which she has pestled in a mortar, she is making a poultice which, she says, will bring the master's abscess to a head.

« Yes, of course we use it in the kitchen », she says, applying the damp linen to the abscess without more ado, while the master, taken by surprise, jerks away with the new pain that suddenly stabs him.

But the old woman takes no notice and carries on as though Sulpicius were not struggling, spitting, roaring and rolling his eyes with pain.

« *Laser* could make you digest stones, but it also brings abscesses to a head. Now, Sulpicius, would you rather fall into the hands of some ointment-pedlar or a rogue of a dentist who might charge you heaven knows how much to pull out a tooth, or worse still, one of those magicians from the East who boast of curing almost anything with their fancy witchcraft? »

« No, of course not, » mutters Sul-picius, who constantly proclaims his disbelief in witchcraft but is not altogether persuaded that plants have beneficial effects (and anyway who can make head or tail of these things?).

« Well then », says the old woman, « this is exactly the medicine you need ».

The master is not completely convinced, especially as he has read something about *laserpicium*, somewhere — but where? Then he remembers; in Pliny, so it can't just be fairy tales, oh if only this tooth didn't hurt so. Then, somewhat anxious, he starts:

« I know of a man in Pliny who had an aching tooth, and they put *laserpicium* in it, and sealed it with a little ball of wax ».

« Well? »

« Well, old woman, the pain became so intolerable that he had to throw himself out of the window ».

« Just the sort of silliness you get from poets! *Laser* is marvellous for anyone with indigestion, anyone who is weak, convalescent, or anaemic. And that is not all: in case you don't know, it heals wounds and sores, sore throats, asthma, dropsy, pleurisy, jaundice, epilepsy... »

« Good heavens! And *laser* has all these virtues? »

« And more besides! It does away with backache, sciatica and all the burdens of old age. It cures the snake bite and scorpion stings, softens corns, sends sheep to sleep, make goats sneeze and snakes explode...! »

« Only the pains of love are beyond it then, » exclaims Sulpicius, lifting his arms in amazement, half ironically, half comically.

He is already half convinced of what the old woman is saying; it may be because the temperature in the room is changing, or because of the *laserpicium*, but the tooth is definitely hurting less. The old woman patiently goes on changing the poultice, taking no notice of the master's irony.

« You don't believe me, master, but when this abscess is ready and has burst... »

« O Jove! Will it hurt... »

« Not more than now. But we shall prepare you a nice little pumpkin poultice with salt and wormwood, and perhaps a little bit of mustard ».

« So you know everything then, old witch? »

« I am old, indeed, Sir, and I know that blessed nature has provided a remedy for every ill ».

« Well, tell me then, if I had the evil eye what would you prescribe? »

« For the evil eye there is one cure, but it would take too long to explain, and for you, unbeliever that you are, I would be talking to no purpose. As for pains in the eyes, each remedy is different: if you had a cold in the eye, I would give you an infusion of violets, myrrh and saffron; for inflammation of the eye, a salve made with poppies or a lotion of wine vinegar; and if your sight is bad, no remedy is better than a cream made of well-pounded myrrh and oil ».

« And for chapped feet? »

« Asphodel ».

« For mushroom poisoning? »

« Mustard ».

« And for a wood splinter that has gone septic? »

« A poultice made of bread, honey and daffodil root ».

« And for the freckles all over my daughter's face? »

« Linseed oil which also makes nails look shiny, whereas barley with salt and honey sweetens the breath, and lupins boiled in vinegar makes scars disappear... »

« Enough, enough! You'll send me mad ».

« Mad, is it? I'll cure you with hellebore! »

(source: The Elder Pliny)

THE THEATRE: ACTORS AND AUDIENCES

It could be said that the Romans invented both the lavish set and the star system. Perhaps these are the most typical and original features of the Roman theatre. The works themselves were nothing more than straight imitations or re-writes of the comic and tragic poetic dramas originally written by the Greeks.

The theatre had one purpose only — to provide the general public with a pleasant way of passing the time. In turn, the public usually fell under the spell of the actor, his personality, his voice and his movements. Consequently, playwrights rarely bothered to see their works on the stage, for the actors altered them to suit their requirements and plot had to take second place in what was left — a massive choreographic spectacle full of costumes, actors, mimes, music, dancers and criminals — condemned to death by the text as well as by the law and executed on stage. The theatre lost all sense of its religious origins and barely managed to survive; the busy calendar of festival days had little room for it. It compared poorly with other entertainments in the eyes of the public. Relegated as it was to an inferior position, performances often took place in the morning, for in the afternoon the crowd was unwilling to be distracted from its favourite entertainment, the bloodthirsty spectacles of the circus.

The incredible number of some hundred and eighty or more holidays devoted to religious festivals, civil occasions, recurring anniversaries and special celebrations, dotted the Roman year at the time of the Empire.

Each month had its festive days fixed around the Ides or at the middle of the Kalends, or in the first quarter of the Nones. By ancient tradition there were forty-five days of public holidays during the year subdivided into the *Lupercalia* in February, the *Parilia*, *Cerealia* and *Vinalia* in April, the *Vestalia* and the *Matralia* in June, the *Volcanalia* in August, and the *Saturnalia* in December. Then there were isolated festivities such as the *Robigalia* on April 25th, celebrated with sack races; the *ludi piscatorii* on June 8th with angling competitions; the *equus october* on October 15th with its horse races, and there were movable feasts depending upon the reigning emperor, in honour of his birthday, his accession to the throne or the apotheosis of his predecessor. Above all there were the great holidays instituted by the Republic in the gravest

hours of its history, to honour the gods and ostensibly to renew requests for their protection, but tacitly to increase the prestige and influence of the reigning leaders. Such festivals were the *Ludi Romani* dedicated to Jove; the *Ludi Plebei*, *Apollinares* and *Cereales* consecrated to Ceres; the *Megalenses* to the great mother Cybele; the *Florales* dedicated to Flora, and finally those feast days organised by victorious generals who sought to attribute supernatural qualities to their own triumphs in such occasions as the *Ludi Victoriae Sullanae*, the *Ludi Victoriae Caesaris* and the Augustan *Ludi Fortunae reducis*.

Yet other celebrations were less official, mainly suburban and popular and very cheerful: they ranged from rural junketings in honour of Anna Perenna, the year goddess, to solemn Latin holidays on the Alban Hills, festivals in honour of foreign but recognized deities, and military commemorations inside the *Castra Praetoria* (the City barracks) to which the plebs were doubtless admitted.

Clearly it was an age of amusements, but not necessarily amusements for amusements' sake. The *feriae* (holidays) had once been religious in intent even if with the years the Romans had lost that association and even forgotten the magical significance of the ritual. For example the angling match on June 8th was dedicated to the god Vulcan. The rally ended with a banquet of fried fish on the altar of the god, the victors being joined there by the city praetor who had supervised the festival and represented the god. The banquet of fried fish appears less prosaic and hearty if one remembers that it was a symbolic representation of the earlier sacrifice to Vulcan of human victims now represented by fish. The real significance of the ceremony was most probably unknown to those taking part, whether competitors or dignitaries. It had become simply a *festa* in which one joined light-heartedly, and where the various competitors were the main topic of conversation.

Similarly the *equus october* with its horse races on October 15th had originally had a double significance: a giving of thanks and a purification for the return of the army from the military campaigns waged from spring to autumn. Once the race used to end with the sacrifice of the winning horse and its decapitation by the priest of Mars immediately on reaching the finishing post. The sacrificial blood was divided into two parts, one part poured on the altar of the *Regia*, the home of the *pontifex maximus*, and the other handed to the Vestal Virgins to be used in purification ceremonies during the year. The head itself was given to the plebs from the *Suburra* and the market gardeners of the Via Sacra, who fought fiercely over it until one party finally gained the right to hang it up in their district.

The very word *munus* as used to define the gladiatorial games implied the ritual sacrifice of human victims to placate the wrath of the gods or to gain their favours. Tertullian speaks of « honours due to the Manes » (the spirits of the dead), but he writes as a learned commentator; people came to these bloody spectacles unaware of their ancient connection with religion. They accepted the preliminary ritual not as a sacred ceremony but simply as a proper and custom-

Actor in a comic mask. On the right the same mask beside a tragic mask. (Vatican Museum and Capitoline Museum, Rome).

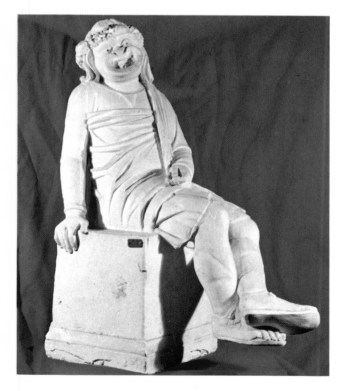

ary practice whose origins had been lost in the mists of time. The toga is another example: it was customary to wear it in public and no citizen would have dreamt of entering the amphitheatre dressed any other way. Yet Augustus had made its wearing obligatory and Claudius had made a decree forbidding it to be covered with a cloak except in bad weather, and never, in any case, before the prince had given the sign to be seated. The decrees reveal that the habit of always wearing the toga was disappearing and that all memory of its being a ceremonial dress in religious rites had vanished completely. But however ignorant a citizen might be he never allowed himself to behave incorrectly at the games, and would never eat or drink during the performance. The etiquette was such that even princes could not be excused, and the people muttered when they saw Caesar at the games still working from his couch, receiving messengers, reading reports and replying to them. Augustus never committed this error, either because he enjoyed the games or because he understood just how important their function was in the life of the State.

THE GAMES AS AN INSTRUMENT OF GOVERNMENT

The games were indeed the modern manifestation of the ancient liturgies, but they became so secular that eventually their function was entirely to improve the image of the emperors, who found the games the main occasion for contact with the people, now that the Senate had abdicated its powers and could no longer transmit public opinion to those in power. At the games the people's feelings could be gauged and sometimes directed into the desired channels; and the fiction of submitting to public pressures was a way of making them participate in, if not initiate, decisions. The games were, for most of the people, the best way of spending free time. The Romans no longer had the means to be interested in politics, and had plenty of spare time since the working day ended very early

Three comic masks from the Wallraf-Richartz Museum, in Cologne, the Kunsthistorisches Museum in Vienna and the Budapest Museum.

153

Mosaic showing actors. (Vatican Museum, Rome).

in the afternoon. There were at least 150,000 unemployed in the city, none interested in finding work since public assistance — regularly distributed under the Portico of Minucius — was quite sufficient to live on. The emperors needed a way of helping the populace to work off its passions and instincts indirectly: in a word, a way of keeping revolution at arm's length. For at this time the Roman people, once accustomed to wielding and delegating power, had fallen into such a poor state that the only way it could assert its power was by threats of revolution.

THE THEATRE

The Roman theatre was a legacy from Etruscan funeral rites, and performed both for the pleasure of the gods and to obtain favours from them; it began by having no fixed abode. Performances took place in the open in public squares, on an improvised stage which could be easily dismantled. The audience stood to watch. Seats appeared only in 145 B.C., by which time the performances had lost their ritual character. There was much objection to the use of seats, mainly on moral grounds. The concept of theatre architecture dates from this time: rows of seats originally put into a rectangular area were now replaced by wooden tiers,

Theatre of Marcellus, Rome. It had 20,000 seats and was begun by Caesar. Augustus dedicated it to his grandson and son-in-law, Marcellus. It was to have a very far-reaching influence on subsequent Roman architecture and on that of the Renaissance. Reconstruction by the architect Fidenzoni in the Museum of Roman Civilisation, Rome.

Mosaic depicting a company of ludiones, *provincial actors who started a fashion for dancing, music and mime in Rome.*

the whole covered in with a roof. If such a theatre had good acoustics it would be also used for musical and choral occasions and was indeed called an *odeum* (the modern Odeon).

The first mention of a permanent theatre occurs in Pliny the Elder who notes that M. Scaurus the *aedile* had had a most luxurious one built in about the middle of the first century B.C., but it is likely that the grandeur described by the writer really belongs to much later constructions. One of Pompey's gifts to Rome was the theatre in the Campus Nastius (55 B.C.) and this is the one that must be considered Rome's first established theatre. Pompey took his inspiration from the Hellenistic theatre at Mitylene.

The second established theatre was built by Cornelius Balbus in 13 B.C. and restored by Tiberius. Little is known about it. The third, the Theatre of Marcellus, was begun by Caesar and finished by Augustus who dedicated it to his son-in-law.

The basic design of a Roman theatre was a circle divided diametrically into the part reserved for the audience (the *cavea*) and the part for the actors, i.e. stage and back-stage. The *cavea* was a semi-circle of stepped seats divided into wedge-shaped sections by staircases and passages arranged radially. At the foot of the *auditorium* was the *orchestra* or *chorus* space, reserved in Rome for senators and important persons.

The stage was a wide and fairly deep raised platform, backed by a wall, treated as an elaborate front towards the stage with columns, statues, niches, decorations in bronze and marble; there were always three doors which opened and closed. Behind this were the dressing-rooms for the actors and for storage of properties and equipment. Farther back there were often gardens with flower beds and paths for walking in the intervals; these were sometimes covered in case it rained. The stage was equipped with elaborate machinery for working the scene changes, for raising and

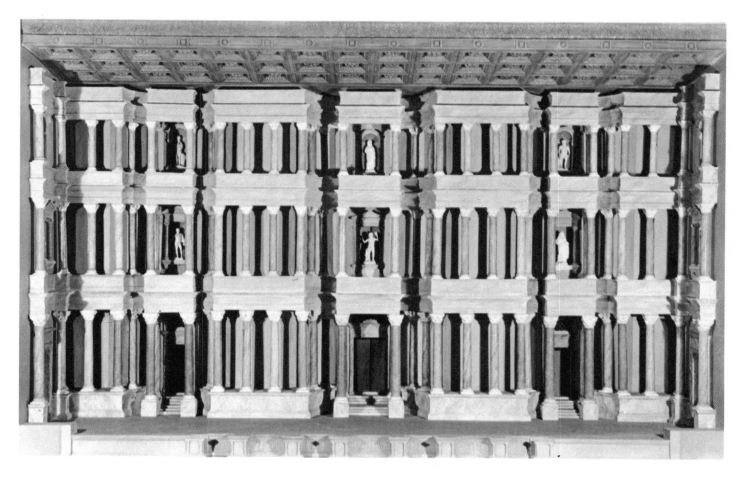

The set of the theatre at Sabratha with the three classic doors, the regalis *in the centre and the two* hospitales *at the sides. The theatre at Sabratha was built under Augustus. (Museum of Roman Civilisation, Rome. Reconstruction by Guidi).*

lowering the curtain into a special underground slot, or for drawing it back to either side as in the modern theatre. The stage had a roof, and the *cavea* could also be covered with an awning against the sun and the rain. In the course of building operations everything was done to assure good acoustics; « echoing bronze vases » were used, but the actual wooden stage which acted as a sounding box was the best acoustic aid.

WHAT THE PLAYS WERE LIKE

At first the plays were by no means original, for the Romans imitated and re-wrote foreign plays, or translated and staged them with no attempt at re-adaptation. They were much affected by foreign influence, which is hardly surprising. The Etruscan showmen and mimic actors who performed in Roman squares from 364 B.C. onwards introduced a taste for dances, music and above all mime to Rome. The *Ludi Fescennini* from the city of the Faliscans, Falerium, brought some coarse scenes of daily life in scurrilous language to Rome and roused a taste for license, whereas the *Atellanae fabulae* from the Oscan city of Atella were already familiar in Southern Italy and Sicily in the cities founded there by the Greeks. They were comedies and mimes and had very few characters, each one wearing a conventionally accepted mask: Dossennus, the cunning hunchback; Maccus, the glutton; Pappus, the silly old man; Buccus, the braggart. In Rome their complicated plots and wordy dialogues often offered a pretext for satirical jibes against well-known political people. Then at the beginning of the first century B.C. with L. Pomponius the mode took a literary form, with Roman town and country life as its subject.

Meanwhile, in the second half of the third century B.C., Greek tragedies and comedies had been translated

The pit of the great theatre at Pompeii as it looks today after restoration, ready to receive the audience.

and produced on the Roman stage. This was largely to the credit of Livius Andronicus of Taranto, who put the first Greek tragedy on the Roman stage in 240 B.C. His constant work for the theatre and his translations of Sophocles and Euripides achieved autonomy and official recognition for the theatrical *ludi*. From that moment onwards, the theatre had a certain number of days apportioned to it in the regular games calendar. In 214 B.C. four days were designated for the theatre during the Roman games in honour of Jove. Thereafter as the number of *ludi* increased, so did the number of theatre performances. These numbered about fifteen at the beginning of the third century B.C., and they increased to more than forty-five during the reign of Augustus.

However, the golden age of the Roman theatre

Theatrical scene in a mosaic from the National Archaeological Museum, Naples. It shows an interval in the performance: the actors have removed their masks and are preparing for the next act.

occupied the 250 years before the coming of Christ. This was the period in which the best Roman authors flourished, and among them Cnaeus Naevius, a younger contemporary of Livius Andronicus, who took his subjects from the myths and history of Rome itself, but without neglecting Greek models. He was considered the founder of the *fabula togata* (comedy with a Roman subject) and the *fabula praetexta* (tragedy with

a Roman subject). Naevius started presenting his own plays in 235 B.C., tragedies, comedies and farces inspired by the Greek theatre, from which he also borrowed the costumes and props used by the actors. They belonged to set characters: thus the soldier always carried a sword, the slave-trader a leather money bag and a straight stick, the master of the house a crooked stick, the cook a large spoon and a bowl full of food.

A performance of mimes, musicians and dancers in a mosaic from the Vatican Museum, Rome.

The masks were like those of the Greek theatre with holes for the eyes and mouth, abundant hair for the female characters and great beards for the males. Gradually these fell into disuse.

To the great period of the Roman theatre belong Plautus and Terence. Plautus, who died in 184 B.C., was the first great comic writer for the stage, and Terence remains to this day an unrivalled master of dialogue. Yet neither enjoyed much success with their contemporaries. The art of Terence was much more elegant and stylised than that of Plautus, and was directed at an aesthetic and cultured type of audience such as hardly existed in Rome.

The plebs much preferred the gladiatorial games and the circus races; society followed their example. Even the younger Pliny was affected by the passion and was forever regretting the attention given to « the miserable histrionics, by an even more miserable audience, and by people who boast of being serious and educated ». In his epistles he wrote: « When I think of this futile, monotonous and silly pastime (referring to the theatre) which glues people to their seats, I feel a certain pleasure at not being a victim of it ». The Emperor Trajan seemed to confirm Pliny's view: wishing to give his subjects extra privileges during the games, he decreed that the public could go in to the circus free for thirty days, and to the theatre free for only fifteen days. The combined number of seats in all three theatres amounted to a fifth of the seats available in the circus. In fact Trajan knew his public, and computed that the people interested in the theatre would be vastly fewer than those anxious to go to the games.

The theatre Pliny speaks of was already in decline. The last major dramatist, Seneca, had been writing his plays mainly for his pupil Nero rather than for the stage. In succeeding ages — and especially in the Elizabethan age — Seneca's plays were often considered as the highest examples of Latin tragedy and became a source of inspiration, yet from the dramatic point of view they lack life, movement and depth. They are in fact more suitable for declaiming in drawing-rooms or for reading aloud than for the stage. This was the fate of the Roman theatre faced with an audience which preferred recitation and songs (*cantica*) to dialogue (*diverbia*) and whose deepest interest was in the actors as individual stars and in the scenery as a fantastic and exotic display.

STARDOM

Perhaps the Roman tendency to adulate the actor prevented the Roman theatre from ever reaching the sublime heights of its Greek counterpart. The chief comedy actors of the Republic had practically abolished the chorus by making it come on to the stage and take part in the action. Under the Empire the chorus became an essential part of the action and completely lost its function of assuring counterpoint. It became just a body of people shifting about the stage as part of the fantastic set decor which rapidly transformed the theatre into a sort of magical realism quite unknown on the Greek stage. The dialogue was cut to the minimum needed to link up the various *cantica* sequences. In these, the actor was given full scope to express his personality, to capture the public's attention with the power of his voice, and the elegance of his gestures and movements. In fact he concentrated all the interest of the drama in his own person. The actor achieved all this by a fairly rigorous discipline. He kept his figure in trim with diet and plenty of exercise to loosen his muscles, and he made careful studies of human nature to find the best and most immediate means of moving his audience with the accent of truth. This is what the Roman theatre lover wanted: he idolized the actor, applauded and acclaimed him wildly, considered him the hero of the day: he invited him to his home and honoured him even though the law continued to call the actor a « histrionic » and label him as « infamous ».

The public wanted the fantasy of the stage scene to grow ever closer to reality, until the theatrical fiction no longer satisfied, however accomplished it was; if a character had to die on the stage, then die he really had to. So, at the last moment, the actor's place would be taken by a man condemned to death who, according to the story on the stage, would be either nailed to a cross, or eaten by wild beasts or burnt alive. All this probably exposed the Romans' basic desire to see on the stage the spectacle they liked best of all: the gladiatorial combats (*munera gladiatorum*).

AN IMPATIENT AUDIENCE

They had been waiting there since the night before, half asleep, but ready for a fight with anyone who might try to sit on a seat already taken. Some started to fall asleep, head in hands, others began to eat and drink but the laughter and arguments never ceased for a second.

If anyone moved, he left a friend to keep his vacant seat, and the wooden step echoed beneath his feet.

They were there long before the beginning of the show. The curtain was still down, hiding the scenery painted on wood; everyone knew it by heart as it was always the same. The back wall had three doors and the actors came and went through them.

Down at the foot of the tiers were the fourteen rows reserved for the relatives of equites and the tribunes, though everyone knew that they preferred to go to the other theatres, those of Marcellus, or Balbus or Pompey which were all built of stone. Important members of the audience always came at the last minute, but the poor who came without paying had to take the upper seats and spent their time complaining because some actor's voice didn't carry or because the theatre manager had not yet given out the free cakes (the *bellaria*) and the usual drinks.

Now that the sun was up and it was beginning to get warmer, the impatient audience loudly asked for the overhead blinds to be let down to protect them against the heat. A few with foresight had come provided with sunshades, but they joined in the general outcry because they liked shouting. The theatre staff had not yet arrived and the watchman would have nothing to do with the blinds.

A new hullabaloo broke out because the show was late in starting. Already some of the best seats had been occupied, a sure sign that it was nearly time to begin. But even when the curtain finally came down into its slot and the play started, the shouts and whistles and catcalls did not end. Some laughed at the performance of the first actor, whereupon his fans (*fautores*) clapped furiously and threatened the others with clenched fists. They were the *fautores* of yet another well-known actor, and had simply come to the theatre to make trouble. Just to make things perfect, the hired claque would start clapping and cheering as hard as they could.

When the actor who played Mercury came down from the sky on a rope looking just like a hanged man there were screams of laughter. The pulley worked rather badly and « Mercury's » fears got the better of him — he waved his legs wildly and the claque began to clap. When the thunder machine broke down the stage staff had to use the old (and not very successful) method of throwing stones into a brass container. This brought . more laughs and the audience shouted insults at the organisers, but the claque, obedient as always, clapped enthusiastically.

The play seemed too thin and commonplace. The dialogue went right back to Romulus, someone said. It all lacked salt and especially pepper.

In any case it was almost impossible to hear what the actors said because of the continual row made by the spectators — their laughs, long and loud, and sometimes belated when someone suddenly understood a joke after all the others, the rumble of footsteps on the boards as those who were tired pushed their way out past those who stayed seated, stumbling along the rows and catching their togas, without a thought for the people they were disturbing or the protests they made.

Those who really were interested in the play, and they were few, tried very hard to catch what was being said.

The characters were obvious since they were dressed according to convention and each in his appropriate garments, which was just as well since the masks simply represented the sex of the character, and were dark for men and light for women. If the gown was white, then the character was old, if coloured, then young. If it was purple-brown the character was rich, if red he was poor. A short tunic signified a slave, a *chlamys* (a short cloak) a warrior.

Most of the crowd protested, not because the play was feeble, but because they were so accustomed to a different kind of show: mass movement, processions, triumphs to the sound of trumpets and a thousand other fantasies which the organisers somehow or other managed to stage. Here there were just words piled on words and the crowd rapidly became bored by its monotony and began to wish they could finish the morning in the amphitheatre or the circus. Only the flute-playing during the intervals pleased that impossible audience, and for this good reason *dominus gregis*, the director of the troupe, escaped having to pay back the money to the organisers of the show.

Just as the final curtain was going up, the rain poured down and the blinds were of very little use. Everyone made a dash for shelter, and it was a miracle that the wooden stairways did not collapse. There are too many of these wooden theatres in Rome — that go up and come down every time there is an election. Supposing the public started knocking them down!

(sources: Statius, Suetonius, Martial and others)

CIRCUS AND AMPHITHEATRE

Lawful sacrifices to the gods, schools for character-building, understanding of foreign military exercises, capital executions: these were some of the functions which the educated Romans found in the munera, *the gladiatorial shows. But for the plebs, the* munera *were simply the show itself and its capacity of giving them a subtle sensation: horror. Centuries of civilisation have not wiped out this sensation, even in our day, and not even the establishment of the Christian ethic of love has succeeded in altering its nature. The basis of the gladiatorial combat was justice and fairness: the gladiators in the* munera *nearly always bore equal arms, and each hoped to survive because of his own courage, his own fighting spirit and his personal belief in his qualities as a warrior. Each fight represented the moment of truth for the gladiator. The Roman soldier-citizen who had already faced several such moments demanded that there should be no make-believe of war in the arena, but real war — no coloured water, but real blood. For the Romans it was natural that the best man should win — and that he should win at any cost.*

The *ludi* or games were of three kinds and each had its own particular setting: the *ludi circenses* in the circus, the *ludi scaenici* in the theatre and the *munera gladiatorum* which also included the *venationes* (combat with wild beasts) in the amphitheatre.

Various types of performances took place in the circus, from sham fights on horseback to elephant charges, from acrobatic feats of horsemanship at the gallop to jumping competitions by horsemen who rode lying down or kneeling. But chiefly the circus was the scene of races for chariots with two, three and four or more horses, the *bigae, trigae* and *quadrigae*, which were immensely popular for their spectacular value and for various economic and political interests attached to them.

The biggest, most important and most beautiful was the Circus Maximus. It served as a model for the other two smaller ones, the circus Flaminius (221 B.C.) and the circus Gai (built by Caligula).

The Circus Maximus fitted perfectly into the site it occupied in the depression between the Palatine and the Aventine hills — the track was in the valley of the Murcia and the seats rose up the slopes of the two hills. Originally the track was simply marked by two columns (*metae*) round which the competitors had to ride or drive. The *meta prima* stood at the foot of the Palatine in the cavity of the altar to the god Consus, an ancient agricultural divinity, which was originally uncovered only during the *Consualia* on August 21 and December 15 at the end of the grain harvest and the start of the sowing but later for the games as well. *Carcerea* or stables were then added to this primitive race-course. First they were crude wooden sheds, but later they were made of tufa and later still of marble. The two *metae* were then joined by a piece of raised ground (*spina*) upon which, in time, were placed the statues of divinities supposedly favourable to sport. An obelisk dating from Rameses II and brought to

Rome from Heliopolis was also set up there, and several other ornaments. Every ruler from Tarquin to Trajan contributed in some way to the embellishment of the circus and the organisation of the games.

THE CIRCUS GAMES

The *ludi circenses* always adhered to a strict ritual and had to take place again the following day if there had been an infringement. This was on account of their sacred origins. They had two parts: the *pompa* and the races. The *pompa* was a ritual procession which began on the Capitol and came down the Tuscus vicus to the Velabrum and through the Boarium Fora into the circus. It went round the track and dispersed in front of the emperor's enclosure after having deposited on the *spina* the effigies of the gods, which had been carried in the procession. The magistrate who presided over the games, the priests of various rites, the competitors and the youth of Rome on foot and on horseback, took part in the procession, as well as musicians, dancers and whole groups of satyrs and burlesque figures accompanying the images of the divinities and their symbols carried in stretchers (*ferculae*) and on carts (*tensae*).

Meanwhile the crowds were gathering in the circus and the first bets (*sponsiones*) were being placed, discussions were started on each charioteer's form and new acquaintances were struck up which might lead to friendships and possibly even weddings, in the case of girls. « ... Of course young men attended the circus », Juvenal writes. « The shouts, the bold wagers, the presence of elegant girls were exactly what they liked ». Ovid actually advises young men to attend the circus because many a pleasant acquaintance could be made there in the course of conversations before the event and especially during the excitement the races engender.

From the moment the magistrate rose to the sound of trumpets, the general excitement grew. Over his scarlet tunic, like that of Jove's, he wore his bordered purple toga: like a living statue, he held an ivory rod crowned with a golden eagle about to take flight, and on his head he wore a golden wreath of laurels, so

The Circus Maximus *was built in the little valley between the Aventine and the Palatine; the seats for spectators rose up the hillside, while the race track was on the flat land below. The course in this Circus was about 840 yards long and 87 yards wide. (Reconstruction from the Museum of Roman Civilisation, Rome).*

heavy that a slave had to help support its weight. Leaning over the arena from his enclosure, the magistrate threw down the white flag, the signal for the start of the races.

Beneath the enclosure just in front of the *carceres* the *quadrigae* (four-horse chariots) had lined up in the order established by drawing lots. The chariots were made of a very light box mounted on two wheels which only a man's weight could keep steady and balanced. Two horses were fastened to the shaft, while the other two were attached to the chariot by thongs. These outside horses had to bear the strain of the race, especially the first horse on the left who raced round the inside, closer to the *metae*. The skill shown at this bend decided whether the chariot would crash, or « shipwreck » as the Romans called it, throwing the driver out and causing a catastrophic collision with many dead or injured. To guard against such mishaps, the drivers wore a metal helmet and protected their legs with pads and bandaging.

At the starting signal the barriers came down and the chariots set off raising clouds of dust. It was a compelling sight: the horses' manes were studded with pearls, their harness decorated with buckles and amulets, the drivers in the bright livery of their stables, standing up with the reins round their bodies, whip in hand, leaning forward desperately trying to keep or gain first place, the incessant shouts of the supporters encouraging the horses from their stable. But it was not only the spectacle which made the crowd tremble with excitement: the honour of each stable was involved in every race, and this was never just a sporting contest. The very colours, white, red, blue, green, if not representing political parties, represented political ideologies and well-defined social positions. The « whites » and the « reds » might be anti-imperial forces, and as they lost place, up would come the « greens » supported by emperor and populace, and the « blues » backed by Senate and aristocracy. So much political passion was associated with a victory, as though it represented a symbol of political ascendancy, that some of the emperors had no hesitation in condemning to death over-vociferous members of the opposing factions.

One hundred and fifty thousand spectators would be following the race intently; the track was eighty-four yards wide and round it raced the four *quadrigae*; the completion of each lap was signalled by the reversing of one of the seven markers on the *spina* (either a bronze egg or a dolphin). Everything might be decided in the last round, when the horses would be asked to make a supreme effort. The anxiety of these last moments and the exultation of victory were reflected in the inscriptions commemorating the charioteer's performance. If he had kept the lead from start to finish, he would write « *occupavit et vicit* »; if he had managed to win by coming into the lead from second place, the inscription read « *successit et vicit* »; if, however, he managed to come right up to the first place from the last, he wrote proudly « *erupit et vicit* ». There were praise and cheers for the victor and his stable from all his supporters and curses from supporters of the losing stables. A preliminary curse might be arranged by inscribing an adversary's name on a plaque together with a suitable curse, and burying it in a tomb. If an unfortunate charioteer was thrown out of his chariot in the last round and dragged round the track because he could not cut through the harness and release himself, death was accompanied by a long cry of mixed exultation and commiseration from the public.

Fatal accidents were very frequent. Some charioteers could boast of more than a thousand victories — Scorpus with 2,048, Pompeius Epaphroditus with 1,467,

Pompeius Musclosus with 3,559, or a certain Diocles with 4,462, but there were also charioteers cut off in the flower of their youth like Fuscus at the age of twenty-four with fifty-seven victories, or Aurelius Mollicius at the age of twenty after 125 victories. Their popularity was widespread. The plebs decorated their houses with effigies of their heroes. Poets sang their praises or lamented their death. People bet on them always, and the rich laid such odds on them as to involve large capital sums, while the poor would passionately risk their last penny. Their popularity, as in every epoch, was tied up with the irregularity of their lives, and the charioteers lived as wildly as they pleased, to the extent of assaulting passers-by and robbing them; their fame guaranteed their immunity. They were also popular because they earned such enormous sums of money, different factions being prepared to pay fabulous retaining fees. It was said that the charioteer Diocles had accumulated a fortune of thirty-five million sesterces. The races increased in number as the years went by, rising from twenty to twenty-four a year, then to thirty, forty, forty-eight, and finally reaching as many as a hundred a year. The festival was not over with the end of a race. The excitement lasted all the day, and, by order of the emperor, a host of gifts and benefits had been distributed to the plebs — sweetmeats, cakes, little bags of money, I O Us which gave the right to a house, a farm or even a boat. The plebs were invited to a banquet;

Under the Empire the charioteers were divided into four factions: the veneta *wore blue, the* prasina *green, the* albata *white, the* russata *red. The colour of the charioteer's tunic gave the name to the faction. (National Museum, Rome).*

 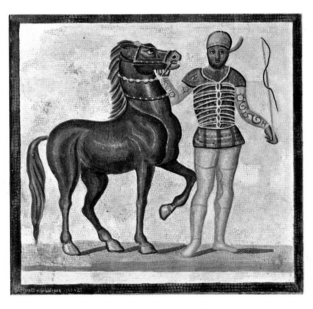 

Roman Amphitheatre at Nîmes. (Museum of
Roman Civilisation, Rome).

the losers were restored to calm and a feeling of balance,
almost lost during the race, was re-established. This
feeling of balance was what the emperors sought: it
enabled them to govern in relative tranquillity.

THE AMPHITHEATRE

In his Tusculanae Cicero maintains that the finest
example of death occurs in a contest between gladiators,
and this seems to have been the current opinion among
the Romans, who attended the frequent butcheries
with savage enjoyment. The *munera gladiatorum*, like all
the other spectacular games, had started in Rome as
a kind of religious funeral rite, perhaps as a relic of
the old Samnite custom of offering human sacrifice on
the tombs of important people. In Rome, in fact, the
first recorded gladiatorial contests took place at the
funeral of Junius Brutus in 264 B.C., but they very
soon lost their sacred character to become mere entertainment, for some even an instructive entertainment
which the younger Pliny wrote « lit the flame of courage by showing that the love of glory and the desire
to win could be found even in the hearts of slaves and
criminals ». The intellectuals might be naïve enough
to justify contests which were really evidence of incred-

167

Reconstruction of the interior of the Colosseum.

The 45,000 seats in the Flavian Amphitheatre otherwise called the Colosseum were not sufficient to seat the crowds of passionate circus devotees. The first seats rose above the arena in order to protect the public from the wild

ible cruelty, but politicians were very clear as to the value of the *ludi*. They actually consolidated their power by means of the *munera* and the fanaticism they roused in the people, for whoever sought a political career and the certainty of being elected had only to organise a gladiatorial contest at his own expense. This practice had reached such proportions that the Senate in 63 B.C. sponsored a law intended to put a brake on it. By this, the election of a magistrate who had organised games at any time during the two years preceding his election, would be declared null and void. Nevertheless Caesar and Pompey continually used the games to increase their own prestige, and it

animals. Consuls, senators and equites had special entrances and special seats. The doorways at the end of the major axis (see detail of the interior on the left) were used for the entry of the triumphal processions during the performance. A low door called the libitinaria *was used for removing dead bodies. (Reconstruction in the Museum of Roman Civilisation, Rome).*

was a friend of Caesar's who invented the amphitheatre.

Previously the *munera* had taken place in the circus or had simply used certain open squares where temporary seating could be erected. But in 53 or 52 B.C. Curio the younger, a friend of Caesar's, was a candidate for the office of tribune and decided to base his electoral campaign on spectacular games and munificence, for which he decided to build two semi-circular wooden theatres set back to back with the curves touching and mounted on pivots. At the end of the show the two theatres were to swivel round to form an oval with the arena in the centre once the two stages had

been removed. The public was to remain seated during the swivelling process.

This was indeed the first amphitheatre. Caesar immediately adopted it and built one in 46 B.C., albeit a temporary one and of wood, to celebrate his four triumphs that year (Gallic, Alexandrian, Pontic and African). The first permanent amphitheatre was built in 29 B.C. by C. Statilius Taurus but was destroyed in the burning of Rome in A.D. 64.

Eleven years later Vespasian drained the marsh of the *Domus Aurea*, between the Velia, the Coelian and the Esquiline hills and filled it in; there he began to build another amphitheatre with blocks of travertine

from the Tibur quarries (near the modern Tivoli) so big that a new road had to be made, eighteen feet wide, to bring them in. After Vespasian's death, the emperor Titus finished the building and inaugurated it in A.D. 80 with a hundred consecutive days of games. Later the emperor Domitian decorated his brother's work with ornamental statues, friezes and bronze shields. Built as it was near the Colossus of the Sun, the Flavian amphitheatre came to be called the Colosseum. It could seat 45,000 people, with standing room for 5,000. There were seventy entrance doors, four for the staff and sixty-six for the public. Each entrance was numbered and seat tickets bore the entrance number and the number of the tier and the seat.

The arena occupied about 3,610 square yards and was surrounded by a protective iron railing. Underneath the arena was a complicated system of canals which allowed the whole area to be rapidly flooded for naumachiae (mock naval battle). There were also underground cages, corridors and ramps up which came the wild animals, when they were needed in the contests.

THE *VENATIONES*

From the first, wild and exotic animals formed one of the main attractions of the programme. The spectacle was not always an exhibition of hunting; sometimes it was simply a show of wild animals which had been tamed: panthers harnessed to a chariot, tigers performing at the order of a ringmaster, clever elephants who wrote with their trunks in the sand of the arena, strange and unfamiliar animals on show to a public that never ceased to be fascinated. Sometimes fights between wild animals were staged, bears against buffaloes, an elephant against a rhinoceros, or else *tauromachiae* of man against bull as in the modern Spanish corrida. The favourite scene was the hunter against the wild beast. Usually the native setting of the wild animal was reproduced; and the gladiator was often unarmed and was expected to use the cover as though he really were in some remote forest at grips

Fight against wild animals with sword and shield. (Bas-relief preserved in the Villa Torlonia in Rome).

Venationes, *the combats either of beast against beast, or man against beast. (Mosaics in the Vatican Museum in Rome).*

with a bear or a lion. Sometimes the show took the form of a mass hunt with archers and armed gladiators. As many as three or four thousand animals might be slaughtered in a hunt of this sort — five thousand were killed for the inauguration of the Colosseum.

But hunts or *venationes* were only a change from the *munera*. The real spectacle of the amphitheatre was armed combat, in which armed men fought and killed in order not to be killed themselves.

THE GLADIATORS

The gladiators were all differently armed, which gave an extra thrill of uncertainty to the encounter and increased the interest in the betting on which the Romans spent as much money as on the circus races, yet what drew great audiences to the amphitheatre was not so much the betting as the lust for real battle at which they could be present and experience with all the appropriate emotions, yet without being involved in any personal risk. The *munera* were organised in imperial Rome by State functionaries who had taken the place of the former *lanistae* (retired professional gladiators), who still ran gladiator schools in the provinces and practically owned the gladiators. These had been acquired as slaves, or else as free men who had temporarily sold themselves to the *lanista* body and soul, abandoning all their human rights.

The Roman gladiators, a small army of fearless men to whom the emperors did not hesitate to turn

in time of need, were largely recruited among prisoners-of-war, men condemned to death and ruined sons of good families who were drawn by the vision of a life without responsibility, and above all by the illusory prospect of instant rewards of fame and fortune without the necessity of having to look for work.

In the two barracks on the Via Labicana (the *Ludus magnus* and the *Ludus matutinus*) the recruits began their training under the supervision and rule of older gladiators of proved valour. They were first

Naumachiae, *fights between small ships took place in buildings of the same name. The fairly large arena of a naumachia would be flooded before the spectacle. (From the map of ancient Rome at Porta S. Silvestro, Rome).*

trained by exercises against a post (*palus*) planted in the ground, and then they were gradually exposed to even greater difficulties until they reached the rank of *primus palus*, the last phase of training; the gladiator was then ready to enter the arena.

On the eve of the contest the gladiators met at a banquet (*cena libera*) which anyone could watch. They were carefully inspected by those who planned to bet on them on the next day. The *morituri* (those about to die) ate ravenously and with cynical amusement, for the meal might well be their last.

The next day they entered the arena in purple tunics, unarmed, and marched across the amphitheatre to the emperor's enclosure calling: « *Ave imperator, morituri te salutant* ». (« Hail, Emperor, we who are about to die salute thee »). Then the arms were examined, the weapons distributed and the fight began. They fought in different ways according to their weapons. The *retiarius* or net-fighter wore a short tunic fastened by a broad protective belt and carried no other weapon of attack but a net (*iaculum*) and a trident (*fuxina*); for defence he had a leather and metal armband terminating in a shoulder piece (*galerus*) up on the left shoulder. The *retiarius* spent his time avoiding his attacker and waiting for a suitable moment to throw his net over him, and then if successful, to stab him with his trident or with a short dagger. Usually the adversary of the *retiarius* was a *mirmillo*, so called because there was a picture of a fish called *murma* on his helmet. The combat was a representation of a fight of a fisherman (the trident was the instrument used by the tuna fishermen) against a fish. There were Samnite gladiators armed with a sword (*spatha*) and a shield (*scutum*), Thracians who fought with a kind of scimitar (*sica*) and defended themselves with a small round shield (*parma*), the *essedarii* who gave battle from a kind of British war chariot (the *essedum*) which they drove around the arena at tremendous speed, and the *dimachaeri* who fought with two swords.

The essence of the combats was to show the people of Rome the way their enemies had fought and the weapons they had used, but the organisers were free to introduce whatever they liked to rouse more interest. So there might be a fight between *andabates* who wore a helmet with a solid visor which was lowered so that

they fought blind, or there might be a *sportula*, a sort of free-for-all for several gladiators — a *munus sine missione*, a fight without a finish which could not end because as one gladiator died a fresh gladiator was substituted for him, and even the most valorous fighter could not hope to survive in such circumstances.

Sometimes the gladiators fought unwillingly and then a monitor would go into the arena accompanied by scourgers (*lorarii*) to incite the gladiators until they fought fiercely. Slaves dressed up as Charon and armed with hammers made certain of death by hitting the skull with a mallet and then their assistants, the *libitinarii*, carried off the body and raked over the bloodstained sand.

Sometimes the contestants were so well matched that neither succeeded in killing the other and the combat would be declared null as they ceased to fight, wounded and tired. Sometimes one of the two, wounded and exhausted, lay down and raised his left arm in sign of surrender. In principle it was left to the victor to decide the fate of the vanquished, but he renounced his claim in the presence of the emperor, who would decide only after consulting the crowd. If the defeated gladiator had fought well, the mob would shout « *Mitte!* » (let him go) raise their thumbs and wave

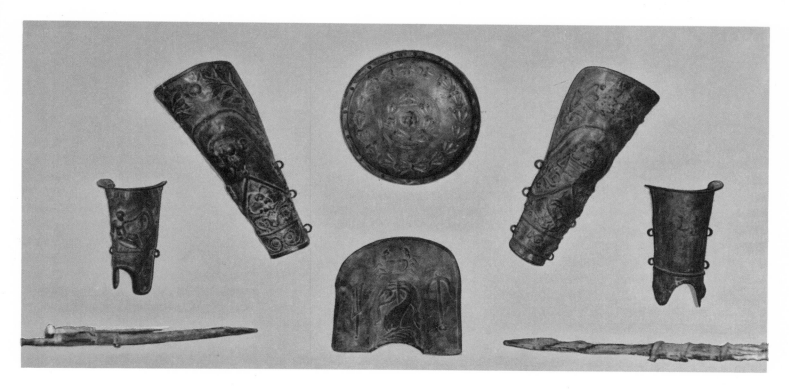

Full-dress helmet and arms of a gladiator. (National Archaeological Museum, Naples).

their handkerchiefs; if the emperor showed his fist with the thumb up it meant that a life was conceded. But if the gladiator had fought badly, the mob would cry « *Jugula!* » (cut his throat) and the emperor's thumb pointing downward would signify his agreement with the sentence. The victor then gave the final stroke amid the applause and cheers of the crowd and was rewarded on the spot by prizes carried into the arena on a silver dish, precious jewels, bracelets and gold coins and sometimes even the *rudis*, a wooden stick or sword which signified that he had become a freed man. From that moment a gladiator could withdraw from the arena and live on his prizes. But very often he would renew his contract with the *lanista* or the Roman organiser and re-enter the ring immediately, probably to die. The epitaph of a certain Flammus tells us that he had received the *rudis* four times and had each time « signed on » again.

Capital sentences were also carried out during the games with all the trappings of a spectacle. Perhaps through a sense of shame or because executions in themselves were not specially interesting, they took place at dawn when the amphitheatre was almost empty or at noon, when the spectators were filing out for lunch.

The dawn executions were for those whom the magistrates had condemned *ad bestias*. This frightful torment was unintentionally invented by Augustus, when he allowed the bandit Seluros to be dropped into a pit of ravenous panthers and leopards. The criminals condemned *ad bestias* would be pushed unarmed into the arena singly or in a group, and on to their defenceless bodies would be unleashed bears, bulls, lions and tigers. This was usually inflicted on Christians.

At noon the *gladiatores meridiani*, those convicted of murder, theft and larceny and condemned to die in the amphitheatre, would enter. The first couple would consist of an armed and an unarmed man. The armed man would kill the unarmed, only to be deprived of his arms and in turn be killed by the next condemned man. This revolting spectacle also had its devotees like the emperor Claudius who preferred missing his lunch to missing the thrill of another's death rattle. In spite of his talent for government, he set aside the duties of the State to stay in the amphitheatre from dawn to dusk. Only with the fall of the Empire and the triumph of Christianity which gave all men, whatever their condition, a hitherto unknown dignity, were the *munera gladiatorum* and the verdicts *ad bestias* suppressed. But that did not happen until the fifth century A.D.

173

CHARIOT AND HORSE RACES IN THE CIRCUS

The great oval arena of the circus is empty but the tiers of seats are buzzing and black with heads, like a restless beehive. Transparent, full, white clouds come in from the west and disperse, hiding the sun from time to time. Like the swell of a great river the cries of the crowd rise high before the chariot race. Any new happening in the arena is immediately reflected in the tone of those thousands of voices. The entry of a servant walking slowly across the hippodrome, the opening of a cage, brings a sudden silence on the tiers followed by an explosion of excited voices.

Then suddenly everyone rises in his seat, from the first seats reserved for the senators and their families, and the second seats where the *equites* and their families sat, to the last high row where the people waited fuming with impatience and excitement. Gigantic applause greets the entry of the emperor and his family. Curiosity in the main drives these 150,000 people to interrupt their chatter and discussions about the horses, the drivers, the Greens and the Blues, the *Prasini* and the *Veneti*, arguments which were capable of bringing supporters to blows.

In the silence that follows the emperor's entry there comes a faint sound of slow music from far away, borne in on the wind. Everyone turns to watch the door of the *carceres*, and now the first part of the procession emerges. It had started a little time ago at the Capitol. The magistrate, donor of these games, heads the procession and greets the emperor from triumphal chariot. He is dressed in purple and carries a long ivory sceptre surmounted by an eagle. A slave supports the golden crown on his head and he is surrounded by young men on foot and on horseback.

Now there is another long outburst of applause. The charioteers enter in their *quadrigae*, dressed in brief tunics bound with leather bands. Here come the Greens who have the sympathy of the whole crowd, and now the Blues whose appearance rouses cries of execration from one part of the circus and mad applause from the other. Finally comes a motley procession of musicians and dancers, attendants raising clouds of incense, bearers sagging beneath the weight of litters laden with gold and silver vases, sacred and imperial statues, and then more superb gold chariots.

As the procession stops and crowds round the altar for the sacrifices, the interest of the crowd ceases and all eyes are on the charioteers. Shouts, cheers and imprecations fly across the overheated atmosphere of the arena. Special interest is focused on the first horse on the left of the *quadrigae*. He will determine the race. He is the best and is therefore idolized. « Look there's *Delicatus*! And that's *Scholasticus*! » Everyone knows the horses' names.

This is the crucial moment when bets are made. Everyone seems to have waited for the *quadrigae* to pass before deciding how to bet. But of course this is not quite true: they just wanted to have one more look at their favourites. And as the horses pass by in a slow trot which shows the play of muscles rippling under the shining coat, the firm tendons and the supple strength in every movement, the passion for racing in the great bright eyes and in the proud curve of the neck, the crowd for once is silent with admiration as it watches. The harness is bright with spangles and tiny bells, the manes plaited and sprinkled with gold dust, the tails tied up well out of the way.

The horses themselves seem to know how much admiration they rouse as they step by lightly, powerfully and under complete control. No sooner has the last horse passed than the bets are laid. Some bet a few coins, others all they have. These are the last moments and odds are mounting feverishly.

Now the *quadrigae* go into the *carceres*, and as the audience goes wild, they reappear, line up and the race begins. Everyone has his eyes glued to his favourite, fists clenched and cheering wildly. The charioteers, too, seem to have gone mad. Fastened to their chariots, with muscles tensed, they urge their horses on with whip and with shouts. They are enveloped in a cloud of dust and the audience glimpses briefly the bodies of the horses and the gold of the chariots.

Cirno's chariot is in front and manages to reach the *spina* which runs for about 200 yards down the course, dividing it in half. This will enable him to make the shortest turn when he reaches the *meta*. Now suddenly Cirno's horses seem to falter. The shrieks of the crowd blame Cirno for having taken the turn too wide so that another chariot overtakes him on his left.

Seven times they must all go round. One of the blue chariots has been pressed too hard against the *spina* by the green chariot, and the charioteer has been knocked down so that eight horses are struggling in a bloody tangle, while the oncoming chariots do all they can to avoid it.

Cirno is in the lead again now and leaving the rest behind. He turns sharply round the *meta* with a skill which wins the admiration of the crowd. Meanwhile the attendants have cleared the track. Three horses were killed and one charioteer has just died. But Cirno, the idol of the crowd, has reached the winning-post and crossed the *calx*, the white line of victory.

The Greens have won, and it is just as well they did, otherwise the city would be in mourning, sad and upset, like the morning after the defeat at Cannae.

(sources: Ovid, Juvenal, Silius Italicus)

RELIGION, RITES AND PRIESTS

The Romans originally conceived their gods in the shape of men, and this anthropomorphic religion absorbed all the other gods in the Mediterranean basin. It was reasonable that, born of a people primarily concerned with the concrete and the everyday, the Roman religion should create this motley array of gods whose powers were manifested within the framework of home and fields and whose influence was kept within carefully defined limits.

It was a family and domestic religion which, because of the Roman's own concept of society, soon became the religion of the State.

Rome, as Cicero says, knew how to absorb other races and this was the basis of her successful rule. With the same hospitality she took into her Pantheon gods of every nationality, romanising them or maintaining their original cult. She opposed only those religions likely to upset the well-established politico-religious structure which had become, in fact and in law, the religion of the State. She sometimes looked with suspicion upon the religions of the East, and for centuries read a message of political and social subversion into the Christian ethic.

In its official structure Roman religion remained abstract and cold, but was practised with sincerity throughout the countryside, in the cult of deities whose genius was admirably suited to the people who created them — the deities of family and fields. As long as Rome itself lived, these cults would survive.

Of all the pagan religions practised by the civilised peoples of the past it can be said that none was less endowed with ethical and spiritual principles than the Roman religion. The religion of the Latins — and moreover of the other Italian peoples, the Umbrians and Oscans — was little more than a form of nature worship or a rudimentary anthropomorphism. It had none of the lively and varied mythology of the Greeks. None of its beliefs or rites had any of the spirit of supernatural mystery which impregnated Egyptian religion and gave rise in Greece to so many doctrines and to the development and cult of the Orphic and Dionysiac mysteries.

There was nothing of the kind in Rome or Latium. Content to clothe in human form the forces and manifestations of a deified nature, the Latin people left these divinities in a state of abstract personification,

with neither name nor sex. Only much later did some among them become detached from the general mass of divinities and acquire a distinct personality of their own.

To these gods, to the greater as to the lesser, all regarded simply as beings with superhuman powers, the shepherds and the peasants of Latium addressed their prayers and their sacrifices in the hope of ensuring the satisfaction of needs. Prayers, petitions and sacrifices would, however, be useless, they thought, if these powerful overlords were not offered the petitions and offerings they demanded — in the prescribed form: this explains the precise formula and meticulous ritual of their invocations to the divinities.

It was at this point that the State intervened to regiment the gods and codify the rituals and the formulas. Numa Pompilius is possibly a legendary personage, but tradition has identified him with the work of the first anonymous legislators of the Eternal City. Religion represented an essential part of the monarchical and later republican constitution of the new Latin city; the priests, surest intermediary between gods and men, as well as the depositaries of religious rites, rapidly gained great ascendancy in the public life of the State.

Such a religion, effective both in juridical affairs and in matters of protocol, whose sphere of action and influence was clearly defined and confined, could easily be invested with a political significance. This is what happened to Roman religion. It was divided into two separate cults: one public and official and the other private and domestic. The first, modelled on the second, fixed and one might say stylised the essential elements. In public, and consequently in private, everything had its place, its rank, its time, rigorously defined: rites, priests, even gods were classified according to rank into major and minor; amongst the former were three of supreme importance: Jupiter, Mars and Quirinus, then the nine others, their order of precedence being reflected in the ranks of the *flameni*, their earthly ministers.

Inevitably contacts with the other peoples of the peninsula, in particular with the Etruscans and the Greeks, brought new gods and new cultural concepts to the notice of the Romans. The State soon intervened to regulate and discipline what it was unable to reject or what it found expedient or opportune to welcome. A special college of priests was set up with ten « ministers of religion » (*decemviri sacris faciundis*) to supervise each introduction of new gods and to codify the new rites within the framework of the official religion.

Thus the Roman religion lacked a « mythology » which, like that of the Greeks, would regulate the reciprocal relationships of friendship or enmity of the gods and codify their fantastic adventures. Yet it often pleased the Romans to bestow the names of *pater* and *mater* upon their gods: epithets which reflected their piety. Later, when the Romans became acquainted with the Greek gods, they assimilated them into their own Olympus and attributed to most of their Roman deities the characteristics and myths of the corresponding Greek divinities. Until then, the Romans had never depicted gods in sculpture or painting, or raised temples to them, except to Vesta, in whose temple the sacred fire burned; they preferred to worship in a sacred place (*locus*) or in an enclosure upon an open-air altar (*fanum*).

THE MOST ANCIENT GODS OF THE ROMANS

At the beginning of the republican era — between 500 and 400 B.C. — the Romans separated their gods into two categories: first came the most ancient divinities, who belonged to the original religion of Rome, and then the more recent gods brought to the Romans by the other peoples of the peninsula, the Etruscans or the Italian Greeks, and absorbed into the state religion. The first were called *di indigetes* (gods of the country) and the others *di novensiles* (gods of recent importation). The greatest of the *indigetes* were Jupiter, Mars, Quirinus, Juno, Janus, Vesta, Lares, Penates, Saturn and Neptune.

Jupiter (*Iuppiter*, from *Jovis Pater*) is the god of the heavens, and from the heavens he dispenses light to mankind or sends down thunderbolts (*I. Fulgurator*) or rain (*I. Pluvius*). He was venerated in Rome from the earliest times, and his principal sanctuary was on the Capitol. In this temple — under the name of Jupiter, Best and Greatest — he was venerated as the divine protector of the State, the god of loyalty and oaths; and the Ides, the thirteenth or fifteenth day in every month, was sacred to him.

Mars or Marsapicus we see under the twofold aspect of god of agriculture and god of war. As god of agriculture he watched over the sowing of the seed and the spring seedlings. The month of March was assigned to him, and ceremonies for the purification of the fields — such as the *Ambarvalia* of the month of May — were performed in his honour. As god of war he protected the country from devastation by enemies and took care of the army in its campaigns. Under this aspect he was venerated in two very ancient shrines — in the Campus Martius and at the *Regia* in the *Forum*, where the sacred arms of the god were kept: shields and spears. The feasts of Mars fell in March and October to mark the opening and closing of military campaigns.

Quirinus, the name of Romulus after his deification, was particularly venerated in ancient times, and then forgotten. He was the god of the *Quirites*, that is the Romans under arms (literally « men armed with lances », derived from *quiris*, a lance or spear). Legend had it that Quirinus was none other than Romulus, and that Romulus went to heaven on his death. Jupiter, Mars and Quirinus constituted a divine triad in ancient Rome, a trinity of the chief deities of the city. Priests were appointed to each cult. These were the *flameni*, recruited among the patrician families, and elected for life. The *Flamen Dialis* attended on Jupiter, the *Flamen Martialis* on Mars and the *Flamen Quirinalis* on Quirinus.

Juno (*Iuno*) was the female counterpart of Jupiter and was venerated as a goddess of the sky, more particularly of the night sky and the moon — *Juno Lucina*. She was, therefore, specially associated with the new moon, which coincided in the Roman calendar with the beginning of the month. Roman months were calculated according to the lunar cycle, and the Calends or beginning of the month was dedicated to her. Later she became like her Greek equivalent, *Hera*, the spouse of Jupiter and the goddess of marriage and conjugal life, as well as the patroness of women in general, under the title of *Juno Pronuba*. Her titles of mother and queen derived from her position as co-protector of the state with *Jupiter Optimus Maximus*.

Janus (*Ianus, Ianus pater*) was the ancient guardian and deity of all gates, portals and arches, having two heads and looking both ways. From being the god of entrances he quickly became the god of beginnings, the beginning of the day, the month, the year and life itself. January, the first month, was therefore dedicated to him, along with the first feast of the year.

Vesta was the goddess of the domestic hearth. She symbolized the sanctity and the eternal quality of family ties. She enjoyed particular veneration as patron of a symbolic national « hearth », an emotional shrine of the state over which she watched with a college of priestesses (the Vestal Virgins) tending an ever-burning flame in a little temple in the middle of the Forum.

There were other ancient family deities, the *Penates* and *Lares*, the former being gods of the actual household affording daily help and protection to the family; the latter were the spirits of departed ancestors watching with especial concern the perpetuation of the family and the race. The cult of these divinities was closely linked with that of Vesta. Just as a state Vesta was venerated, so state *Lares* and *Penates* were created whose worship was also conducted in the temple of Vesta.

Saturn (*Saturnus*) was the god of the fields. He was said to have derived his name from sowing (*sero,*

Head of Mercury from Veii. Etruscan influence was strong on primitive Roman religion. (Villa Giulia Museum, Rome).

sevi, satum). He protected the grain seed in the earth and distributed health and well-being to men. His feast — the *Saturnalia* — began on December 17th and lasted seven days, a time of great rejoicing in which even the slaves participated freely, forgetting if only for a few hours the heavy yoke of their masters.

Neptune (*Neptunus*) was the chief marine divinity of the Romans, and like his Greek counterpart Poseidon, the protector of sailors and navigation. The first horse, Scyphius, was supposed to have been created by Poseidon, so Neptune was also the protecting divinity of horses.

FOREIGN DEITIES

During the reigns of the last kings and the early years of the Republic, the first foreign deities were introduced into the state religion of Rome.

The temple at Tebessa believed to have been dedicated to Minerva. It was built on a high podium and was particularly richly decorated with eagles, trophies, victories, garlands and rosettes. (Reconstruction by Gismondi in the Museum of Roman Civilisation, Rome).

King Tarquin was reputed to have purchased certain collections of oracular books from the Italo-Greek city of Cumae. These Sybilline (*libri sybillini*) books were believed to have been dictated by a prophetess or sybil who lived at Cumae. A college of twelve priests (*decemviri sacris faciundis*) was instituted to consult the books, read and interpret the oracles, and conduct the appropriate sacred ceremonies.

The books being of Greek origin, their ceremonies and prayers were addressed to the Greek gods. It was therefore necessary from time to time for the *decemviri* to have to ask the government to include Greek gods in Roman ceremonies. In this way Apollo and Demeter entered Roman mythology, the latter as goddess of agriculture and harvests, after her native Greek name of Ceres had been changed. Hermes, the Greek god of commerce, became Mercury. Aesculapius, god of health and the medical arts, was the Greek god Asclepios. Pluto, or Dis, was the Greek god of the lower world and of wealth. The Greek mother of the gods, Cybele, joined the Roman mythology much later, about the time of the second Punic war.

Roman gods on Trajan's Arch at Benevento: Minerva armed with helmet and lance, Jupiter bared to the waist with sceptre and lightning, Juno veiled. In the background Hercules, Bacchus, Ceres and Mercury with his wand or caduceus.

In the course of time new foreign divinities received special temples built for him or her beyond the sacred area of the city. Only the temples of the original Roman or Italic gods were allowed within this area.

Soon foreign religious beliefs of doubtful nature and practices began to invade Italy, and when freedom was demanded for cults of this kind they were banned absolutely. Those who had been won over to the orgiastic rites of the cult of Bacchus at the beginning of the second century now paid dearly for their devotion to the god. These cults had established themselves in

Etruria, coming north from the Greek colonies of Southern Italy, and had spread throughout the peninsula, with many adherents in Rome itself. Alarmed by the current rumours, no doubt exaggerated, about Bacchic practices, the Senate ordered the dissolution of all Bacchic societies and condemned all who were found guilty of damaging public or private morality to the most severe penalties, including death. The famous Senate committee on the Bacchanalia was formed. It suppressed any associations practising the cult in Rome and throughout Italy. Immediately after

The child Bacchus. (Mosaic from the National Museum, Rome).

The child Hercules strangling serpents: from the Hercules legend on frescoes in the House of the Vettii, Pompeii.

the Bacchanalian affair came the massive expulsion from Rome and Italy of all the oriental astrologers, the so-called Chaldaeans, in the year 130 B.C.

However, the Senate, in assuming the responsibility for defending the integrity of the state religion against influences deemed to be irreconcilable with its nature, and in its determination to uphold the place of a state religion in the constitution, had taken on a task beyond its strength. Ever-growing contacts with Asia Minor, Syria and Egypt increased the number of those attracted by the mystical and the orgiastic elements in these religions. Here was something not to be found in the formalism of the ancestral creeds. Actually the most ardent among the propagandists of the oriental religions — in the last centuries of the Republic — were the heads of the State, the great captains and dictators who came to power during the troubled times of the civil wars, and chief among them Sulla, who also brought the works of the Greek philosophers to Rome.

To the disrupting influences of the oriental cults was now added that of the philosophical schools: the philosophers taught that the gods were unreal and abstract figments of the human imagination, creations far removed from, and foreign to, the life of man or nature. They denounced the practice of cults as a purely conventional activity. It mattered little to the philosophers that their beliefs were accepted only amongst the most cultured classes of society, for almost all public offices and the priesthood were the exclusive privilege of patrician families. The common people followed only the oriental cults. So in the last period of the Republic it was the priests who were the first to give up acceptance of these divinities and cults, which made them smile so condescendingly in secret. One can see how it came about that the high posts in the great priestly colleges of Pontiffs, Augurs, and *Quindecemviri sacris faciundis* were filled purely for their

The purpose of the Mysteries was to be united with the gods and seek the salvation of the soul through special rites and ceremonies. Here is a detail from a series of wall paintings in the Villa of the Mysteries in Pompeii, exquisitely painted and showing some part of the initiation ceremonies. These religious practices came from the Orient and had a considerable following in Rome.

political importance, while the lesser sacerdotal positions, carrying no influence on public life, often remained empty.

In the lower classes the striking collapse of the official religion, the scepticism and scorn that were shown for rites, temples and ceremonies caused growing despair. Where would it all end? How would the gods take vengeance on this impious people who had once conquered the world with their help and who now cast them aside?

The answer to this agonizing doubt seemed to lie in the ruins and massacres of the civil wars that raged in Rome and throughout the Republic between 50 and 30 B.C. Pious souls saw divine retribution in the terrible events of these twenty years: they longed for a return to calmer times which they feared they might never see unless the meaning and practice of religion were restored to their places in the minds of people and government.

DOMESTIC CULTS AND THE CULT OF THE DEAD

Public worship, the worship led by specially appointed priests in honour of the protecting gods of the State, was developed from domestic cults and primitive forms of religion practised in the humble dwellings of the Latin cities and in shepherds' huts. The state religion gradually became quite separate from its origins.

Domestic cults probably had their origins in the sacred character of certain objects or acts closely associated with family life. The hearth round which the women busied themselves was looked upon as the very centre of the household and the family: there the family prayed and made sacrifices to Vesta, the goddess of hearth fire, and the fire itself acted as her image. Close to her they kept the statues of the Lares and Penates and the god Genius (the daemon or spirit of the family).

The Lares were probably at first local protecting Genii or good spirits who watched over the land and dwelling of the tillers of the soil. Their annual feast, the *Compitalia*, was celebrated at the *compita* or crossroads where several neighbouring properties met. In time the Lares of the highways came to be distinguished from the Lares of the hearth. The latter had their cult within the house and were held to be the surviving spirits of the dead who, though now beneath the soil, did not altogether forget their former surroundings and friends. Writers **also** mention a single *Lar familiaris*, probably indicating a collective spirit personifying all those once belonging to a family but now wandering in the mysterious regions beyond the tomb.

Since the protection of the Lares extended to the whole family, including the slaves, in large properties the cult was entrusted to the wife of the farmer (*villica*) who worshipped them formally three times a month: at the Calends, Nones and Ides, and on the occasion of other feasts of the master's household: births, marriages, leavetakings, homecomings, deaths, and also when a baby spoke its first word.

It is difficult to define the idea of the Genius, that other member of the domestic pantheon. The very

The goddess Roma. (Museum of Roman Civilisation, Rome).

root of the word — *gen* — means the vital principle underlying birth, surviving death, and passing from one man to another, a spiritual essence perpetuating itself unchangingly whilst the form itself changes; a divine spirit who accompanies and protects the individual and to which the individual offers homage, calling upon it to witness his oaths. The Genius of the *pater familias* inside the family circle later became the Genius of the Emperor for the State and for his subjects.

A mural painting in Herculaneum shows us a *pater familias* who, with veiled head, which was customary when praying, holds in his hands the Genius's horn of plenty and scatters its offerings upon the altar, close beside the hearth. Facing him is a flautist, and on each side, a child — probably his sons — dressed in tunics and acting as servers. One holds in his left hand the sacred discus and in his right hand beribboned garlands for the sacrificial victim, a pig which the other boy is urging toward the altar.

The after-life and its problems were of small concern to the Romans. Their religion contained none of the rites and special prayers which, in other religions, were thought necessary to accompany the dying and escort them on their difficult and painful journey beyond the tomb. They did not believe in an after-life of rewards or punishments geared to the earthly life of the deceased. The souls of the dead were held to be pure and holy beings (Manes — good spirits) whose presence sanctified their sepulchres. Their tombs contained neither chapels nor statues to any other god; the tomb was recognised by the funeral inscription which often included invocations to the Manes or to other

Reconstruction of a mausoleum at Ghirza in the Fezzan, near Tripoli. Shrine built on a podium with Doric frieze. (Museum of Roman Civilisation, Rome).

Altar of the Lares in the House of the Red Walls in Pompeii. It is built in the form of a stall. The Genius of the family stands between the two Lares.

celestial or infernal deities. The religious sense of the Roman people held only one certainty: that the soul liberated from the body acquired a divine nature. Cicero said: « Know then that thou art a god ».

It is clear that to the Romans the cult of the dead and the cult of the gods had much in common. The surroundings of the sepulchre were sacred and sacrifices were offered on the tomb, which sometimes took the form of an altar. It was believed that the soul of the deceased found peace only after the funeral rites and the burial. He who neglected to wrap the corpse in a winding sheet was guilty of a grave sin, to be expiated by the sacrifice of a sow before the harvest. The burial was followed by a funeral feast, and foods appropriate to the occasion were served. After eight days the *sacrificium novendiale* (service of the octave) was celebrated near the tomb and ended the period of mourning.

Later, public homage was rendered to the memory of all the dead, with the participation of State and priests. These were the feasts of the *Parentalia* and the *Feralia*, a kind of Feast of All Souls, held from the 13th to the 21st of February. Throughout these days temples remained closed, magistrates discarded their insignia of office, the fires of altar and hearth were extinguished; they were the days of public and private mourning.

Small bronze figures, probably representing Penates. (Secular Museum, Vatican, Rome).

184

SACRED PLACES AND PRIESTS

The juridical spirit innate in the Romans led them to distinguish rigorously between, and define precisely, their sacred places and objects. Whatever belonged to the gods, such as temples, altars, religious adornments, were called *sacrum*. *Sanctum* on the other hand was used to define things like city walls and gates which by long usage and tradition had become inviolable in law. *Religiosum* was used to define what was neither dedicated to the gods nor inviolable in law, but which by its very nature would come to be considered immune from violation — a tomb, a private shrine, a place where lightning had once struck, etc. The word *fanum* was used for a piece of ground with well-defined boundaries, dedicated to the services of the state religion whether or not it contained sacred buildings, whence the word « profane » for whatever was outside the boundaries of the *fanum*. A wood believed to be sacred could be a *fanum*, and there is reason to believe that sacred woods were the first natural centres of religion.

The first temples were built at the time of the kings of Rome, but the generic name « temple » does not cover all the sacred buildings in Rome. The Latin *templum* corresponds to the Greek *temenos* and the common root is found in the Greek verb *tempein* meaning to cut. Thus *temenos* like *templum* indicates a piece of ground cut out or separated from the rest. The Latin *templum* was in fact a clearly defined area with a visible boundary. This demarcation called for rules and special rites which formed a part of the art of augury. The area of the *templum* was contained within a square or rectangle of which the sides had to face the four cardinal points. The ground thus « inaugurated » became *templum* and no secular building could ever stand there. If a sacred building were put up, it would have to be orientated in the same way. Thus in Rome and in Latium the word *templum* necessarily applied only to square or rectangular buildings « inaugurated » according to the rules. Round buildings could not be « inaugurated » and were called *aedes*, not *templa*.

The sacred building was consecrated as soon as it was finished and given a particular set of rules (*lex*) setting out which cults could be performed there and the rights, privileges and income of the temple. Sometimes such privileges included the right of asylum, allowing anyone accused of any crime whatever to take refuge there with impunity.

Temples in Rome were usually closed. They opened on the days dedicated to their own divinities and for exceptional occasions. Priests attached to the temple saw to their maintenance and received a salary from the State, which appointed the staff necessary for the care of the building (*servi publici*).

The ceremonies of worship were performed by several priests: besides the *flameni* and the *decemviri sacris faciundis*, the most important were the priestly colleges of the pontiffs, the augurers, the *fetiales*, and the *fratres arvales*.

There was no priestly class in Rome. Priests were ordinary citizens elected for life or for a fixed period, attending prescribed religious ceremonies in certain well-defined circumstances.

The pontiffs (*Pontifices*) derived their name from the fact that in very ancient times they supervised the construction and upkeep of the *Pons Sublicius*, once

Altar at Ostia with bas-reliefs showing details of legends about the origins of Rome. (Terme Museum, Rome).

185

the only bridge all of wood linking the two banks of the Tiber. They controlled all sacred matters. At the head of the college was the *Pontifex Maximus*, supreme head of the religion of Rome.

The role of the *Augures* was to interpret the will of the gods. They observed certain signs such as the flight and song of birds, thunder and lightning, prodigious events such as a « rain of blood and stones », the birth of human or animal monsters, etc., all of which were believed to manifest the will of the gods.

Another body of sacred interpreters was that of the soothsayers or *Haruspices* who read the wishes of the gods in the entrails of the sacrificed animals. This particular art (*haruspicium*) had been learnt from the Etruscans.

The *Fratres Arvales* were a brotherhood of twelve members dedicated to the cult of Ceres. In May they celebrated the *Ambarvalia*, feast of the purification of the fields, during which they sang an ancient religious chant, the *Carmen Arvale*, dating back to the fifth century B.C.

The *Fetiales* were regarded as speakers for the Roman people in all matters concerning foreign affairs, declarations of war or treaties of alliance.

Priestesses were not unknown in the religion of Rome, but apart from the wives of the priests, who were called *flaminae*, the only true Roman priestesses were the *Virgines vestales* of the cult of Vesta. Their task was to tend the eternally burning flame in the temple, virtually a symbol of the continuing existence and destiny of the Roman people.

Six in number, they were ruled by the oldest (*Virgo Vestalia Maxima*) and were subject to the authority of the sovereign pontiff.

A vestal virgin found guilty of negligence in allowing the sacred fire to go out was beaten, but a more terrible punishment awaited the vestal who had broken her vow of chastity. She was buried alive in the *Campus Sceleratus* near the Colline Gate.

SACRED RITES: OMENS AND DIVINATIONS

In pagan religions, three forms of rite normally regulated the relations between men and gods: prayer, sacrifice and the interpretation of the divine will, practised in a variety of ways.

Since no texts have survived, little is known of Roman prayers: though there is the one Cato the Elder quoted in his work on agriculture. Enough is known, however, to be certain that Roman prayer consisted essentially in meticulous *formulae* whose exactness aimed at the realisation of what was prayed for.

The Romans did not kneel to pray like the Orientals, but remained erect, the hands raised and open, the

A Vestal virgin. (National Museum, Rome).

head covered by a fold of the toga. Prayers, or more usually « supplications » were recited not only to beg for graces or favours, but also as thanksgiving for benefits received. Naturally, private individuals said their prayers and supplications in private; but in Rome public prayers were by no means rare. They were organised officially by priests or magistrates. To render them more efficacious they were often accompanied by fasting, or more accurately by abstinence from certain foods or certain activities.

The temple of Vesta, held to be the centre of religious worship for the Roman Empire.

Sacrifice was added both to private and public prayer, that is to say the offering to the gods of vegetable products or sacrificial animals of the highest quality and price. Incense, little cakes of meal, honey, milk, wine, lambs, pigs, cows, of which the age, colour and quality had to fulfil certain conditions, were all offered.

One of the most frequent sacrifices was the *suove-taurilia* — the offering of a pig, a sheep or a bull.

A mixture of ground cheese and salt called· *mola salsa* (whence the term « immolate ») was spread on the head of the victim ready for sacrifice. When it was killed, only the internal organs, the liver, lungs, heart and kidneys, were offered to the gods. They were cooked in a casserole, cut into pieces and laid upon a dish, then carried to the altar to be consumed by the flames. The remainder of the meat was used for the religious banquet.

The gods took a more tangible part in the sacrifice called the *lectisternium*. In this case, sacred offerings were arranged on the table round which were statues

Part of the procession on the bas-relief of the Ara Pacis of Augustus in Rome.

of the gods reclining on beds in the manner of Greco-Roman guests.

The most complete and terrifying sacrifice of all must not be forgotten: the sacrifice of life itself which certain Romans vowed to the gods in order to ensure the success of some enterprise or to expiate a fault. This sacrifice was called *devotio* and those who made it *devotus*.

Special rituals interpreted the will, the intentions and the desires of the gods with respect to man's actions. In all he did, the Roman felt intimately and acutely the presence and the influence of the divine being. A set of rules was drawn up by which the intentions and the will of the gods could be known and the signs interpreted. The latter were called « auspices » (*auspicia*) and constant reference was made to them. The observation and interpretation of these auspices were called *augurium*, and the art of divination was in fact a theory which taught the rules of reading the signs.

The Romans learnt from Etruria another method of interpreting the divine will: by examining the entrails of sacrificial victims in search of omens. This art, called *haruspicium*, was entrusted to the Haruspices.

THE SACRED CALENDAR OF THE ROMANS

There is still no solution for all the problems raised by the study of the most ancient Roman calendar; but in any case it is certain that it was based on the solar year divided into lunar months, from which arose the necessity of introducing intercalary periods to balance the two cycles. The year was probably divided into twelve months and opened in March, as witness the names of the months from July (*Quintile, Sextile, September, October*, etc.). Three days of every month corresponded to three essential points in the lunar phase: the first day of the month corresponded to the new moon, the seventh day to the first quarter, the

A sacrifice. (Bas-relief in the National Museum, Rome).

15th (or the 13th) to the full moon. The first day was called *Kalendae* because on that day the king (and later one of the pontiffs) summoned the people and announced the beginning of a new month or a new lunar phase, of which the days were called *Nonae* and *Idus*: *Nonae* because that day was nine days before the Ides (inclusive, according to the Roman system). The Ides were so called because they divided the month into two parts (*iduare* — to divide, in ancient Latin).

Later, the Romans subdivided the months into eight-day periods, the *nundinae* (from *novem dies*, since, if the first day is counted, there are nine days); markets were held on those days, so the word *nundinae* came to mean market. The sacred calendar originally held few fixed religious holidays, but the number of feasts grew considerably as new foreign gods took their places in the Roman Olympus. Each month saw its own religious festivities during which the various gods were feted: Carmenta in January, the dead in February and May; Mars and Minerva in March;

Ceres, Pales and Flora in April; Vesta in June; Juno in July; Consus in August, and so on.

The most popular and most boisterous was always the *Saturnalia*, consecrated to the god Saturn, guardian of the crops and revered above all others by the peasants of Latium. Saturn awoke the memory of the Golden Age he had granted to mankind, so in December (from the 17th to the 23rd) the people stopped work and took a holiday: celebrations, games and banquets gave splendid opportunities for gaiety, debauchery and orgy, but also for acts of fraternity and sympathy towards neighbours. Slaves, for instance, were treated with unaccustomed generosity: their masters invited them to a banquet at which they themselves served.

The modern feasts of Christmas and the New Year are like extensions of these festivities. In Italy *Ferragosto*, on the 15th of August, perpetuates the feast in honour of the emperor (*Feriae Augustae*). It remains the most popular annual festival in Rome's Trans-Tiber quarter.

189

RELIGIOUS REFORM UNDER AUGUSTUS

Augustus, who was a politician through and through and in no way a mystic, had no alternative but to restore the state religion to its proper place and to rescue it from weakness and neglect: he could not be other than the Numa Pompilius of the Empire. From the outset, he set himself three simultaneous courses of action: a merciless struggle against the religions (dubbed superstitions) of the East; restoration of the religion of ancient Rome; and finally, since the imperial dignity represented a novel doctrine to the Romans, he had to introduce into the state religion a new element which would enhance his political genius.

There is little to say about the first point in his programme: it consisted mainly of police measures. The oriental religions, including the Egyptian religion, could be practised only by natives of that country, but only outside the bounds of the sacred area of the city. Agrippa was later to extend this prohibition to the suburbs, a mile outside the sacred area.

No one has described this religious restoration better than Augustus himself in what has been incorrectly called a political testament but is rather an authentic commentary on his work in the *Res gestae*: « Being Consul for the sixth time and having taken the advice of the Senate, I decided upon the restoration of eighty-two temples in the City of Rome, neglecting none that needed to be restored.

« I built the temples of Jupiter Feretrius and Jupiter Tonans, of Quirinus, Minerva, Juno, Queen of the Sky, and of Jupiter Libertatis on the Aventine, the temple of the Lares on the summit of the Sacred Way, the temple of the Penates on the Velia, and the temple of the Great Mother of the gods on the Palatine ».

And also: « I was the Sovereign Pontiff and Augur, I belonged to the Colleges of the *Quindecemviri sacris faciundis* and of the *septemviri epulones*, I was an Arval brother, the companion of Titius and Fetialis ».

Long before he was named Sovereign Pontiff, Augustus had revealed his long-term policy by restoring the state religion; he guided it along fresh paths to new destinies — no longer those of the Republic but of the new Empire. When the supreme religious authority was vested in him in 12 B.C. he succeeded in bestowing a regal character on the traditional Roman ritual.

Acting on these principles he began to carry out his intentions. The cult of Vesta and the college of the Vestal Virgins came directly under the Sovereign Pontiff, and for this reason his official residence was located in the *Forum*, close to their temple and dwelling. Now that he had become Sovereign Pontiff his first step was to transfer the seat of the Pontificate to the Palatine, into the imperial palace itself. Next, to maintain the traditional proximity of the Pontiff's residence to the temple of the goddess, he built a new temple for Vesta on the Palatine and joined it to the imperial palace. In this way, the hearth and Penates of the emperor became the hearth and Penates of the State. The emperor was thus enthroned on the Palatine between Vesta and Apollo, almost a god among gods.

However, Augustus was not to consider his task complete until he had found some new element by which religion would become for the Empire what it had once been for the Republic. He needed a principle which would mirror in religion the place which the kingly ideal and the person of the emperor held in the new constitution. So he instituted the imperial cult under two distinct aspects: the adoration of the emperor as a god, the deification of emperors after death.

Augustus decided to associate the imperial cult with that of the goddess Roma and he organised it in the provinces by creating temples, priests and feasts, assemblies and annual synods — pretexts for the celebration of solemn games and for displays of loyalty on the part of the provincials towards the Head of State. On the other hand, he systematically forbade throughout the whole peninsula the paying of those honours to the emperor which belonged to the gods alone, and he authorised only the cult of the deified Julius Caesar — the *Divus Iulius*, first of a long series of *divi*, emperors deified after death.

Of all the elements contributing to the immense achievement of Augustus, his religious reform was soon to prove the most fragile and ephemeral. When the first enthusiasm waned, this restoration of ancient deities and rites, though carried out with genius, was seen to be an anachronism incapable of surviving the shock of reality. The imperial religion, which ought to have brought men the good tidings they awaited, perhaps satisfied those who were eager for some new ideal while Augustus was alive, and represented an almost miraculous being who gave the world what they had never thought to obtain from any man. But on his death this religion remained what in fact it really was — purely human, knowing nothing of man but his earthly life. It was basically an essentially political religion whose aim was to ensure the obedience of the citizen and the subject to the Head of State.

In this religious reform can be seen the fatal symptoms of the future conflict between the Empire and Christianity. By creating the imperial religion which constrained all the peoples of the State to respect and worship the monarchy, Augustus partially broke with the traditional tolerance of the Roman government in religious matters. The imperial cult, obligatory for everyone, was the real point of friction between the Empire and a nascent Christianity.

The Christians were prepared to recognise the authority of Caesar; they could not adore him. Their refusal to subscribe to the imperial worship was the original cause of the persecutions and martyrdoms which gave to the new Christian society its heroic impetus.

THE ROMAN CALENDAR

DAYS OF OUR MONTH	JANUARY AUGUST DECEMBER			FEBRUARY			APRIL JUNE SEPTEMBER NOVEMBER			* MARCH MAY JULY OCTOBER		
1	Calends			Calends			Calends			Calends		
2	a(nte) d(iem)	IV	Nones	a. d.	IV	Nones	a. d.	IV	Nones	a. d.	VI	Nones
3	» »	III	»	»	III	»	» »	III	»	» »	V	»
4	Pridie		»	Pridie		»	Pridie		»	» »	IV	»
5	Nones			Nones			Nones			» »	III	»
6	a. d.	VIII	Ides	a. d.	VIII	Ides	a. d.	VIII	Ides	Pridie		»
7	» »	VII	»	» »	VII	»	» »	VII	»	Nones		
8	» »	VI	»	» »	VI	»	» »	VI	»	a. d.	VIII	Ides
9	» »	V	»	» »	V	»	» »	V	»	» »	VII	»
10	» »	IV	»	» »	IV	»	» »	IV	»	» »	VI	»
11	» »	III	»	» »	III	»	» »	III	»	» »	V	»
12	Pridie		»	Pridie		»	Pridie		»	» »	IV	»
13	Ides			Ides			Ides			» »	III	»
14	a. d.	XIX	Calends	a. d.	XVI	Calends	a. d.	XVIII	Calends	Pridie		»
15	» »	XVIII	»	» »	XV	»	» »	XVII	»	Ides		
16	» »	XVII	»	» »	XIV	»	» »	XVI	»	a. d.	XVII	Calends
17	» »	XVI	»	» »	XIII	»	» »	XV	»	» »	XVI	»
18	» »	XV	»	» »	XII	»	» »	XIV	»	» »	XV	»
19	» »	XIV	»	» »	XI	»	» »	XIII	»	» »	XIV	»
20	» »	XIII	»	» »	X	»	» »	XII	»	» »	XIII	»
21	» »	XII	»	» »	IX	»	» »	XI	»	» »	XII	»
22	» »	XI	»	» »	VIII	»	» »	X	»	» »	XI	»
23	» »	X	»	» »	VII	»	» »	IX	»	» »	X	»
24	» »	IX	»	» »	VI	»	» »	VIII	»	» »	IX	»
25	» »	VIII	»	» »	V	»	» »	VII	»	» »	VIII	»
26	» »	VII	»	» »	IV	»	» »	VI	»	» »	VII	»
27	» »	VI	»	» »	III	»	» »	V	»	» »	VI	»
28	» »	V	»	Pridie		»	» »	IV	»	» »	V	»
29	» »	IV	»				» »	III	»	» »	IV	»
30	» »	III	»				Pridie		»	» »	III	»
31	Pridie		»							Pridie		»

* In March, May, July and October the days of the Nones and the Ides were set respectively on the 7th and 15th, instead of the 5th and the 13th as in the other months.

A VISIT TO THE UNDERWORLD

There was a great cave with a vast yawning entrance, set amid crags by a lake of black water, deep in the forest's gloom. Here the priestess set in place four bullocks black of hide, and poured wine over their foreheads. From high up on their brows she plucked bristles, and these she laid as a first offering on the sacrificial flame. Meantime she cried out in invocation to Hecate. Her attendants slit the victims' throats and caught the warm blood in bowls. Aeneas himself took his sword and slew a black-fleeced lamb in offering to the mother of the Furies; for Proserpine, Queen of the Underworld, he sacrificed a barren heifer. Then, when night had fallen, he set up an altar to the King of the Underworld. He laid whole carcasses of bulls upon the flames and poured rich oil over the glowing entrails. The sun was just about to rise when, behold, the ground bellowed beneath their feet and the forested hills began to shake, while through the gloom dim shapes like dogs ran howling: the goddess Hecate was drawing near. « Away ! » shrieked the priestess, « Away, all that are unhallowed. Begone from all the grove. But you, Aeneas, quick, on your way ».

With these words, the priestess plunges into the cave, and Aeneas with her. Down the path that leads to the river Acheron, where they find Charon, who ferries the dead to the farther shore. Charon's hostility to the visitors from the land of the living is allayed by the sight of the golden bough which they carry as a token of Proserpine's protection. On the other side they are confronted by the howling, three-headed watch-dog Cerberus, his neck a mass of twisting snakes. The priestess pacifies him with a drugged sweetmeat, and as they hurry on they pass by the place where Minos, supreme judge of the Underworld, holds court and assigns to each soul its due place in the kingdom of the dead. A little farther on they come to the Mourning Fields where dwell the shades of those who died for love. The farthest field in this neutral region between Tartarus, the prison of the damned, and Elysium, the abode of the virtuous, is inhabited by the renowned in war. The way now divides; to the right the road leads to Elysium, to the left, the path of the wicked to Tartarus. Aeneas takes the path to the right, but looking back, catches sight of a massively fortified place girt about with a river of flame from which issue the dismal sounds of pain and punishment. Here Rhadamanthus, stern judge, holds sway and Tisiphone the avenging lashes the guilty. The lower depths of Tartarus hide those who sinned most grievously against gods or men and who now suffer punishment as terrible as their crime was monstrous. Aeneas and the priestess hasten on to the entrance of Elysium, where Aeneas sprinkles himself with fresh water and plants the golden bough. They enter a pleasant land of shady groves and well watered meadows where happy souls spend their days in singing and dancing, in peaceful recreation, in feasting and in mirth. Here dwell the noble dead, the priests, the poets and those who led an upright life. Deep in a green vale they find Anchises and there is a tearful greeting between Aeneas and his father. Nearby is a great throng of souls waiting to ascend into the world above and be reincarnated. Anchises explains: « First: the heaven and earth, the oceans, the glimmering face of the moon, the sun and stars, are all sustained by Spirit working within them; and Mind, pervading every part, is infused through the whole mass and gives it life and movement. From Spirit and Mind arose the whole race of men and beasts, all flying creatures and the strange monsters that Ocean brings into being beneath its bright surface. The strength of Spirit and Mind is a pure strength as of fire: they are lifeseeds whose origin is in heaven, but their heavenly part is hampered by the body's imperfections and dulled by earthly limbs and mortal frames. It is the body that is the cause of fear and desire, of griefs and joys, and because of it the soul, trapped in its windowless prison, has no clear perception of the free air. Even when on the last day of life its mortal sojourn ends, the soul, alas!, still is not wholly freed from misery and bodily evils; inevitably, many faults have long been hardening mysteriously within it and become embedded there. Accordingly, after death, souls are schooled with retribution and pay the penalty for their old offences. Some hang stretched out for the empty winds to blow on; from some the stain of guilt is washed away deep in swirling waters; from others it is burnt out by fire. Thus each of us after death undergoes what is appropriate to him. Then afterwards we are released into the wide freedom of Elysium, and we few inhabit the Fields of the Blessed, until length of days, as time's cycle is completed, has removed the hardened corruption and leaves, all untainted, a perception pure and bright and a pure flame of spirit. All souls such as this, when time's cycle has revolved a thousand years, are summoned by the god in a great throng to the river Lethe, so that they may reascend into the upper air with no memory of what has gone before (for drinking the water of Lethe induces complete oblivion) and may conceive a desire to reenter bodily life ».

Presently the time came when Anchises must bid his son farewell. Together they went to one of the Gates of Sleep, whence dreams and visions ascend into the world of men, and here Anchises sent Aeneas and the priestess on their way.

(source: Virgil's Aeneid)

POLITICAL INSTITUTIONS

The institutions of the Roman State which developed through the experience of centuries were the firm foundations of the largest political edifice of the ancient world. They started life in a rural village, they developed in a capital city which rapidly conquered the whole of Italy, and they came to full maturity in a metropolis which was to become the capital of the whole known world, and they kept under their authority the most varied and distant peoples, religions, civilisations and traditions. If it is true to say that they were the instruments of a rule which used extreme severity, it is also necessary to acknowledge that thanks to them this conquered world knew peace and security. Under the protection of the laws and institutions of Rome, commercial activity flourished, economic life developed, cultural expression and art took on new and more mature forms whilst vital elements of the great civilisations of antiquity met and united under their auspices. Thus for about five centuries, in a world almost wholly Roman, this political unity made possible the last great intellectual achievements of the classical world; the constitution of the earliest Romans which began in the community of ancient Rome and ended with the gigantic structure of the Empire, became in truth « the constitution of the human race ».

The Greek historian Polybius, who was detained at Rome for political reasons between 167 and 150 B.C., there became convinced that the Roman constitution was the key to Rome's phenomenal success. « Yet », he complains, « it is not at all easy to explain the present working of this constitution owing to its complicated character; only careful attention can reveal its distinctive qualities ». It was not, he added, the work of a single lawgiver, like Lycurgus at Sparta; on the contrary it had grown up gradually, by a process of trial and error, carried out amid the discipline induced by many struggles and troubles — yet the result was the same as at Sparta, a mixed constitution in which elements of monarchy, aristocracy and democracy were nicely balanced to resist the natural tendency of all states to decay.

There is a good deal of truth in this. The Roman constitution contained all these three elements; but behind the façade which Polybius sketches of three powers neatly dovetailed we can detect the reality: at all times the Roman Republic was predominantly an aristocracy. Constitutionally the Roman people, which passed laws and appointed magistrates in its various assemblies, possessed ultimate sovereignty, limited only by the control exercised by those magistrates themselves. But in Polybius's time the State was mainly run by 300 senior statesmen, ex-magistrates, who were appointed to the Senate for life; and within the Senate itself power was concentrated in the hands of a narrow group of noble families.

The strength of the Senate lay in the fact that it contained representatives of all the major family groups (*gentes*) who dominated political life, and of the two orders into which from the earliest times the Roman people were divided — the patricians and the plebeians. For nearly two and a half centuries, from 509 to 287 B.C., Rome had been torn by a long struggle between these two orders, whose differentiation is hidden in the obscurity of time. The patricians formed an élite, a group of aristocratic clans, who originally monopolised the membership of the Senate, the magistracies, the priesthoods and knowledge of the *formulae* governing judicial procedure. But in time the less privileged clans, supported by the common people, had gradually gained access to all these, and had acquired an assembly of their own, the *concilium plebis*, and a special body of officers, the ten tribunes of the plebs, *tribuni plebis*; a law passed in 287 B.C., the *lex Hortensia*, laid down that henceforward decisions taken by the plebs in its *concilium* should be binding on the people as a whole, plebeians and patricians alike.

The tribunes formed a remarkable feature in the Roman constitution. It was their task to defend the lives and property of the plebeians, and by an oath the people had declared them inviolable, *sacrosancti*. By custom they would render any act of any magistrate, and any law, election or decree of the Senate null and void merely by interposing their veto. They had in course of time gained access to the Senate itself and eventually possessed the right to convene it. The tribunate thus represented a unique, revolutionary office embedded by custom in the Roman constitution; but by the second century B.C. the tribunes had shed their revolutionary role, and we now find them acting as the useful instruments of leading politicians, who exploited their veto as a political weapon.

The tribunate was an office without parallel. But the veto which the tribunes could exercise against other magistrates and against each other was inherent in the Roman concept of politics. Long ago Rome had been governed by kings; and ever since the dynasty of the Tarquins had been expelled (traditionally in 509 B.C.) and a republic established in its place, the Romans had attached great importance to the principle of collegiality — that is, the electing of magistrates in groups of two or more, each with the right to veto any act of his colleague. These two principles of collegiality and veto together acted as a brake on all radical magistrates. They created that atmosphere of slowly moving conservatism which makes Rome such a contrast to the more volatile states of Greece.

The kings of Rome had left behind them a lasting fear of unchecked authority and of any office of importance unrestricted by a time limit. In their place annual magistrates were appointed to carry out strictly defined duties of which we shall say more later. These magistrates were essentially amateurs, rich landowners who devoted their lives and energy to the political game, and as politicians were sometimes liable to temper patriotic enthusiasm with a sober regard for their own future careers. The Romans recognised the need for authority; and their magistracies fell into two classes, those carrying *imperium* — supreme power embracing the right to command troops, administer the law and if need be inflict the death penalty — and those that did not. Authority, however, was jealously watched and *imperium* was the object of a specific grant, independent of the actual election to the magistracy. This jealousy of authority served as a check on unconstitutional actions and slowed down the processes of change. But it neither encouraged flexibility nor easily allowed the creation of the new political machinery which became necessary once Rome was the capital of a large empire.

THE DECLINE OF THE REPUBLIC

The first century B.C. revealed cracks in the edifice. Problems arose — overseas wars, piracy, slave revolts — which called for more protracted commands; and when a general like Julius Caesar had enjoyed the almost unlimited exercise of *imperium* in Gaul for ten years, he did not take kindly to being disciplined by jealous senators.

Caesar was one of a series of politician-generals who stretched the old constitution to breaking-point. Commands were extended to five and ten years and made to cover vast areas; the tribunate was stirred into new life as the radical weapon of popular leaders; and the many problems connected with overseas administration were subordinated to the private ends of ambitious men.

When in 31 B.C. Julius Caesar's adopted son, C. Caesar Octavianus, by defeating his rival Mark Antony, and Cleopatra, the queen of Egypt, in the sea-battle at Actium, made himself ruler of the Roman world and the first Roman emperor, the constitution was ripe for revision. The imperial system represents both a simplification of that of the Republic and a gradual substitution of professionals for amateurs. The change was possible because its true nature was concealed. Octavian, who in 27 B.C. took the awe-inspiring name of Augustus, was careful to disguise his true position. He claimed to have restored the Republic, but in fact remained master of almost all the important provinces where legions were stationed. He accumulated powers, all of which separately could claim good republican

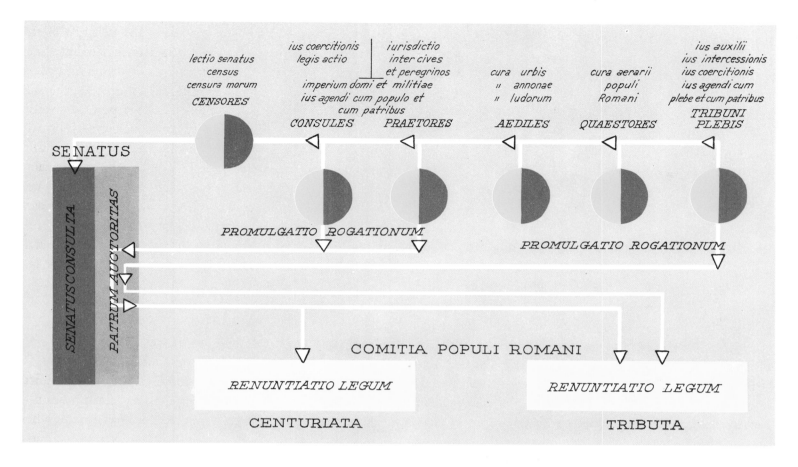

Plan of republican political institutions, their functions and their relations with each other.

Plan of republican political institutions, their functions and their relations with each other.

precedent, but in combination added up to a position quite unparalleled since the time of the kings. In one sphere after another he and his successors took over administrative duties hitherto exercised by the Senate and put them in the hands of imperial servants. Thus the Roman government became increasingly monarchical, resting on the power of the legions, and employing an even greater staff of professional administrators, taken from every rank of society from the senators themselves down to liberated slaves. The imperial constitution was both more simple and more elastic than that of the Republic; it furnished the skilled professional attention necessary to run a vast empire, and it created a political structure which was to last, in Constantinople at least, for fifteen hundred years.

SENATE AND SENATORS

The Senate was the most highly regarded and influential body at Rome. Its 300 members (increased by Sulla in 81 B.C. to 600 and later by Caesar to 900) were easily distinguished in the streets by the broad purple stripe on their tunics and their special red leather shoes, as they went about their business in the Forum and the law-courts attended by many clients; and at religious ceremonies and in the theatre they occupied special seats. By an act passed in 218 B.C. senators were debarred from all commercial activity; but although no property qualification for membership of the order existed until the time of Augustus (who imposed one of a million sesterces) their large estates usually ensured that they were among the wealthiest men in the land. Originally the Senate had formed the advisory council of the kings, and tradition assigned its creation to Romulus himself; under the Republic its duty was still theoretically one of advising the magistrates. But for several reasons it soon acquired more extensive functions. In the first place, it contained the most eminent citizens both patrician and plebeian; the former were the *patres*, the latter were *conscripti*, but the combined expression *patres conscripti*, used in

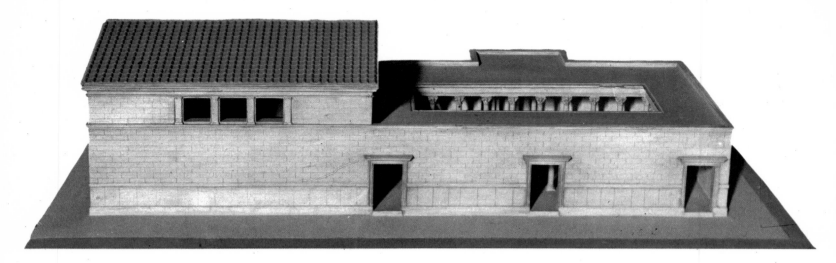

The Curia reconstructed by the architect, Italo Gismondi. The Curia was the building in which the Senate usually met. (Museum of Roman Civilisation, Rome).

addressing the Senate, symbolised the Senate, and symbolised the close collaboration of the two orders from about 300 B.C. onwards. Appointment to the Senate was in the hands of the censors (see below); but they normally chose new members first from those who had held the chief magistracies — the curule magistracies as they were called, from the *sella curulis*, the ivory folding chair without back or arms, which was the attribute of all magistrates possessing *imperium*. Thus the Senate was in close rapport with the magistrates; and popular election to a magistracy became the usual route into the Senate by the time of Sulla, who made membership depend on the holding of the quaestorship, the magistracy concerned with the administration of the law.

The Senate normally met in Rome in a special senate-house (curia) on the north side of the Forum. Its meetings, which had to take place between dawn and sunset, were summoned by the presiding magistrate, a consul or some other magistrate with *imperium*, or a tribune; written reports were presented, and the senators were invited to express their opinions in a definite order of rank, starting from those who had been designated consuls for the next year or, if the elections had not yet been held, from anyone who had already held the consulship. When discussion had gone on long enough, the senators divided and voted. Their decision was called a *senatus consultum*, and was recorded in the Treasury (*aerarium*) by the urban quaestors. Though under the Republic this possessed no legal force in itself, it often served as a basis for legis-

lation; and within the large sphere of administration controlled by the Senate, it laid down policy and led to action. As we have seen, a *senatus consultum* could be vetoed by a tribune.

From the third century onwards, when Rome was involved in almost continuous wars, the Senate grew more and more powerful through its close association with the magistrates, thanks to the acquiescence of the people, whose leaders were now absorbed into the ruling class. It gave advice to magistrates on all aspects of policy, on finance, religion and legislation, and normally assigned the provinces to their governors and voted the necessary equipment and supplies (*ornatio*). Questions of peace and war were usually decided by the Senate, though technically the people had to pass the war-measure (and sometimes were known to create difficulties). In addition the Senate conducted all negotiations with foreign powers by sending and receiving embassies, and by its control over the organisation of conquered territories.

Inside the Senate particular influence was wielded by a narrow group of noble families, defined as those who had a consul among their forebears. The noble families, the Claudii, the Cornelii, the Metelli and others (many of them plebeian), regarded the great offices as theirs almost by prescriptive right; and they used all the means at their disposal to keep out new men, such as the elder Cato or Cicero, from entering the privileged circle. Real power at Rome thus circulated within a very small oligarchic group. From 133 B.C. onwards the Senate was exposed to the challenge of the *popu-*

lares, men of ambition and capacity and sometimes themselves of noble origins, who resented the exclusiveness of the oligarchy. The struggle was joined on two constitutional issues in particular — the claim of the Senate to give the approval of its *auctoritas* to bills before they were submitted to the assembly, and the question of the validity of the so-called « ultimate decree of the Senate » (*senatus consultum ultimum*), which summoned the consuls to see to it that the State suffered no injury and thereby (in the view of the nobles, though not in that of their opponents) empowered them to execute citizens without trial, if need be, in the interests of the Republic. These issues were unsolved when the Republic and the nobility both fell before the assault of Caesar's legions, which opened up an era of violence and civil war.

THE PRINCIPALITY

The civil wars led to the setting up of an autocracy, the Principate, by Augustus. Under the Empire the Senate's role was changed. Instead of being the unofficial ruler of Rome the fathers became a hard-working body of men to whom the emperor turned for his administrators and governors. Membership of the Senate became officially what it had always tended to be, a hereditary privilege (though the emperor always could and did introduce new men); and the most important administrative posts like the governorships of provinces were in the hands of senators. Public life provided the young man of senatorial class with a clearly defined career, beginning with a minor post and service as a military tribune in a legion, and culminating in the consulship and the senior posts to which this led, such as the governorship of an important military area like Syria or the Rhineland. As a body, the Senate acquired new prestige, for it was essential to the running of the state as Augustus envisaged it. It still controlled the more peaceful provinces, and in addition it became a court of law; by A.D. 200 its *consulta* had full legislative force. But with real power and decision in the hands of the *princeps* its deliberations grew increasingly unreal, and emperors found it more and more difficult to obtain a reasonable attendance and to elicit bold and informed discussion. In a speech of the emperor Claudius (A.D. 41-54) senators are reproved for merely agreeing with the view of the magistrate proposing the motion and imagining that they have thereby done their duty.

The extension of Roman citizenship to overseas communities increased the area from which senators could be chosen. The civil wars had taken toll of the noble families, while others simply died out; under the Principate each new dynasty rewarded its supporters with political preferment. By Trajan's time (A.D. 98-117) over a quarter of the senators came from outside Italy and many of these from the eastern provinces. Thus gradually the Senate came to be representative of the wealthiest class of landowners throughout the whole Empire; and right down to the fourth century A.D., it maintained its importance, often defending the old ways against such trends as the adoption of Christianity, and asserting its role as a bulwark against the growth of absolutism.

THE *COMITIA*

Such was the Senate's position, one — under the Republic at least — largely based on custom and popular acquiescence. But Rome was a free state, and its freedom found expression in the powers of the people, exercised in the various assemblies, known as *comitia*. These formal assemblies contained all adult male citizens, patrician and plebeian. They were summoned on an appointed day, on a site inaugurated with due religious formality, and after the taking of the auspices to determine whether the omens were favourable (as they almost invariably were declared to be). The people assembled not as individuals but in special groupings, and they were convened by a magistrate endowed with due authority.

The groupings were of three kinds. In early times the Roman people had been divided into three primitive tribes, the Ramnes, the Tities and the Luceres, and each of these into ten *curiae*, groups of neighbouring families, sometimes named after some prominent constituent *gens*. The earliest Roman assembly was based on these *curiae*, and was called the *comitia curiata*; but by the

first century B.C. it had become obsolete and its surviving duties, such as the voting of military power (*imperium*), were carried out by a small committee of thirty *lictors* (who were simply attendants on the magistrates).

More important was the *comitia centuriata*. At some early date — traditionally under one of the kings, Servius Tullius — the Roman people were divided up into classes based on wealth, and each class had to furnish the army with a specified number of units of roughly 100 men, known as *centuriae*. In time the assembly formed out of these *centuriae* acquired political powers and began to act as an assembly of the people and to be used for legislation, the election of the major

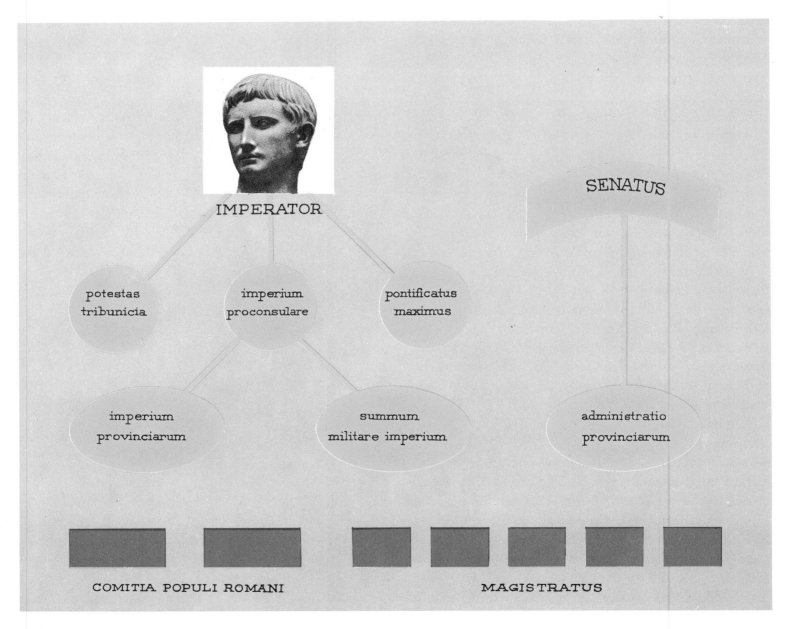

Augustus gradually concentrated in himself those powers which had previously belonged to the Senate and the assemblies. The institutions remained, but only as consultative bodies for the ruler who had become a complete autocrat.

198

magistrates, the declaration of war and the hearing of appeals against a capital sentence. It contained 193 centuries, of which eighty belonged to the highest property class and a further eighteen to the knights (*equites*) who formed an élite among the rich. Since these two classes voted first, they could, if unanimous, control a majority, and since voting halted once a majority was declared, the less eminent citizens had rarely any say in matters coming before the *comitia centuriata*. Voting took place in enclosures set up in the Campus Martius to the north of the city, and was presided over by a magistrate. From 139 B.C. onwards voting was by ballot, and the voters placed tablets marked for or against the motion into urns. The votes of the members of each century were counted, the decision of the majority being returned as that of the century.

As we saw, the plebeians had their own assembly, the *concilium plebis*, under the presidency of the tribunes. Here voting took place by units based on the thirty-five local tribes into which the Roman people were divided since the third century B.C., when the last tribe was made in 241. After 287 B.C., when resolutions passed in the *concilium plebis* (*plebiscita*) acquired the force of law, the plebeian *concilium* was in effect an assembly of the people. It continued to elect tribunes and aediles of the plebs, but its resolutions were often a convenient form of legislation, and it provided a useful body to try minor cases. There was also an assembly of the whole people modelled on the *concilium plebis* and voting by tribes, which met under the presidency of a consul or praetor. This tribal assembly (*comitia tributa*) elected quaestors and curule aediles (see below), and also enacted laws and tried cases. It is not always easily distinguishable from the *concilium plebis*, so similar were the two bodies in organisation and many of their functions, and the ancient sources often confuse these two tribal assemblies. It was an advantage that both could meet within the city walls, avoiding the cumbersome procedure of the *comitia centuriata*, which required notice of twenty-four days to be given before a meeting could be held. Sometime during the second half of the third century B.C. the *comitia centuriata* was reformed in such a way as to co-ordinate the centuries with the local tribes within each class; exactly how this was done is not known for certain, but it involved reducing the number of centuries assigned to the first class from eighty to seventy,

presumably to enable two centuries to be allotted to the members from each tribe. The total probably remained at 193. This new system must have made it necessary for voting to continue down to the second class before a majority could be registered; but the weighting still favoured the rich.

The assemblies had three main functions. They legislated — usually after the proposed measure had received the Senate's approval (*auctoritas*) — they acted as courts of law and they elected magistrates. With the growth of Roman territory and the extension of citizenship first to all Italy and then to people inhabiting provincial territory overseas, since the *comitia* were attended mainly by the populace of Rome itself, they ceased to express the views of the whole citizen body. No serious proposals were put forward for the remedying of this defect, and with the setting up of the Empire the *comitia* seemed to have outlived their usefulness. From the time of Tiberius (A.D. 14-37) onwards election of magistrates was transferred to the Senate; and the latest law known to have been passed in the *comitia* dates from A.D. 98. Nor did the *comitia* function any longer as law courts, since their judicial duties had been largely taken over by the special *quaestiones*, which appear from the second century onwards (see below), and subsequently by the assumption of judicial functions by the Senate and by the emperor himself sitting as a court. Thus the history of the *comitia* furnishes a further illustration of the gradual concentration of power in the hands of the

Augustus. (Museum of the Terme, Rome).

The Capitol in a nineteenth-century painting which faithfully reconstructs the scene. In the centre, below the miliarum aureum, *the rostrum on which the orators harangued the people.*

emperor and his close advisers and of the simplification of political institutions.

THE *CURSUS HONORUM*

Under the Republic the magistrates form a link between the assemblies and the Senate. It was they who presided over both bodies; and if the Senate gradually became a council of ex-magistrates, it was to their election by the people in its *comitia* that the latter owed their office. The magistrates were the executive part of the government, and their powers (*potestas*) were limited both by restricting the length of tenure of any magistracy, and by ensuring that authority should be shared or alternated between the two or more colleagues in each office. Regulations governed

the order in which the various magistracies should be held, in some cases the interval of time that had to elapse between the holding of them, and the minimum age at which a candidate might be permitted to stand for each. This *cursus honorum*, as it was called, provided a kind of chronological touchstone of political achievement: to be elected consul *suo anno*, that is, at the earliest date permitted by the law, was every Roman senator's hope.

For the young man with either noble forebears or political ambition the first rung on the ladder was election to the quaestorship at the age of thirty. Each year the tribal assembly elected the quaestors, varying in number under the late Republic from four to twenty (after Sulla's legislation in 81 B.C.), with a short period under Julius Caesar when there were as many as forty. The quaestor's duties were mainly financial, and he

The Senatus consulti *were decisions taken by the senators at Senate meetings. They did not have the force of law, but served as a basis for legislation. (National Museum, Vienna).*

201

was often closely attached to some higher magistrate, a consul or a provincial governor, who treated him like a father and by personal precept instructed him in the art of statesmanship. On occasion a quaestor might even be left in charge of a province (*quaestor pro praetors*), when he would have judicial duties and the command of troops, all excellent training for the future. Two quaestors, the *quaestores urbani*, were responsible for the state treasury, the *aerarium*, where funds and state documents were stored. In the first century B.C. the quaestorship carried with it admission to the Senate.

After the quaestorship (the powers and duties of which might be extended beyond the year of office) came the curule aedileship. Originally two aediles were elected each year by the *concilium plebis*; but in 367 B.C. two curule aediles were created, and along with their plebeian colleagues they soon formed a single college, in which the curule members were elected in the *comitia tributa* from patricians and plebeians in alternate years. Though not a compulsory step in the *cursus honorum* the aedileship was popular among the ambitious, since its supervision of the public games furnished splendid opportunities for munificence and self-advertisement, which could be exploited in subsequent election campaigns. Besides the responsibility for the games, the aediles supervised the city of Rome itself, including the care of the roads and traffic, the water supply, and the regulation of weights and measures, and markets; they also had jurisdiction in minor matters carrying petty fines.

The aedileship was not held before the age of thirty-six. Meanwhile an ambitious plebeian could already have held the tribunate, for which no minimum age is recorded. The ten tribunes were the officers of the plebs in their struggle for recognition against the patricians; but once this fight was over they were in practice accepted as magistrates, with membership of the Senate and the right to convene it. Their power of veto (*intercessio*) has already been described; they also possessed personal inviolability (*sacrosanctitas*) and the authority to enforce plebeian decrees and carry through their own actions, if necessary, by force, which could even be exercised against a consul. During the second century the tribunes were largely employed by the Senate to curb refractory magistrates; but from the tribunate of Tiberius Gracchus in 133 B.C. they again began to be associated with popular legislation and they are found supporting revolutionary measures

introduced in the interest of men like Pompey and Caesar in opposition to the noble domination.

At thirty-nine a politician would next stand for election, by the *comitia centuriata*, as a praetor. The *praetor urbanus* was especially concerned with the administration of justice, and the *praetor peregrinus* with cases involving transactions between a foreigner and a Roman citizen. By the early second century the number of praetors had been increased to six, and four of these were used to govern overseas provinces; but in 81 B.C. Sulla increased their number to eight and made them presidents of the permanent courts (*quaestiones*) (see below). Thus the early association of the praetor with law was renewed. The edicts which successive praetors published at the beginning of their year of office were an important source of public law.

The minimum age for the consulship was forty-two, but only the most favoured noble could hope to achieve it *suo anno*; since for eight praetors there were only two consulships available, competition here was keen and ruthless. The consuls were the highest executive officers. The year was officially designated by their names, and they normally presided over meetings of the Senate or the *comitia*. However, the passing of the years had eroded their powers. Newly created subsidiary magistrates had annexed many of their duties, and the growth of the Senate's authority from the late third century onwards had shorn them of other powers; thus the assignment of the provinces was a senatorial prerogative from the time of the war against Hannibal (218-202 B.C.). The consuls' civil jurisdiction was early transferred to the praetor and from the second century B.C. onwards special courts appropriated their powers of criminal jurisdiction. Finally Sulla made it the normal procedure for the consuls to be restricted to the administration of Rome and Italy, while overseas commands with their control of armies were assigned to the ex-consuls and ex-praetors, who went out at the end of their year of office. The great reputations of the first century B.C. were won by proconsuls, not consuls, and from them came the threat to the constitution. Yet for all that the consul's prestige remained high: he was, wrote Cicero, « the good father and faithful guardian » of the State.

The holder of the consulship became a *consularis* on the completion of his year of office: and the *consulares* were the most highly respected members of the Senate. From them, every five years, two censors were elected

CASILLIVM
A OF

M·LEPIDIVM·SRP
AEDVRT

MODESTVM
AED OF

L·XISVCIVND

M·SAM
IVVENEMIR·D·R·

CEISVND

Election propaganda from Pompeii. Names of candidates were usually followed by the formula OF, signifying oro faciatis (we ask you to elect). (Museum of Roman Civilisation, Rome).

in the *comitia centuriata* to carry out special duties which required some eighteen months to perform. The censor made up the official citizen lists, examined the records and filled up the numbers of the cavalry (*equites*) and similarly made up and revised the rolls of the Senate, a function once performed by the consuls. Offending knights or senators could be struck off their respective rolls, though the principle of collegiate veto operated if the two censors disagreed. Each censorship ended with a performance of the lustrum or purification of the people. Censors possessed no *imperium*, but their office commanded high regard, and to hold it was the greatest ambition of the *consularis*. Unlike the consulship, to which a man could be re-elected after a ten-year interval, it could be held once and once only; and though the decisions of one college of censors might be reversed by the next, five years later, a censor could not be called to account for his decisions. During the last years of the Republic, after Sulla, the censor's powers declined and often none were appointed; at this time the auctioning of public contracts and other financial duties which belonged to the censorship were left to the consuls to perform.

In times of crisis the Romans reverted to a carefully controlled autocracy. On the nomination of the consul, acting on the recommendation of the Senate, a magistrate called a dictator was then appointed. The dictator was normally a *consularis* of tried reputation, and he in turn nominated a subordinate called the master of horse (*magister equitum*). The tenure of the dictatorship was limited to six months or the duration of the crisis, and during that time all other magistracies were subordinated to it. After the war with Hannibal (218-202 B.C.) the dictatorship fell into disuse, but it was revived as an autocratic office without any time limit by Sulla and Caesar in the first century B.C.

These were the main magistracies of the Roman Republic. Linked with them were the priesthoods, the pontificate, the augurate and the various minor religious colleges, which were also held by statesmen and helped to increase the prestige of those occupying them. As we have seen, the setting up of the Empire changed the Senate's role. As it became a pool of imperial administrators and a hereditary order, the *cursus honorum* was changed to fit the new conception. The minimum ages for holding the offices were reduced: the imperial

senator could be quaestor at twenty-five, aedile or tribune (now alternatives) at twenty-seven, praetor at thirty and consul at thirty-three.

Before the quaestorship came one or more years in the vigintivirate, a board of twenty men entrusted with minor judicial duties (ten men), the cleansing of the streets of Rome — previously a task of the aediles — (four men), the supervision of prisons and the execution of criminals (three men), and the minting of copper coins (three men). A would-be senator had also to serve in the army as a military tribune of whom six were assigned to each legion, five of equestrian rank and one from a senatorial family. This military service usually fell between the vigintivirate and the holding of the quaestorship. The republican offices retained most of their previous functions (though those of the aediles and tribunes were much reduced); but increasingly administration fell to the chairmen of special boards appointed by the emperor, and the importance of the *cursus honorum* lay in providing the status necessary for appointment to such chairmanships and to various other administrative posts in government service. Examples of these are the commissioner for roads (*curator viarum*) throughout Italy and the prefect responsible for distributing grain to those entitled to a free allowance (*praefectus frumenti dandi*), both normally men of praetorian rank; while the consulars, who were now quite young men, could look forward to a long career successively governing major provinces, and taking the chairmanship of boards for the preservation of temples, the conservancy of the Tiber and the sewers of Rome, or its water-supply. In this way the *cursus honorum* became the foundation of a training for a career which offered every opportunity for service in whichever direction a man's capacity or inclination might lead him.

POWER OF THE JUDICIARY

An important sector of Roman political life was that concerned with the administration of justice. Here, as elsewhere, evolution was unplanned and empirical solutions were adopted as problems arose. As we saw, the praetor had a long-standing connection with the courts, for it was normally before him that the preliminary hearing for the definition of the legal issue in a lawsuit took place. The tribunes likewise had an important role as the prosecutors of peccant magistrates before the popular assembly. Similarly other magistracies had rights of jurisdiction in specific situations. Where a capital charge was involved, the hearing had originally to take place before the *comitia centuriata*, since in such cases a Roman citizen had the right of appeal to the people. From the second century B.C. onwards, however, this appeal to the whole people was largely superseded with the introduction of special courts (*quaestiones*), which partly drew on the procedure used in civil cases. These courts were treated as equivalent to the whole people, so that no appeal lay against their verdict. The first such permanent *quaestio* to be set up dealt with charges of extortion levelled against provincial governors, and following precedent the judges were senators. However, G. Gracchus, in his tribunate of 123-122 B.C., in order to secure allies against the Senate, assigned the control of the extortion court to a new class which had recently developed on the basis of foreign trade and large-scale contracting, and which came to be known by the same title as the old cavalry of the Republic, namely the knights (*equites*). During his dictatorship (82-79 B.C.) Sulla instituted a number of other permanent criminal courts to cover a wide range of public offences such as poisoning, violence and fraud; and he restored the control of these to the Senate. Thus possession of the criminal courts became a pawn in the struggle between the two orders, which was only brought to an end in 70 B.C., when the composition of the judges in these courts was in effect shared between Senate and knights, with a preponderance of the latter.

Under the Empire new forms of justice were evolved. The special courts continued, but were now wholly manned by equestrian panels. In compensation the Senate itself became a high court for the hearing of certain cases, especially those involving a senator or a charge of high treason (which was often very loosely interpreted). The emperor likewise sat in his own court, which also acted as a general court of appeal for citizens facing capital charges throughout the Empire. Appeal to Caesar took the place of appeal to the sovereign people: the famous case of St. Paul is one familiar to all. Both the senatorial and the emperor's court were final; there was no appeal.

Boundary stone between the townlands of Padua and Este erected on the orders of the proconsul Lucius Caecilius in accordance with a senatorial decree.

205

Frontier stone marking the border between the people of Atteste (Este) and those of Vicenza, placed there, following a Senatus consultum, *by the proconsul Soranus. (Maffei Museum, Verona).*

PROVINCES, MUNICIPALITIES, AND COLONIES

The Roman constitution had its origins in a small city and was with difficulty adapted to the needs of a state which controlled first Italy and later the whole Mediterranean world. In this process of expansion the political institutions of Rome were subjected to much strain and the Roman capacity for borrowing and innovating was stretched to the utmost. The political crises of the last century of the Roman Republic are largely a reflection of this problem; ultimately one-man rule with its more simplified forms and procedures was the answer. In the meantime each stage of Roman expansion had evoked new constitutional forms. A good illustration of this process is the organisation of Italy itself.

Between 509 and about 270 B.C. the Romans extended their control throughout the whole peninsula, which contained a mixture of peoples of differing degrees of civilisation, from the Greek cities in the south and the Etruscans between the Tiber and the Arno, to the still primitive highlanders of the Apennines and the Abruzzi, tribes such as the Paeligni or the Samnites. As the Romans pushed outwards, they planted colonies at strategic points, to control dangerous coast-lines, mountain-passes and river-crossings. These colonies were originally of two kinds. Roman colonies proper were small, compact military settlements of about 300 men on land owned by Rome; these men retained full Roman citizenship. Elsewhere larger colonies were sent out to form independent states with so-called 'Latin rights' (*ius Latinum*) — that is, states in close association with Rome but not actually participating in Roman citizenship. From the second century B.C. onwards, however, only Roman colonies were set up, now often quite large, and equipped with the municipal machinery of the former Latin colonies. After 89 B.C., as the final settlement in a war of revolt waged by the allies against Rome, Italy received Roman citizenship and these colonies, along with the so-called *municipia* — Italian towns which had hitherto possessed only the private rights of Roman citizenship (*civitas sine suffragio*) — became the administrative units of a united Roman Italy, each a small copy of Rome with annual magistrates (*duoviri* or *praetores*), a council (*consilium*) and priesthoods.

Under the late Republic and even more under the early Empire colonies were sent out to the overseas territories. The first successful colony to be established outside Italy was at Narbonne in Gaul in 118 B.C., and like many later colonies it was manned by veterans from the legions. Later Augustus set up many such colonies in Spain and the south of France, as well as in Africa and the eastern provinces, and in this he was followed by his successors down to Hadrian in the early second century A.D. These colonies were outposts of Rome overseas, and centres of Romanization: they paved the way for the eventual extension of Roman citizenship to the whole of the Empire.

Another field in which the Romans were obliged to devise new administrative machinery was in the provinces themselves. A *provincia* was originally simply the sphere of activity of a Roman magistrate, but in time it came to mean the overseas territory which he governed. The first province was Sicily, acquired in 241 after the Roman victory in the first war against Carthage, Rome's North African rival; it was soon followed by Corsica and Sardinia, and after a second war with Carthage by Spain (in 197 B.C.), which was divided into two provinces. By 146 B.C. both Macedonia and « Africa » (i.e., the area around Carthage) were added, and in 133 B.C. « Asia », the western part of Asia Minor, was bequeathed to Rome by the last king of Pergamum. The first century B.C. saw a vast increase in the number of provinces, and by the time of Augustus's death (A.D. 14) the Empire stretched from Portugal and the English Channel to the Syrian desert, and from the Rhine and the Danube to the Atlas Mountains and the borders of Ethiopia.

Under the Republic provinces were governed by magistrates or ex-magistrates sent out normally for a single year (two years in distant Spain). In the first century B.C. a governor went out to his province the year after his praetorship or consulship, and carried the rank of proconsul. But in 52 B.C. a five-year gap was instituted between the holding of an office and going out to a province as a promagistrate. This was intended to discourage large-scale bribery at elections by postponing the possession of a profitable province from which the successful candidate might hope to recoup himself for his heavy expenditure by exploiting the provincials. Under the Republic a governor had no salary: but even a scrupulous man had to make an effort not to become rich from his province, and a rogue like Verres, whom Cicero successfully prosecuted in 70 B.C. for his depredations while governor of Sicily, might plunder the unfortunate provincials without restraint. If we can believe Cicero, Verres asserted that a governor must win three fortunes from his province, one to pay his defenders, one to bribe the jury in the inevitable trial for extortion, and a third for himself.

When a province was established, a charter of government or *Lex Provinciae* was normally imposed by a Roman general with the help of a senatorial commission. This provided a code for subsequent governors, modified only by the edict which each published upon going out, and which would contain much traditional material but could also incorporate innovations. Under the Republic the governor had no paid staff. He was assisted by a quaestor, who controlled the money chest and, as we saw, might command troops in his absence. A provincial governor also took out several older staff called *legati*, and a semi-official corps of *comites*, chosen from among his friends to act as a council to whom he could refer problems. The fairly generous expense allowance often compensated for the absence of a regular stipend.

Here as elsewhere the Empire brought great improvements. Augustus divided up the provinces into two groups. The more peaceful and settled provinces like Sicily and Cisalpine Gaul continued to be governed by ex-praetors or ex-consuls sent out normally for a year at a time, with the rank of proconsul; but with a few exceptions those nearest the frontier, which required the presence of troops, were under Augustus's own direct control and were governed by senators sent out with the title of *legatus Augusti pro praetore* (Augustus's representatives with rank of praetor), while minor imperial provinces were put under an *eques*. Such imperial governors often continued in their posts for several years on end: one senator, Popaeus Sabinus, is known to have moved from one major province to another for twenty-four years. One province was treated exceptionally. Egypt was so important for the emperor that he banned it to all senators, putting it under an equestrian prefect in command of a legionary force. In imperial provinces finances were separately controlled by an equestrian procurator; and in general an imperial governor had a more adequate staff than under the Republic as well as a salary related to the importance of the post. His task was partly reduced in complexity by some degree of decentralisation, which left many local decisions to the many municipal towns throughout the provinces.

Marble relief representing a round purse belonging to a viator aerarium. *The* viatores *were State treasury officials. (Vatican Museum, Rome).*

First-century imperial gold coins. (Museum of Roman Civilisation, Rome).

TAXATION

Under the Republic state expenditure was small and budgeting was one of the duties of the censors, who arranged every five years for contracting, public works and the like, and allotted monies for this purpose. Taxation was mainly indirect. A direct tax, called *tributum*, had been levied spasmodically on citizens down to the early years of the second century B.C., but it tended to be regarded as a compulsory loan to be repaid later; and after 167 B.C., when Aemilius Paullus brought back vast booty from the third Macedonian war, Roman citizens in Italy were exempt from paying this tax, and most others except one on the manumission of slaves.

This did not, however, apply to the many overseas provinces. Here the Romans found systems of taxation already in existence and saw no reason to exempt their provincial subjects from the payment of tax. Partly through inertia they preferred taking over and adapting what was already there to creating new machinery; consequently there was no universal taxation system applicable to the whole Empire. Cicero mentions three main categories of province — those like Spain with a fixed tax, of which the various communities paid their share direct to the governor, those like Asia, where the collection was put up for auction and knocked down to the highest bidder among several competing companies, and finally those like Sicily where the previous system, based on payment of tithe, was taken over intact. When the taxes were auctioned at Rome, the censors were responsible; and as early as the second century B.C. large companies (*societates*) of tax-collectors (*publicani*) drawn from the ranks of the *equites* were formed to bid for the collection and, if successful, to carry it out with the maximum profit. These activities could have political repercussions; and the attempts of the *publicani* in 60 B.C. to secure the revision of a contract in which they had overbid was one of the events which contributed to the setting up of a political alliance between Caesar, Pompey and Crassus, which played a great part in the fall of the Republic. Already since 123 B.C., when G. Gracchus transferred the extortion court, in which governors were tried, from the Senate to the knights, the latter had become a political force, though they never, under the Republic, entered the direct service of the State. It was, however, from the ranks of the *equites* that the rare newcomer, like Marius or Cicero, broke the noble monopoly and rose to eminence as a magistrate and a senator.

Under the Empire taxation was treated more systematically, and the conditions of the provincials were greatly improved. Augustus and his successors drew on the financial experience of the *equites*, and from this order they recruited a large part of the imperial civil service; especially, as we saw, the collecting of taxes was entrusted to equestrian procurators, who were also to be found in the provinces still governed by senatorial proconsuls. There was a growth and systematisation of direct taxation, and here the *publicani* continued to be used even as late as the early second century A.D.; the excessive oppression for which they had won an evil name under the Republic was now curbed, and in

Limestone bas-relief showing tax payments. Some peasants, easily recognisable by their hooded coats, are paying their tax to the tax-gatherers seated behind a table. (Provincial Museum in Trier).

Money-changer's counter as it appears in bas-reliefs. (Museum of Roman Civilisation, Rome).

due course here, too, government officials took over the whole of their work. Under the Empire most provincials, including citizens living in the provinces, paid tax levied on their land (*tributum soli*) and on their other property (*tributum capitis*); in addition there were customs duties on certain frontiers (*portoria*), a five per cent duty on inheritances, and a one per cent tax on the manumission of slaves. All this, together with the proceeds of the mines and quarries, which were now mainly in the hands of the State, brought in a considerable revenue — though perhaps never enough to meet the growing needs of the vast Empire.

MONEY

The Latin word for money, *pecunia*, takes us back to an age when barter was predominant and cattle (*pecus*), were used as a basis of value. Compared with the cities of Greece, Rome was slow to adopt a currency; but by the first century B.C. she had had one for close on two hundred years (though its early history remains obscure). Under the late Republic both silver and copper and occasionally gold were minted in the Temple of Juno Moneta; the main silver coin was the *denarius*, which often showed Bellona and the Dioscuri but also other patterns, frequently relating to the family history of the *tresviri monetales* or other magistrates, who had minted them; throughout the period from 100 B.C. to the end of the Republic an important part is played by military coinage issued by Roman commanders abroad. Augustus introduced a new coinage employing gold, silver and copper. The silver *denarius* was tariffed at a twenty-fifth of the gold *aureus*, and was itself worth sixteen copper *asses*; in addition to the copper *as* there were copper coins representing four *asses* (*sestertius*), three *asses* (*tripondius*), two *asses* (*duopondius*) as well as half-an-*as* (*semis*) and a quarter of an *as* (*quadrans*). Brass coins were also used. Gold and silver both had their own independent values, and in the later Principate suffered from debasement, both in size and in metal content; both these metals were struck by the emperor's slaves and freedmen, while the *tresviri monetales* continued to strike copper in the name of the Senate and the emperor acting in collaboration. This was supplemented by the issue of a great deal of provincial copper coinage, which went on in the eastern provinces until the third century A.D., and city coinages, much of it silver. During the early Empire, Lyons was the site of an important mint under the emperor's control.

For two centuries this monetary system carried the trade of the Empire. It reflected the collaboration of Senate and emperor in the administration and formed a universal system corresponding to the vast Empire which had sprung out of the small city-state beside the Tiber. Its later vicissitudes, which cannot be traced here, also reflect the fortunes of the Empire itself; and when coins cease to appear in the relevant excavation layers, their absence provides a sombre indication of the approaching break-up of imperial government in the West.

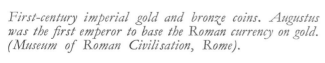

First-century imperial gold and bronze coins. Augustus was the first emperor to base the Roman currency on gold. (Museum of Roman Civilisation, Rome).

THE ELECTION CAMPAIGN OF MARCUS TULLIUS CICERO

That year Marcus Tullius offered his candidature for consul, the highest office in the Roman State. He was one of the « new men » in politics: he was the first member of his family to aspire to the supreme magistrature. For anyone who did not belong to the nobility such an attempt seemed doomed to failure, since it had to overcome the solid opposition of the nobles' party. They would always unite to exclude an outsider, and with their wealth, their alliances and their lack of scruple they were very powerful.

But he had high hopes, because he had previously won the confidence of the Roman electors. He had, in fact, been elected quaestor and in that year had been entrusted with the governorship of western Sicily, where he had uncovered and denounced with spirited oratory the robberies and other misdeeds of Verres. Then he had been elected curule aedile and later praetor. Now, after three years, he was standing for this highest of all dignities, a simple knight whose only merits were the offices he had held, and which his opponents would certainly try to play down.

His only weapon was his professional legal skill: the power of launching a sensational trial if he discovered that someone was using money to get votes from the electors, which in Rome was forbidden by law.

For the rest, the attempt to win such votes as the alignment of his adversaries would allow meant that he would have to act for himself and very shrewdly at that. There would have to be slow, continuous and exhausting attention paid to the voters of Rome and Latium, and to the leading personalities of other regions such as Apulia, Etruria, the Sabine, Brutium and Campanian areas, now that Roman citizenship had been extended to the whole peninsula, and

with it the right to vote. So he would have to go to these places to gain the confidence and sympathy of these unknown and distant people, but at least there was no need to make any public speeches. These distant peoples, who had the right to choose their administrators but could only vote in the centurion gatherings in Rome, found it difficult to bear the heavy cost and the discomfort of such a journey.

Marcus Tullius began approaching the electors in Rome, while keeping well in mind the three considerations which his brother Quintus had made: that he was not a noble, that he wanted to be elected consul, and all this *in Rome*. Therefore, whenever he pleaded in any lawsuit, even the simplest and dullest, he showed the greatest diligence, as though on each of them depended the judgment of people as to his value as an advocate. The prestige he gained in this way would serve, at least in part, to compensate for the fact that he did not belong to the nobility.

At the same time he arranged to let everyone know that his supporters belonged to social classes such as the nobles rarely had on their side: men in high finance, rich bourgeoisie, entire city municipalities united in his favour, many electors he had defended in the courts, many societies and finally a very large number of young men who followed his cases passionately in order to acquire the art of oratory. And he never forgot to ask all these people to vote for him, for they were all in some sense his debtors, and this, he would say, would be the best way for them to pay their debts; or if they wanted some service from him, then this would be the way to put him under an obligation.

Then he began to visit the noblemen themselves, the statesmen, ex-consuls and high magistrates to convince them of his political intentions and show that

he concealed no revolutionary ideas, but was a conservative like themselves. To get over this great obstacle of not belonging to the nobility he also made use of easy comparisons between himself, not a noble, yet of obvious stamina and courage, and certain candidates of the nobility who were good-for-nothing if not actually ruffians or worse.

There was no time to make new friends, but possibly those he already had would suffice. He had acquired them little by little by making himself useful in any way he could and by his friendly, agreeable manner. By friend Marcus Tullius meant somewhat elastically anyone who greeted him or smiled at him in the street or came often to visit him.

At that time he became very expansive and cordial, even with those who roused his antipathy.

Nor did he forget to cultivate his relations, even very distant ones, whom he had not seen for a very long time, and the neighbours, the clients, the freedmen, even the slaves, remembering that even the humblest opinion has its uses.

He also recruited a small army of electoral agents to win votes for him from the electors of their clan. He gladly promised to grant any favours asked of him; he said yes to everyone — he would have given the moon if anyone had asked for it.

Although he concentrated on those who might be really useful to him, he never refused outright those whom he knew were not much help. He had no scruples about letting those whose cases he had pleaded know that if he had asked them no favours up to now, this was the moment he wanted them to settle their moral debts.

And thus Marcus Tullius Cicero won the election and became consul.

(source: Letter from Quintus Tullius Cicero to his brother Marcus)

THE ARMY THAT CONQUERED THE WORLD

In general the soldiers of Rome in her greatness bear little resemblance to those martial figures of praetorians, centurions and tribunes that adorn the bas-reliefs on triumphal arches and commemorative columns. Most of the soldiers were shepherds and peasants from Latium, Samnium and Marsica, who for years and years were compelled to endure interminable marches and terrible battles in foreign lands. Strapping black haired men, with labourer's shoulders and muscles, their physical features typified that southern stockiness which Caesar names brevitas.

Patient and tenacious, they found compensation for homesickness for their families and distant villages through constant activity, for they were always being required to build camps, put up fortifications, span rivers, repair roads, or sow the fields with the seed that they frequently carried with them from the home country.

They were shepherds and peasants trained in the discipline of arms for the common good, citizens enlisted to fulfil a task or a mission voluntarily undertaken in the interest of the Republic, which embodied the interest of all. As long as the army numbered them in its ranks, even as professional soldiers, the prosperity of the Empire remained on a firm footing; but when recruitment for the legions had to be ensured by contingents of provincials and barbarians, to whom Roman patriotism meant nothing, it was for Rome the beginning of the end.

There is no more fascinating subject than the way in which the Romans built up, maintained and controlled their military force. In discussing this aspect of Roman life, it is appropriate to quote from the well-known nineteenth-century German historian Theodore Mommsen, who opened one of his lectures with the words: « Gentlemen, in speaking of ancient Rome, I could not have chosen a more modern subject ». And indeed, on examining more closely the wonderful system of the Roman army, on observing its mechanism and studying its functions, it must be admitted that here indeed was a system of the same type as that of the great European armies of the nineteenth century. Naturally this system was not created in a day, but this is not the moment to elaborate on the various stages of development in the military organisation of the Romans.

The Roman army was based on recruitment of Roman citizens, for in Rome as in many modern nations every citizen was a soldier. Yet the fundamental difference between military service at the time of the Romans and in modern times must be noted. Today armies are « permanent » in the sense that they have a peace-time structure and organisation, and recruitment goes on fairly steadily all the time; the change-over to a state of war is achieved by expanding the numerical strength through calling up former military personnel — the reservists. The Roman army had only a war-time organisation; its officers and troops were created only for the purpose of undertaking a specific military task, when a state of war had been declared or was considered to be imminent. But in practice the call to arms took place each year, for in the pre-Augustan period nobody had ever known the doors of the temple of Janus to be closed; that would have meant that the Republic was in a state of absolute peace — a situation that had occurred only once — in 235 B.C.

Liability for military service began at the age of seventeen, and did not cease until the age of forty-six. However, the Roman citizen could not be called up for more than twenty campaigns in the infantry, or ten in the cavalry. In the period just before 100 B.C., when the number of enlisted citizens had considerably diminished, the system of voluntary enrolment was introduced by C. Marius, the famous conqueror of Jugurtha (in 107-105 B.C.), the Cimbri and the Teutons. From then until the time of Caesar volunteers played an increasingly important role in the army, and under the Empire they formed the greater part of its effective strength.

Thus the Roman army, while theoretically retaining its old organisation, gradually underwent a profound modification: from a « nation in arms » it changed to « an army of volunteers ». These volunteers, introduced by Marius, had to be Roman citizens, which meant that they were Italic. If in the stress of the civil wars provincials were occasionally enrolled, these generally received the title of Roman citizens as a reward in the course of their military service.

If the recruitment of volunteers depended directly on political troubles and even on civil wars, this was because enrolment (of the contingent as well as the volunteers) was not a function of the State as it is in a ministry of modern times but was undertaken by the heads of the forces — consuls or proconsuls who had been charged with the conduct of a military campaign. Consequently, once the volunteers had been enrolled, they regarded themselves as committed not to the Republic itself but rather to the general who had established their rate of pay and had promised them rewards. In the military sphere this voluntary system considerably enhanced the technical value and efficiency of the Roman army as compared with the time of the war against Hannibal, when there was a militia composed of men recalled to the colours.

Each year after the elections (which until 153 B.C. took place in March, thereafter in January) the consuls, acting as commanders-in-chief of the army, appointed twenty-four senior officers as military tribunes — corresponding to our colonels or generals. Some of these were personal nominees, while others were elected by the people's assemblies. Then came the gathering on the Capitol of the men who had come to Rome in response to the mobilization orders transmitted to all districts (*tribus*) of the Roman territory, which specified the classes to be called up. The twenty-four tribunes formed the complement of officers of the four legions that normally constituted an army (six tribunes to a legion); and from the mass of men who had presented themselves were drawn at random the 4,200 required for each of the four legions. Those who had not been selected returned to their homes. The same procedure was used to enrol the four contingents of cavalry, one for each of the legions.

The Roman legion, with its 3,000 infantrymen equipped with heavy arms and its 1,200 *velites*, lightly equipped troops who wore no armour, constituted a complete combat unit (comparable to our « divisions ») capable of acting independently or in association with another legion. Each of the two consuls had under command a force consisting of two legions, with twelve subordinate commanders (the tribunes). But the two legions could operate separately on two different fronts, one remaining under the direct command of the consul, while the other came under the orders of one of the tribunes, who then assumed the title and rank of legate.

When the needs of war increased, Rome multiplied its legions and also the number of the military commanders.

The Italic allies of Rome had to make a contribution in men to the Roman army. For each of these peoples the treaty of alliance stipulated the size of the contingent to be placed at the disposal of the Roman generals. These « auxiliary contingents » were then allocated to the various legions and fought by their side.

When Marius achieved the military reforms that have already been mentioned, he transformed the legion (now consisting mainly of volunteers) into a powerful body numbering 6,000 men, divided into ten « cohorts » organised so as to be capable of operating separately as small autonomous units.

OFFICERS AND MEN

It has already been mentioned that Rome possessed no permanent army before the time of Augustus, and consequently there could be no career officers with permanent commissions.

In Rome the supreme military command was vested in the highest political authority, namely the consul, and when necessary in the magistrature or the praetor, who came directly under the consul. On election at

Roman insignia: in the centre, between the eagle of the legions and the labarum, *the imperial standard surmounted by victory, the insignia of a cohort in the imperial period. The insignia of the legions were entrusted to warrant officers of proved valour and experience* (acquiliferi); *those of less important units were given to warrant officers called* signiferi. *(Museum of Roman Civilisation, Rome).*

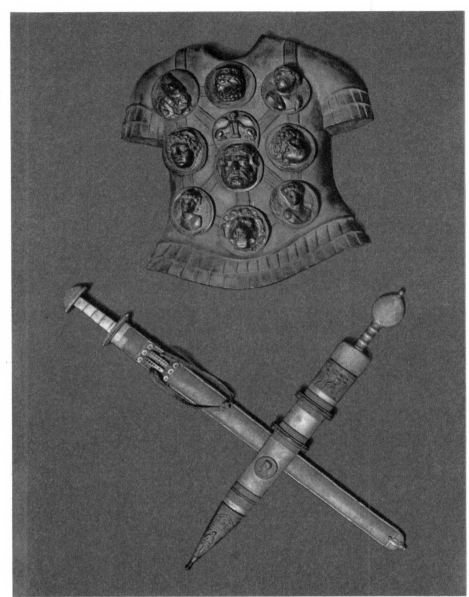

Roman centurion of the first century B.C. The helmet is capped by a transverse plume, an indication of rank. The decorations (phalerae) are prominent on the moulded leather breastplate. (Museum of Roman Civilisation, Rome).

the beginning of the year the two consuls ordered the call-up of a certain number of « classes » and proceeded to assume command of the legions thus created. If more than four legions were to be formed, the praetors were required to command them, and if this were inadequate, the consuls and praetors of the preceding year were retained in their commands as proconsuls and propraetors.

The senior officers of the legions were called « military tribunes » (tribuni militum). There were six of these in each of the four legions, and they were elected by the comitia tributa. Normally recruited from the young men of noble family who had already completed their military service, they at once acquired senior rank without having to pass through the subordinate grades. The tribunes succeeded each other in the general management of the legion; they nominated the centurions and apportioned the various responsibilities among themselves.

At a later period the command staff of a legion was made up of legati, a word that denotes « charged with a mission ». In practice these were citizens chosen

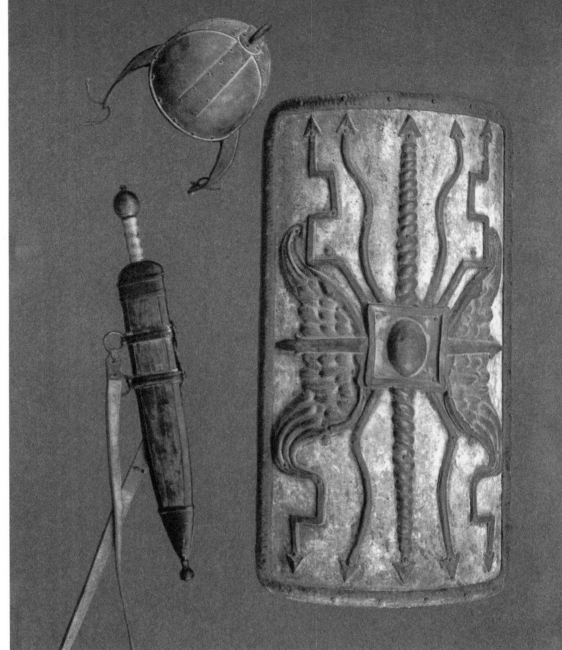

Roman legionary of the first century A.D. The equipment of the legionary consisted of a sword and buckler, together with the javelin, the throwing of which was the signal to start battle. (Museum of Roman Civilisation, Rome).

by the Senate for their proved competence in political or military affairs, who accompanied the commanding general and under his authority carried out all the functions that he could not himself attend to.

The junior officers, of whom there were sixty in every legion, bore the title « centurion », and each commanded a company of 100 men. Centurions were selected from the ordinary soldiers; they were nominated by the tribunes and appointed by the commander-in-chief. They had several grades, corresponding to a modern army's captains and subalterns. Those of the

highest rank were entitled to be mounted when on the march, but not for combat.

Between the centurion and the common soldiers (*gregarii milites*) were the « warrant officers » (*principales*) who had important functions in training as well as in active service. Among these Caesar frequently refers to the *aquiliferi*, who carried the silver eagle, emblem of the legion, and the *signiferi*, the standard-bearers of the maniples, a unit of men varying from 120 to 200 in strength, who were noted for their bravery. Then there were the *beneficiarii*, who like our

Battle between Romans and barbarians. On the left can be seen an aquilifer, *a Roman horseman and an allied horseman. Bas-relief.*

modern orderlies attended to the personal needs of the officers and were exempt from fatigue duties.

The legion's cavalry came under a senior officer, and was divided into squadrons (*turmae*) which were commanded by three decurions.

The allied contingents were directed by their own chiefs under the authority of a Roman senior officer (*praefectus*).

Insignia were worn by the officers and warrant officers to indicate the rank and the different specializations. The military tribunes of the equestrian order wore the golden ring that was the distinguishing mark of horsemen and the « angusticlave » tunic (the tunic worn by those starting an equestrian career); those belonging to the senatorial order wore the « laticlave » tunic (the one reserved for men embarked on a senatorial career).

EQUIPMENT AND ARMS

All legionaries had the same clothes and equipment, which could on this account qualify as a uniform. It consisted of a woollen *tunica* without sleeves and worn next to the body, a field cloak, also of wool (*sagum*), which was secured on the right shoulder by a clasp; it gave protection against cold and rain, but was discarded in battle. The footwear consisted of high closed boots (*calcei*) laced with four thongs.

The defensive arms consisted of the breastplate, helmet and buckler. The breastplate (*lorica*) was shaped from strips of leather, and over the breast it was covered with a sparkling metal badge. The metal helmet (*galea*) was kept in position by a chin-strap; it was capped by a plume of red or black feathers. The buckler (*scutum*) attached to the left arm was rectangular and convex;

Helmet, breastplate, buckler and bare legs for better control of the horse. This was the basic equipment of the Roman cavalryman. Below: an archer. The majority of the archers were in the allied contingents. (Museum of Roman Civilisation, Rome).

it was about four feet long and two and a half feet wide and consisted of two parallel curved panels of wood bound together with an outside covering of grey leather, the centre having a metallic embossment, called the *umbo*.

For purposes of attack the legionaries carried the short double-edged sword of the Spanish type (*gladius hispaniensis*) and the big javelin (*pilum*); the skirmishers or *velites* were equipped with a small round buckler (*parma*), a light leather helmet and a bundle of light javelins. The horsemen carried the same weapons as the *velites* — light javelins.

THE ENCAMPMENT

The Romans attached the greatest importance to the organisation of the fortified camp. They took every

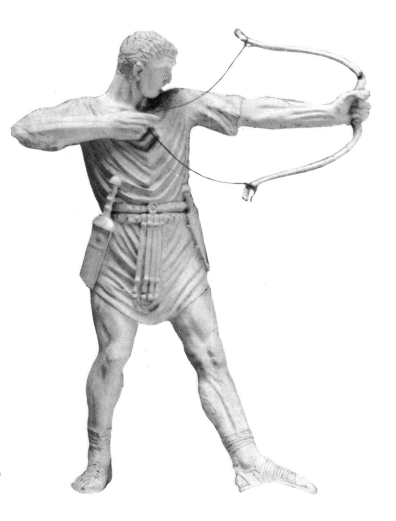

Detail of the defensive system of a camp. In front of the palisade, which had a watch-tower, a ditch was dug, and this was protected by the levee of earth formed by the excavation. (Model in the Museum of Roman Civilisation, Rome).

THE CAMP OF A ROMAN ARMY OF TWO LEGIONS
(DIAGRAM IN THE MUSEUM OF ROMAN CIVILISATION, ROME)

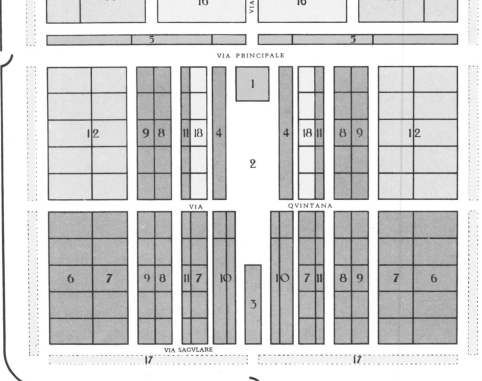

1. **Praetorium.**
2. **Forum.**
3. **Quaestorium.**
4. **The General's bodyguard** (Selected cavalrymen and infantrymen, recalled to the colours).
5. **Senior Officers** (*praefecti socium, tribuni, legati*).
6. **Infantrymen.**
7. **Cavalrymen.**
8. **Principes.**
9. **Pikemen** (*hastati*).
10. **Men recalled** (*evocati*).
11. **Soldiers of the third rank** (*triarii*).
12. **Allies** (*socii*).
13. **Auxiliary infantry.**
14. **Auxiliary cavalry.**
15. **Complementary infantry.**
16. **Complementary cavalry.**
17. **Light infantry** (*velites*).
18. **Romans.**

Roman legionary in campaign uniform. The Gallic style tunic and the short trousers are made of leather. (Reconstruction based on a find in Germany. Museum of Roman Civilisation, Rome).

care in setting it up, even in cases of an interrupted march, which meant exhausting work for the troops each evening.

A suitable site was chosen, preferably on the gentle slope of a hill, and in such a way that the front of the encampment corresponded to the lowest part of the slope. Ideally the terrain would possess at the foot of the hill, and always in front of the camp, some natural obstacle, such as a stream, a valley or a marsh, which would make it difficult for the enemy to launch a surprise attack. The troops were accommodated in a quadrilateral surrounded on all sides by a specially dug ditch. The excavated earth was thrown to the inside to form a rampart (*agger*, or *vallum*) sufficiently large to post the defenders behind it. The organisation of the various camp parties and the fixing of the dimensions began in the interior of the camp and spread outwards. The tribune charged with supervising the building of the camp started by selecting a site for the general's tent (*praetorium*), a square with sides of sixty yards, at least 200 yards away from the *porta praetoria*; this gate opened into the middle of the rampart protecting the entrance to the camp. The *via praetoria* ran from the gate to the general's tent, and extended beyond it to the opposite rampart. It was lined on both sides with the tents of the officers and warrant officers, the tribunes and legates, and also the horse-lines. In front of the *praetorium* was the sacrificial altar, whence the *via principalis* ran at right angles to the *via praetoria*, terminating at the ramparts on each side at the principal gates, right and left. Behind the *praetorium* were accommodated the legionaries, the horsemen and the auxiliary troops. Naturally the dimensions of the quadrilateral varied greatly according to the number of troops to be accommodated — two, four or even eight or ten legions. We know, for instance, that in Gaul, in the region of the river Aisne, an army of Caesar's with numbers equivalent to some ten legions occupied a camp covering forty-one hectares, or just over a hundred acres. It should be noted that between the ramparts and the tents a broad boulevard ran all round the camp, thus allowing the troops freedom of movement and at the same time protecting them from enemy projectiles.

At the far end of the camp in front of the *porta decumana* was situated the tent of the quaestor, who ran the supply services. On each side of this tent was ranged the heavy baggage, and probably the engines of war.

While the camp was under construction, and whenever it was occupied by troops, extensive security measures had to be taken, especially if an enemy was in the vicinity. Strong detachments of cavalry patrolled all around the camp while the soldiers of the cohorts worked intensely to raise the rampart. (This could be constructed as a first priority as soon as the approximate preliminary calculations had been made for the dimensions of the camp). Once the rampart had been completed the bulk of the cavalry took up its quarters within the enclosure; but a few squadrons remained outside, taking their turn in all-night patrols, while a cohort from each legion was posted at each gate and supplied guards for the *praetorium* and the *quaestorium*: in addition, sentinels were placed along the entire perimeter of the terrace. Night duty was counted from 6 p.m. to 6 a.m. and was divided into four « watches » (*vigilia*) of three hours. The change of guards was announced by the sounding of trumpets. The very strict rounds of inspection were usually performed by the centurions, and occasionally by the tribunes, the legates and even sometimes by the commander-in-chief.

LIFE AROUND THE ENCAMPMENT

Numerous persons with a far from military bearing were busy around the ramparts, and sometimes camped in the locality. These were the small traders who invariably follow in the wake of an army, peddling all those wares that soldiers always need and buy at a high price — change of clothes, spare parts for weapons, more or less empirical medicaments for ailments and minor injuries, titbits to add relish to dishes that were abundant but plain and monotonous. There were also huts in which diversions of every kind were on offer, and dealers ready to buy back from the soldiers the precious objects they had received as their share of the booty, which sometimes included slaves.

THE ARMY ON THE MARCH

In addition to his arms, the Roman legionary had to carry with him a quantity of grain sufficient for fifteen to twenty days, a scythe, a basket, a spade, an axe, a cooking pot and two or three stakes for the palisade; these accoutrements were far more cumber-

some than the notorious pack and haversack of which our modern infantrymen complain.

Caius Marius tried to ease the marching conditions of the legionary by making him fasten all his baggage to a stick carried over the right shoulder, which enabled him to hold the javelins in the left hand.

The Roman infantryman of the republican era, being burdened with some sixty-six pounds of baggage, was not called upon to march too far; he would march for four or five hours each day, halting at intervals of seven to ten miles, which in the time of Caesar was extended to twelve to fifteen miles. If the enemy was not in the vicinity, the legions and the convoys usually occupied the centre of the marching column, while the advance guard and the rearguard consisted of the infantry and the cavalry of the allies.

Depending on the general's concept of the initial development of the impending battle, the legion adopted one of the following marching orders: the simple column (*agmen pilatum*), the order of combat (*acie instructa*), or the square (*agmen quadratum*). In the first, the cohorts followed one another in numerical order. In the second case, the march could be made in *lines*, that is, in as many columns as there were lines of battle (which was usually three) or alternatively by *wings*, that is, in three columns formed by the three cohorts of the left wing. In the third case, the arrangement consisted of a detachment of troops marching *by wings* followed by the supply train, with a similar formation as a rearguard, while the two flanks of the supply train were protected by a third and fourth formation marching in « flanking line », with the cohorts disposed in columns of maniples.

The marching order of a cohort being used as an autonomous tactical unit could be in the form of a « column of maniples » or a « column of centuries ». The change from marching in maniples to combat

Diagram of a legion of the first century B.C. *deployed in battle order.*

formation was effected by ordering all of them to turn right or left, whereby they assumed their place in the battle. The change from marching in centuries to combat formation was more complicated.

THE ARMY IN BATTLE

In the period between the reigns of Marius and Caesar (about 107-44 B.C.) which represents the golden age of the Roman army, the plan of battle was based on the tactical unit of the cohort, where troops were arrayed on a front of fifty men and a depth of eight ranks. (Here we are assuming that the actual effective strength of a legion was nearer 4,000 than the stipulated 6,000 men). There was a space of twenty-one yards between each rank, and each man was about a yard from his neighbour. These distances enabled the men to march without impeding one another and allowed them to throw the javelin, but not to wield the sword. When the cohort had to change from offensive tactics in close order to defensive tactics in extended order,

With the reforms introduced by Marius, the thirty maniples that constituted a legion were re-grouped into ten tactical units, called cohorts. Each cohort had three maniples with names dating from ancient times: hastati, principes *and* triarii; *their armament and equipment were now standardized. In the diagram each square represents a cohort, each legionary a maniple. On the wings the figures represent the Roman cavalry and the allies.*

the front became nearly twice as long, with about two yards between individual legionaries.

The legion assumed combat formation in one of two ways, depending on whether it was to carry out an offensive or a defensive operation. For the offensive plan it was deployed either in two ranks with five cohorts in each rank, or in three ranks with four cohorts in the front rank and three in each of the other two ranks. Naturally the distance between the lines varied according to the tactical requirements and the nature of the terrain, but usually it was from twenty-six to thirty-seven yards. When on the defensive the legion could be drawn up either in a single line or in a circle (*orbis*). The single line was valid in particular conditions, as when defending the ramparts of the camp. In such cases it sufficed to dispose the troops along a line in five ranks, two of which were on the ramparts, the other three forming a reserve at the foot of the rampart. The tactics of the circle (in reality a square was formed) were adopted when protection was required on all sides, as when withdrawing in the face of the enemy. The cohorts were positioned so as

to safeguard a central area of about 124 by 102 yards, which was sufficient to contain the thousand or so beasts of burden with their allotted loads.

But the Romans always preferred offensive tactics, which compelled the enemy to conform to the place and time of the battle. For the actual attack the legions were drawn up close to each other in three lines which were successively sent in to the assault. Thus when the cohorts of the first wave became exhausted they could withdraw by passing through the gaps between the cohorts of the second line, which took over the assault, and so on.

The cavalry units, the *alae* or regiments, each consisting of squadrons of thirty-two horsemen, were usually deployed for combat on both wings of the army to protect it against the enemy's flanking movements, and to allow them in their turn to carry out flank attacks in order to envelop the enemy's wings, or to rush in pursuit of a fleeing enemy.

The light infantry was often mixed in with the cavalry. The auxiliary infantry troops were employed according to the tactics permitted by their weapons, the

Covered battering-ram. The big beam with a bronze head, used for making a breach in the enemy's walls, was moved about on wheels, and controlled from within the machine by two teams. (A model made by the Historical Section of the Italian Army Engineers, in the Museum of Roman Civilisation, Rome).

archers (*sagittarii*) and the slingers (*funditores*) doing the preliminary fighting while in open order.

The commanding general, always accompanied by his praetorian cohort, would inspect each legion, exhorting it to do battle; then he would occupy his command post, usually on the right wing, and order his trumpeter to sound the charge. The fanfare would be repeated by the trumpeter of each legion, and would be answered by the war cry of all the troops.

FORTIFICATIONS AND SIEGE WARFARE

In ancient times as in the Middle Ages, fighting in open country was usually hand to hand. It was not until the discovery of gunpowder that infantry and cavalry could manoeuvre during the battle in association with the large and heavy pieces of artillery, which had to be moved by means of special vehicles, or were fixed at bases or strong-points hurriedly set up near the battle line.

The military art of the ancients included knowledge and frequent use of machines of war, but these were used as part of siege technique. Indeed, sieges and assaults against towns were common occurrences in the military history of antiquity, even after the development of the art of fortifying agglomerations in the interior of the territory, on the coasts or at strategic points vital to the defence of a particular region.

A long-beam battering ram in a sling. It was fourteen yards long and its handling required twenty teams, each consisting of ten men. (A model by the Historical Section of the Italian Army Engineers, in the Museum of Roman Civilisation, Rome).

In the year 52 B.C. Caesar ordered the construction of a substantial system of works against the walls of Avaricum (now Bourges), making it possible to dominate the marked topographical depression surrounding the town. A terrace built of tree-trunks, measuring about 115 yards in length, sixteen yards wide and twenty-five yards high, carried the soldiers up to the level of the enemy's walls. (Model in the Museum of Roman Civilisation, Rome).

The techniques of fortification and siege attained a remarkable degree of perfection amongst the Greeks of the Hellenistic era. The Romans studied them at close quarters and to their cost, since they had to deal with the formidable powers of resistance of the Mediterranean's most impressive fortresses at Syracuse, Lilybaeum (Marsala), Carthage and Corinth.

In the course of his numerous campaigns Julius Caesar constantly assaulted or fortified towns and places of military significance; in his *Commentaries* he has left detailed descriptions of these works. Moreover, the remains of several of these fortresses have been carefully explored by archaeological excavation.

One of the most difficult sieges undertaken by Caesar during the penultimate year of the Gallic War was that of Avaricum (the present-day Bourges). The town was surrounded by a wall of masonry reinforced with beams. Caesar ordered a rampart to be constructed around the perimeter of this wall at a height of twenty-six yards, on which a covered gallery (*vinea*) was erected, the roofing consisting of fresh hides, so that it would not be set alight by the blazing materials hurled at it by the enemy. Other transverse galleries built on similar lines facilitated the bringing up towards the wall of the wooden siege towers from the tops of which the defenders could be attacked with projectiles.

In general, siege operations developed in four stages: (*a*) selection of the point of attack and stationing of the troops at the most suitable emplacements, (*b*) encirclement of the strong-point, (*c*) approaching

225

A frontier watch-tower. Such towers were located at points where the frontier had no walls or ramparts. The watchmen's method of signalling by day was with red flags, by night with torches. (Model in the Museum of Roman Civilisation, Rome).

the walls whilst evading the reactions of the besieged, (*d*) the opening of a breach and the assault.

ENGINES OF WAR

During the siege two types of engines were used: those which hurled large projectiles, corresponding to the artillery of modern times, which were called *tormenta*; and those designed to shield the attackers from enemy blows delivered from behind cover. In the first category were included the *catapultae, ballistae, scorpiones* and *onagri*; in the second, the *plutei, testudines, vineae, musculi, arietes, falces* and *turres*.

The catapults can be compared to large crossbows; they fired projectiles with an almost horizontal trajectory and were of light weight. On the other hand the *ballistae* could hurl stones or large arrows along a trajectory whose steepness depended on the weight of the projectile. They could be fixed at an angle of forty-five degrees, when their curved track enabled them to pass over walls and other obstacles, as with modern howitzers and mortars. The *scorpiones* were small catapults capable of being carried by a man, and consisted of a steel bow fitted with a string of tendon or gut. The *onager* consisted of a kind of wooden coffer, empty in the middle, fitted with a horizontal bundle of tendons, to which a lever was attached, whose outer end was spoon-shaped to hold the projectile. To discharge it, the lever was lowered by means of a winch from the vertical to the horizontal (cocked) position, and then released.

The *pluteus* consisted of a wicker mantle of semi-circular shape covered with hide. It was moved towards the walls by rolling it on three wheels, the soldiers

The onager was a machine for catapulting large stones, with ballistic properties giving a trajectory of up to forty yards in height and a range of thirty-two yards, thereby enabling indirect fire over the top of obstacles, rather like the present-day mortar. (Model in the Museum of Roman Civilisation, Rome).

keeping under cover behind it. The « tortoise » (*testudo*) was the name given to a robust wooden gallery mounted on four or six wheels which allowed the soldiers to reach the walls and remain under cover while levelling the ground, filling in the ditches or undermining the foundations. The *vineae* (trellis) had the appearance of a wooden hut on wheels, with a sloping roof made of planks and wattles. By placing several *vineae* end to end it was possible to form a kind of porch at the level of the wall of the enemy city. Under cover of this the soldiers could work with the battering-ram or other engines to loosen the foundations of the

rampart. The *musculi* (mice) resembled the tortoises, while the *aries* or battering-ram consisted of a large beam with an iron-bound end, anything from twenty to sixty yards long, which was suspended by a set of chains from a solid scaffolding; several soldiers (varying in number with the length of the ram) swung it from rear to front to batter the wall where a breach was required. The *falces* were long poles fitted with iron hooks with which to loosen the walls of the enemy fortifications.

Finally, for carrying the besiegers up to the level of the ramparts, use was made of mobile towers (*turres ambulatoriae*) mounted on wooden wheels and covered with iron plates or with hides. The towers were built with from three to ten floors, the lower floor containing the ram, the upper floors carrying drawbridges.

THE ENGINEERS

A large part of the Roman soldier's day was spent working. The scythe, the spade and the hatchet were an integral part of his equipment and were always in use. The camp or siege works and the construction of bridges often required the Roman infantryman to turn himself into a jack-of-all-trades.

The commanding officer had at his disposal thousands of hands whose work was planned and supervised by teams of technicians and specialists, collectively known as *fabri*, a system that originated in very ancient times. During the imperial period teams of this type were assigned to each group of the legions stationed in the different territories, and they came under the authority of a *praefectus fabrum*, that is, a general of engineers.

Thus the vast works of fortification achieved by Caesar in Gaul, and the bridges thrown across the Rhine, were constructed by men from all the cohorts with the assistance of groups of specialists.

The enlistment of the *fabri* was probably based on the voluntary system, and included contingents of slaves selected from those working in civilian shipyards and workshops.

In addition to this function the *fabri* concerned themselves with the construction and maintenance of the heavy and complex engines of war, which had to be built at the place of use, since they could not easily

Detail of a bridge about four yards wide and over 420 yards in length which Julius Caesar threw across the Rhine. (Model by the Historical Section of the Italian Army Engineers, based on the description in the Commentaries*).*

be moved any distance. Labourers were assigned to work with the *fabri* in the building of the heavy engines and especially the large battering-rams on slings. Indeed, the legions were accompanied by a considerable number of non-combatants, the *calones*, who were charged with maintenance and especially with the care of the horses, and the *muliones*, porters for transporting the tents.

BRIDGES

In time of war it has always been a major problem of an army on the march to cross rivers, especially if

The framework of the bridge was supported by trestles formed of two big stakes secured by a master cross-beam. The stakes were driven into the bed of the river and sloped inwards. The beams supported the planking of the bridge. Upstream, small palisades in the shape of a « V » protected the stakes from objects thrown into the river by the enemy. (Museum of Roman Civilisation, Rome).

they are wide and deep. In general, bridges were less common in ancient times than today. They are frequently destroyed to prevent or delay the advance of a hostile army.

Whenever possible the Romans preferred to ford a river, and they sometimes had to do this under difficult conditions, as in the Punic wars, with water coming up to the shoulders or even the chins of the soldiers. But when fording was impracticable they had to build bridges, which Caesar frequently did in the course of his numerous campaigns, although he had no specialized corps of engineers.

The simplest bridges were made by laying a number of tree trunks close together across the river and covering them with wattles to facilitate the march of soldiers and horses. But a bridge of that type could only be used over narrow streams or canals, and although easy to erect, it was merely a foot-bridge.

In marshy regions or on muddy ground the method was to use trunks or thick planks laid over faggots, which were secured to the bottom by means of large piles. In order to cross the larger rivers it was necessary to build proper bridges; they rested on pontoons or on piles, according to the circumstances.

In foreign countries it was not always easy to find an adequate number of suitable boats, and it was considered undesirable to give the allies the impression that the progress of the legions really depended on help from them. Hence the most usual solution was to build the bridge on piles; Caesar has left a detailed account of this in his *Commentaries*. The two bridges described by him were built at different points on the Rhine between Cologne and Coblenz in 55 and 53 B.C. They were works of great merit, erected in record time, the designers having allowed for the variable state of the current and water level, as well as for the possibility of hostile attacks from the river. Thus the piers were protected from possible damage from drifting objects by using trellis shields; any material thrown into the river by the Gauls thus being deflected under the bridge without difficulty.

The Roman army included a considerable number of competent swimmers. All officers had to know how to swim. All men capable of swimming crossed the rivers by their own effort, while their comrades and the convoys used the bridges, thus shortening the overall time for the crossing.

SUPPLIES

This problem was closely linked with the movement of troops from one point to another in the operational zone, or from one district to another in the occupied territory. For many hundreds of years up to the middle of the nineteenth century the problem remained almost unchanged, for it must not be supposed that the question of supplying munitions arose only after the adoption of firearms. In ancient times, too, armies required stocks of offensive and defensive arms to be readily available; every battle that involved large numbers of troops consumed thousands of javelins, spears and swords which had to be replaced immediately. Replacements were also needed for helmets and breastplates rendered unserviceable through blows, for pierced or broken bucklers, for horses' saddlery and harness, soldiers' uniforms, and the stock of projectiles for the engines (stone ballshot, large arrows, etc.).

It is evident, then, that a legion on the march included a large quantity of material (*impedimenta*),

Details of a reconstruction of the Rhine bridge. Note the pile-driver for positioning the big stakes. (Museum of Roman Civilisation, Rome).

Remains of Hadrian's Wall, the extensive Roman fortification in the north of England.

which was usually carried on the backs of horses or mules (*iumenta*, *sarcinaria*). These were used as beasts of burden rather than as draft animals because of the scarcity or complete absence of roads. Yet attached to each legion there was always a certain number of wagons to carry the fodder or the wounded, while other vehicles were owned by the merchants who accompanied the troops.

The tents, made of hide (*pelles*), accounted for a large proportion of this baggage. There was one tent for every ten soldiers, while the centurions had one each, and the senior officers were allowed several. On the basis that a horse or a mule could carry the material for one tent, a legion's 6,000 men and their officers would thus require between 700 and 800 pack-animals, and this number would be trebled for a consul's army of two legions with auxiliary troops. If to this are added the thousands of beasts of burden and the wagons needed for transporting the *impedimenta*, it is evident that the army of a consul on the move would form a column extending to several miles.

THE TRIUMPH

For any military chief who had been victorious in a pitched battle with the enemy, the most coveted reward was the triumph. It was the prerogative of the officers and soldiers themselves to declare their general worthy of this supreme honour by acclaiming him on the spot as *imperator* (victorious commander), but the army's verdict had to be ratified by the Senate, which alone could order the triumph.

Greek and Roman writers have given colourful and detailed descriptions of the triumphs of victorious Roman generals.

A military commander returning from the scene of operations as victor, who had either received the honour of a triumph or was anticipating a senatorial pronouncement on the subject, did not pay off all his troops, as was the usual practice, but kept a considerable number under arms so that they could exercise their right to participate in this demonstration of appreciation and joy, when their presence would add to

The triumph. The legionaries have secured for Rome some distant lands. Now they follow the imperator, *who is on his way up to the Capitol, preceded by the lictors. For these soldiers, the future holds the prospect of a new field to till and of a little booty to pay off the debts incurred by the family during the campaign. Alternatively there is the possibility of re-enlistment and a new departure to other frontiers. Reconstruction based on the bas-reliefs on the Trajan Arch at Benevento. (Museum of Roman Civilisation, Rome).*

the solemnity of the triumphal ceremony. According to the constitutional rules in force during the last century of the Republic, a military chief could not enter the sacred confines of the city until he had laid down the insignia of his command and had disbanded his army. Moreover, the *imperator* had to remain outside Rome until the appointed day of the ceremony. At dawn on that day the cortège was formed on the parade-ground (corresponding approximately to the present-day urban district that is bounded by the Via del Corso, the Corso Vittorio Emmanuele and the Tiber). When all was ready, the long procession was set in motion, entering the city through the *Forum Boarium*, passing through the *Circus Maximus* at the foot of the Aventine, thence along the entire length of the Via Sacra and up the slope (*Clivus Capitolinus*) leading to the Capitol.

It might be supposed that the cortège was accompanied by a military band, but the military units taking part used only their service instruments — the *lituus*, a long trumpet with a curved extremity emitting a sharp and sonorous tone, which was peculiar to the cavalry; the *tuba*, a long, straight trumpet terminating in a funnel, giving a rumbling and noisy sound; the *cornu*, a kind of circular horn with a harsh and hollow sound which was used by the escort of the *signiferi* or colour-bearers; and the *bucina*, similar to the horn, which was used mainly to pass signals at night to the sentinels.

Of all the triumphal processions that filed through the streets and squares of Rome, one of the most spectacular was probably that of Aemilius Paullus after his victory over Perseus, the last king of Macedonia, in 167 B.C. The ceremony lasted three days and the

belonged to the soldiers of various countries who had fought in the armies of Persia and her allies. These were followed by 3,000 men in columns of fours carrying 750 urns filled with pieces of silver, totalling 2,250 talents, equivalent to about 75,000 pounds sterling or $ 240,000. The third day's procession, which was heralded by the blare of trumpets, offered the most religious and perhaps the most noble spectacle: twenty oxen, garlanded and crowned with flowers, and destined to be sacrificed as a thank-offering to Jupiter; then the young people connected with the divine service in the temples, displaying urns filled with gold and jewels captured from King Perseus, and the king's own war-chariot with its coat of arms and the royal crown;

The Triumpher's Chariot. (Model in the Museum of Roman Civilisation, Rome).

memory of it had endured for over a century, when Livy described its magnificence in a few notable pages of his *History of Rome*. The populace, clothed in white, occupied the benches that had been installed in the Forum and all the squares on the route of the procession, for most of the streets were too narrow for seats. The smoke of incense poured through the open doors of the temples; the lictors and the guards for maintaining order had their hands full preventing the crowds from spreading into the streets and so obstructing the march of the procession. The first day was barely sufficient to permit the display before the admiring crowds of all the works of art, statues and pictures seized from the palaces and towns of Macedonia and Greece, which were exhibited on 250 chariots. On the second day the same number of chariots was used to display the arms of all types that had and lastly the mass of prisoners, including the king, queen and all the royal princes accompanied by their slaves and preceptors, their courtiers and friends, all manifesting profound despair. Immediately behind the prisoners came the triumphal chariot with the *imperator*, on his head a crown of laurels, his robe a purple toga embroidered with gold, his feet in gilt sandals, and clasped in his right hand the ivory sceptre capped by the eagle — the sacred bird of Jupiter. Following behind his chariot were the mass of the victorious soldiery, surrounded by a troupe of performers executing comic dances to the sound of a lyre. The soldiers, too, chanted couplets composed for the occasion, with words that praised their leader but also made fun of any ridiculous or reprehensible characteristics he might have.

MILITARY REWARDS AND PUNISHMENTS

On the day following a victorious battle the commander-in-chief, hailed by the troops with the title of *imperator*, ordered a roll-call. All the officers and non-commissioned officers and the greatest possible number of soldiers gathered before the *praetorium*, where from a platform (*tribunal*, *suggestus*) the commander congratulated the troops for their courage and discipline in the fighting, and complimented the officers on their understanding and skill. He then announced the rewards — material benefits in the form of booty due to each one, sums of money and increase in pay for individual acts of courage or for valorous conduct by entire maniples or cohorts; and the honorary awards which the Roman soldiers prized above all others. Inscriptions dating from the imperial age indicate that these latter awards were regarded seriously, and not as mere rhetorical forms. There was the award of a *hasta pura*, consisting of a symbolic spear without the iron point, or of bracelets made of gold or silver chains, of collar chains and of bronze on gold medals to be carried on the breast-plate, and for the officers various crowns, which could also be awarded to common soldiers. Thus the *corona civica* could be awarded to a person who in the course of a battle had saved the life of a Roman citizen; the *corona muralis* was reserved for

the first man to scale the walls of an enemy city, and the *corona vallaris* went to the first to cross the rampart of a fortified camp.

But the general, who already possessed reports from all commanders of legions and cohorts, did not dismiss the assembly until he had announced the more important punishments bestowed on soldiers for grave derelictions. The most serious of these was when a sentinel fell asleep or deserted his place of duty. The offender was immediately tried and condemned to death by a court-martial composed of tribunes, and the execution was entrusted to his comrades, who beat him to death with sticks and stones. In milder cases of insubordination the punishment consisted of a simple beating; those guilty of cowardice were deprived of pay or of booty, and this punishment could be bestowed collectively on a whole cohort or legion. Minor faults incurred various punishments that were regarded as humiliating (*ignominia*), such as being sent on duty without wearing uniform or with bare feet, exercising with full equipment, drawing rations of barley bread instead of wheat bread, or being deprived of arms for a specified period.

Disciplinary penalties were imposed on the legionaries by the military tribunes, and on the allied soldiery by their respective chiefs (*praefecti sociorum*). The commander-in-chief scrutinized only the offences committed by officers and those liable to the death penalty.

Despite the profound changes in the Roman army that resulted from the reforms of Marius, who introduced voluntary recruitment as a parallel system to compulsory conscription, and the subsequent abolition of conscription through the measures taken by Augustus, the Roman legions continued for a long time as paragons of organisation, discipline and military efficiency. Nor did they lose their excellence after the Social War (89 B.C.) when almost all the Italic allies were incorporated in the ranks of the legions, for these brothers-in-arms with their long service had become familiar with the rules and traditions of the Roman army. Those rules and traditions not only survived the evolution and transformation of other aspects of social and political life, but endured for a longer period than any other military organism known to history. Indeed, apart from certain purely superficial details,

On the door of his house the ex-soldier sometimes hung the civic crown. It was made of oak, and was awarded to those who had saved the life of any Roman, whether soldier or citizen. (Museum of Roman Civilisation, Rome).

The first soldier to scale the walls of an enemy city under siege was awarded the corona muralis, *circular in form and made of gold. (Museum of Roman Civilisation, Rome).*

The golden corona vallaris *was the decoration bestowed on the first man to get across the enemy's trench and enter the fortified camp. (Museum of Roman Civilisation, Rome).*

The standard of the Third Praetorian Cohort, with decorations attached to the pole. The corona muralis *can be identified. (Museum of Roman Civilisation, Rome).*

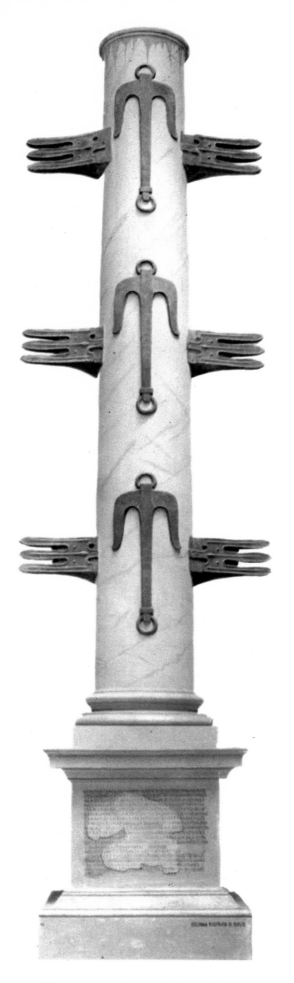

The rostral column of Caius Duilius.

the admirable bas-reliefs on the Trajan Column still illustrate the scenes of Roman military life, which have also been portrayed no less admirably by the historian Polybius.

THE ROMAN NAVY

Like other Latin peoples the Romans never showed much enthusiasm for maritime enterprises, and in this respect they were quite different from the Greeks, the Etruscans and their rivals, the Carthaginians. Not until rather late in the second Samnite war (328-304 B.C.) did they acquire a war flotilla of twenty small units — the *triremes*. It needed the conflict with Carthage — the great maritime power of the third century B.C. and absolute mistress of the Western Mediterranean — to induce the Romans to invest in a large fleet capable of standing up to the redoubtable squadrons of the Carthaginians. Under this pressure an important navy sprang up miraculously from nothing, to record its triumphs over the enemy's fleets and establish Roman predominance at sea.

Once Carthage was defeated, the Romans had no other maritime power to contend with, and they so neglected their fleet that in the second century B.C. it was possible for pirates to roam the Mediterranean with impunity, capturing and sinking merchant ships and their crews both at sea and in the ports. To put an end to this state of affairs the Romans built a fleet of 500 vessels, which under Pompey swept the corsairs from the seas that they had infested (67 B.C.). Thereafter battle fleets figured in actions during the second and third civil wars, when naval operations assumed a considerable and even decisive importance — as in the battle of Actium in 31 B.C.

The warships most employed in ancient times, commencing with the fourth century B.C., were the *quinqueremes;* the Romans copied the type from the Carthaginians and the Greeks, who named it « pen-

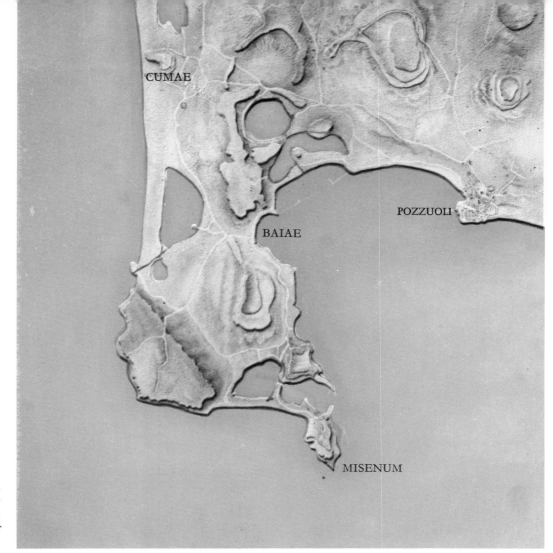

CUMAE

BAIAE

POZZUOLI

MISENUM

Of exceptional commercial and military importance were the ports of Pozzuoli and Misenum, created and developed by Agrippa and Augustus. (Museum of Roman Civilisation, Rome).

Long and with a low freeboard, the Roman bireme was very easy to handle. It was built with a curved rostrum which formed part of the hull. On the rostrum was a mobile battering-ram. Along the sides ran a passage-way which could be used by the combatants. Mounted on the poop was the covered cabin of the captain, and above it were displayed the emblem of the fleet and the flag of the vessel. The overall length of the ship was thirty-three yards, beam six yards, and draft about 5 feet. (Museum of Science and Technology, Milan).

View from above of a monoremis. This was a light vessel with a central mainmast, an inclined foremast and square sails. The sides of the ship were fitted with brackets which carried the extensions to the thwarts to increase the effectiveness of the oars. Each oar was handled by two or three men. The poop had no cabin. The prow with its curved rostrum contained a grapnel which was handled from the foremast. Length forty-one yards, beam six yards, draft one yard. (Museum of Science and Technology, Milan).

Roman freighter. The ship was designed to carry the maximum possible load in men or goods, and with hull features enabling it to be easily beached in the event of landings on an enemy coast. (Museum of Science and Technology, Milan).

ters ». A more ancient and smaller type of vessel to be kept in service was the trireme. The Roman quinqueremes were fast and robust vessels, over forty yards in length with a beam of six to seven yards, manned by a crew of 300 men including seamen and oarsmen, and a detachment of 120 soldiers with twenty officers and N.C.O.s. Although fitted with sails, they normally proceeded under oars, furling or even jettisoning their sails before an action. With a well-trained crew they attained speeds up to five or six knots. On the other hand cargo ships relied exclusively on sails and had a reduced crew to provide more space for passengers and cargo.

During a campaign the quinqueremes were accompanied by smaller vessels with two banks of oars (*miopari, catascopi*). As the rudder had not yet been invented, the ships were steered with two large oars, placed one on each quarter near the poop. The sail was fitted to a yard on the single mast (*malus*). At the start of a battle the sail was furled and the mast lowered. All ships possessed iron anchors with rope cables.

The crew consisted of oarsmen (*remiges*) and seamen (*nautae*) who were usually provided by the allies (*socii*) of the maritime colonies or recruited among the freedmen (*liberti*). They were not slaves; and if occasionally slaves were allowed to be enrolled, these were subsequently promoted to the state of freedom. The crews obeyed the orders of the *magistri* (chiefs of the oarsmen) or the *gubernatores* (pilots and chiefs of the seamen), while the command of the ship was entrusted to a tribune or a centurion. The commander of the squadron was a legate.

It was only in the imperial epoch that permanent bases were organized for the fleet. Two were established at Misenum and Ravenna, with ancillary bases at Fréjus and Aquileia.

241

ONE AGAINST TEN

The forest was filled with the sound of axe-blows; the voices and the laughter, barely distinguishable in the cold air, were in an unknown dialect of soft accents and sibilant end-syllables that bore no resemblance to the harsh and rugged language of the local population, who until now had always come here to gather supplies of wood. This was a detachment of the Roman legion whose quarters lay a few miles distant, men, who, judging by their speech, came from central Italy — Umbrians, Tuscans, and mountain people from the Abruzzi. They had been in the forest since the morning, selecting and cutting timber for the camp buildings; as usual there were some who did the work of four men, while others thought of every excuse for doing none: a blunted axe, or maybe an old scar that gave trouble with the change of weather — a pretext for endless tales of battle and heroism.

As usual they were gossiping about pensions, the food in the camp, the rumours of failures and military reverses. No precise information was available in the camp, but the adjutant had mentioned it, and long experience had shown him to be well informed.

« The devil take them, provided all ends well », exclaimed an infantryman of the escort, wrapping himself in his woollen cloak. A huge Umbrian, who had lived through many campaigns and always with the same general, winked at the infantryman as if to second this imprecation, then proceeded to wield a mighty axe-blow at an old fir tree whose tip soared up to the pale winter sky.

At that moment the Gauls suddenly surged up on all sides in this part of the woods; they and their great horses seemed to materialize out of the trees. Their attitude left no room for doubt. One does not brandish swords and lances or bend bows merely to spy upon people.

The first to move was the centurion commanding the detachment, who fell flat on his face with an arrow in his back. Since resistance was out of the question, the Romans signified their intention to surrender; hurriedly they regrouped, throwing their swords down under threats from the enemy, who brutally drove them forward with prods from spears and blows with the flat of their swords.

In the camp it was the same story. The enemy's infantry had advanced towards it, yelling as they poured out of the wood on all sides in their hundreds, like ants. But at the camp they had been halted, for in such cases the Romans were never taken by surprise. The warning shouts from the sentinels on the ramparts were enough. In Gaul there is no fooling about; an alarm is not sounded without good reason. The air was now filled with cries of excitement and the blare of trumpets. They sprang upon the ramparts just as the alarm had found them, breast-plates half buckled; hurriedly seizing the javelins and spears from the racks, they reached their posts without confusion, eyes fixed on the ensign-bearer. Within a few moments they were ready to face the assault.

The attack had developed simultaneously from all four sides, indicating that the Gauls had done a thorough job in silently liquidating all the cavalry patrols that had been outside the camp. They were evidently clever, though without the most elementary idea of tactics. That was the opinion of Quintus Cicero, second-in-command and brother of the orator, who had climbed to the observation-post, burning with fever but dressed with parade-ground smartness. Shielding his eyes with his hand, he tried to make out what kind of people had attacked in this way. All he knew was that they seemed to be wild with some extraordinary fury. Perhaps that was all they were capable of, these barbarian Gauls.

Writing material was brought to him so that he could compose an urgent message for Caesar's headquarters; and when his attention was called to the uselessness of this step, since all the routes had been blocked for some time, he did not bother to reply, but merely advised the clerk to show no discourtesy towards the couriers who, contrary to all expectations, would succeed in returning with a reply.

Now the battle raged on all sides of the camp with unimaginable violence. The attackers hurled themselves against the Romans with no thought of personal safety; wave after wave of them came out of the shadow of the woods. It was as if the whole of Gaul had gathered here, obsessed with the desire to storm the entrenched camp of Lieutenant-General Cicero.

The general cast an anxious look at the sky; he was afraid the troops might not last the night, all the more so since in this hitherto quiet spot the work of fortification had been somewhat relaxed.

Just as a pale glow in the sky announced the dawn, the general was distracted from his anxieties by the arrival of four centurions escorting a Nervian noble, who had been forced to accompany his fellow-countrymen, but had at the last moment and for personal reasons preferred to remain loyal to the Romans. In this way Cicero received certain intelligence which gave him a rude shock, although he was careful to appear unaffected by it; his attackers were peoples of *Gallia Belgica* — Nervii, Eburoni and especially Aduatuchi. They had wiped out all the inhabitants of the area so effectively that there was no longer any talk of the Romans for a hundred leagues around, while Ambiotrix, king of the Eburoni, was resolved to liberate Gaul once and for all from Roman domination.

While the Gallic deserter and the interpreter were talking, an impressive silence fell on the camp and in the trenches, broken only by the faint cries of the wounded. The battle had suddenly ceased, and Cicero, having judged and dismissed the Nervian, withdrew to the praetorian tent with his senior officers. But he spoke mainly with the staff of the *fabri*. Before long the camp was echoing to the sound of a thousand hammer-blows.

Intrigued by this commotion and by the flickering light of fires, the Gauls sent some patrols close up to the rampart, but were none the wiser; and with the coming of dawn their surprise was all the greater. Rising above the whole length of the terreplein, more than 120 wooden towers could be seen, massive and threatening even if only partially completed. Some miracle had made them sprout during the night.

The Gauls hurriedly regrouped amidst the noise and confusion characteristic of them, and hurled themselves into a new attack, dragging behind them faggots and tree-trunks intended for filling the ditches. But the Romans, having got over their surprise, trusted in their own organisation; they stood their ground on that and the following days.

How frightful those night attacks can be! Before they started the men could sleep on the ground at night, forgetting or perhaps dreaming with half-closed eyes of some small village in the Apennines with its scent of mown hay and hot bread. In the evenings there was time to cultivate a discreet bit of garden where the centurion could not see, a bit of cabbage or chard to lend a homely flavour; those were the nostalgic days. But now there was commotion everywhere. It was even said that the commander, still smitten with fever, had been on his feet all through the night inspecting everything — the fortifications, the newly finished platforms of the towers, the stakes with their heat-tempered points which were planted all along the rampart, the javelins that would be hurled at those wild creatures when they rushed forward roaring like a herd of bulls, the parapets of wattle being endlessly woven by skinned hands.

On this day, however, something new happened at the camp. A group of unarmed Gauls, who appeared to be of some importance, presented themselves to the general. Evidently they had some plan in mind, now that they saw it was useless to persist in opposition. And Sestius, Caius and Claudius, the humble infantrymen who in the past week had never been separated from their javelins or swords, began to hope that the affair would soon be settled, so that they could again sleep in peace and eat their food without running the risk of some sudden alert, which always seemed to come as they settled down for a meal.

It was not long before the Gallic emissaries withdrew, their sullen looks seeming to show that they were not satisfied. The know-all adjutant told his friends that there had been a complete deadlock: « Just imagine », he said, « they offered to spare our lives if we surrendered, telling us that we could expect no help from our own people, that we were surrounded; they would make every possible concession to us, provided they were not required to maintain a single one of these cursed fortified camps ».

« As for Cicero », he continued, « he behaved like the great general he is! He received them in his ceremonial uniform, as calm and motionless as a tree; he allowed them to speak quite freely, then addressed them in a voice to chill the blood: ' It is not our custom to receive terms of peace from an enemy in arms. First you must surrender, and then I shall not fail to refer the matter to Caesar. Bearing in mind his profound sense of justice, it is not impossible that he will look at your request with favour '. Now you know what he told them; tomorrow you will see what happens ».

The Roman patrols, which on that night had advanced beyond the rampart, observed an unusual commotion round the camp of the Gauls — a continuous chatter of Celtic voices, the incessant sound of foot-steps and of earth being scraped. Next morning it was the turn of the Romans to be surprised.

During the night the Gauls, working like beavers, had dug an enormous ditch with its corresponding bank which covered about two and a half miles. They had put into practice lessons learnt from the Romans during years of occupation. But lacking the requisite tools, they had to dig the soil with their swords, and carry the earth away in their hands or their cloaks.

Once the trench was finished, they started building towers, again according to the Roman technique but far more crudely — a poor copy, in fact. For six days they too never relaxed, being fully occupied in the task of enclosing the Roman camp in a vice, as if to say: « Here you are, and here you stay ». For six days they worked without stopping. At dawn on the seventh a strong wind sprang up from the north, an icy, howling wind that lashed the trees. The eyes of the Roman sentinels were fixed on the trench and on the edge of the wood. The rugged infantrymen from the Sabines and Samnites, the sun-tanned highlanders from the Abruzzi uttered no word but gazed on this disturbing silence and calm, anticipating the Gallic war-cry that would free them from the strain of waiting. At last something suddenly stirred among the trees. The Gauls were advancing in silence, carrying some strange objects — a round smoking pie-shaped object, and javelins transformed into torches. As they came down the side of their rampart, the Romans took action stations. When the Gauls had reached a certain distance they began to hurl into the Roman camp these strange pies that exhaled a black and nauseating smoke.

The Romans kept still, arms at the ready, while the roofs of the barracks, being thatched with straw as was customary, began to catch fire, while the pies, containing a mixture of coal and incandescent peat, emitted thousands of sparks which wove a flaming pattern in the sky. The wind fanned all the fires, and flames shot up on all sides, while a dense, black and acrid smoke enveloped the combatants.

Then the Gauls scaled the terreplein, climbing over one another's shoulders; the men of the legion stood their ground under a hail of arrows, steadfast to a man as if on manoeuvres. Behind them was the roar of the conflagration; they felt the terrible heat from the flames that were devouring their few possessions, the little that they had managed to accumulate in years of campaigning, the wherewithal, as they hoped, to settle debts when they returned home to become ordinary citizens again like the others, with a house, a patch of land and a wife. Everything was burning; yet the infantrymen never once turned round to look.

At a point on the rampart where the blaze had already subsided the Gauls had brought up a mobile tower. The centurions of the third cohort now agreed among themselves to order their men to withdraw slightly. Then with a great many gestures and their small vocabulary of Celtic words they invited the Gauls to advance. The Roman infantrymen, who by now understood the centurions' purpose, which was to ridicule the Gauls, burst into laughter and likewise made signs to them to come down from the earthwork. But the Gauls suspected a trap and did not budge, whereupon the infantrymen drove them back in disorder by hurling stones, and set fire to their tower.

The legion is almost exhausted. The survivors resist, but they have all been wounded, whereas the numbers of the Gauls are increasing alarmingly every day. But they know that the general has succeeded in getting a message to Caesar, because the deserter from the Gauls had placed one of his servants at the disposal of the Romans. Concealing the message under the iron point of a javelin, he managed to get through by mixing with other Gauls, and this morning the reply arrived in a curious manner. A soldier of the fifth cohort found it attached to a javelin that had got stuck in the wall of a tower. It was in Caesar's hand, written in Greek, and must have been there for several days.

From now on the sentinels eagerly watch the only clearing in the forest through which the smoke of Caesar's army would be seen as it advances across enemy territory. Who will be the first lucky man to spot that wonderful smoke?

(source: Julius Caesar's De Bello Gallico)

VOYAGES, ROADS AND VEHICLES

With their words strada, *street and* strasse *the Italians, British and Germans of today commemorate one of Rome's greatest civil achievements — the substantially constructed permanent highways designed to link the City with the most distant towns of the immense Empire. Yet these words do not spring from the Latin name for route, which is* via, *but from the most important technical feature of its construction, namely the* stratum, *the layering, the paving and flagging that distinguish the great Roman arteries from the dusty tracks of antiquity.*

That is not all. The rational concept of the great highways of land communication often involved — in Italy as in the most remote provinces — the setting up of large-scale public works, the tunnelling of mountains, the cutting of rocks, the building of huge bridges with multiple arches. The spokes of the great stellar network, whose symbolic hub in the Forum of Rome was the golden milestone of Augustus, carried soldiers and merchants, ideas and merchandise. Along the roads the civilisation of Rome also passed, followed by Christianity, and then the barbarians who brought to an end a vital phase in the world's history.

« To travel is a hard necessity ». This saying, which reflects the opinion of the ancients and especially of the Romans, sounds strange in our ears. These days how can one regard as a « hard necessity » those journeys we long to make all round the world in the best comfort and with the greatest speed? Yet one has only to see how the Romans did their travelling, how they ate and were accommodated and what vehicles they used, to realize that for the ancients, travelling was a far from pleasant occupation.

Travelling is and always has been done for four reasons, which can be enumerated in chronological order, so to speak, since that was how they successively manifested themselves in the course of modern civilisation: (1) to establish commercial relations with peoples and countries that are more or less remote; (2) to act politically, and (3) to enrich scientific knowledge and to explore unknown or little known lands; (4) lastly, for amusement, in other words, to be tourists.

It is obvious that the ancients could never have imagined a tourist trip. As for voyages of scientific

exploration, several were accomplished by Greek scholars and navigators; but very few were made by the Romans. That leaves the voyages imposed by commercial, political or military considerations. By force of circumstance these became longer and more frequent as the Roman expansion engendered economic, political and military relations with all the countries dependent on the Mediterranean basin. So much was this the case that in order to secure a public office, especially from the start of the Augustan period, one had to be prepared to travel far from Rome and Italy, trailing here and there amidst dangers and difficulties of every kind. From then onwards even military service was almost always outside Italy, in the provinces of the vast Empire and in regions that were often barbarous and inhospitable.

The need to transport so many people, officials, diplomats, military personnel and entire armies, to increasingly remote countries induced the Roman authorities to construct a great network of roads (*viae*) which were unparalleled in the ancient world, with the exception of the rudimentary arterial roads that the Persian kings threw across certain parts of their extensive domains.

THE GREAT HIGHWAYS

The first of the great roads was the *Appia*, built three centuries before Christ. Through the initiative of the censor Appius Claudius the Blind, this route linked Rome with Capua, following the most sensible route; later it was extended as far as Brindisi in the extreme south, passing through Benevento and Taranto.

The other routes were built in the succeeding centuries; to start with they linked Rome to the neighbouring regions. Thus the *Via Clodia* led to Etruria, the *Aurelia* to Liguria, the *Flaminia* went to Rimini, and from there the *Aemilia* ran along the plain of the Po to Piacenza. Then there was the *Latina* along the interior of the peninsula, which crossed the Apennines and ended at Capua; the *Popilia*, which branched off the *Appia* and crossed Lucania to reach Reggio di Calabria. New routes were extended into the conquered provinces, such as the *Egnatia* in the Balkans, and the extension of the *Aurelia* into Gaul, which ran along the coast in Provence and turned up the Rhone valley to Lyons. There were many other ramifications towards the frontier of the Rhine.

The roads, whose greatest width was about five yards, were covered with gravel (*glareatae*) or, as in the case of the Appian Way, with big pebbles or blocks of basalt stone quarried in the shape of regular polygons.

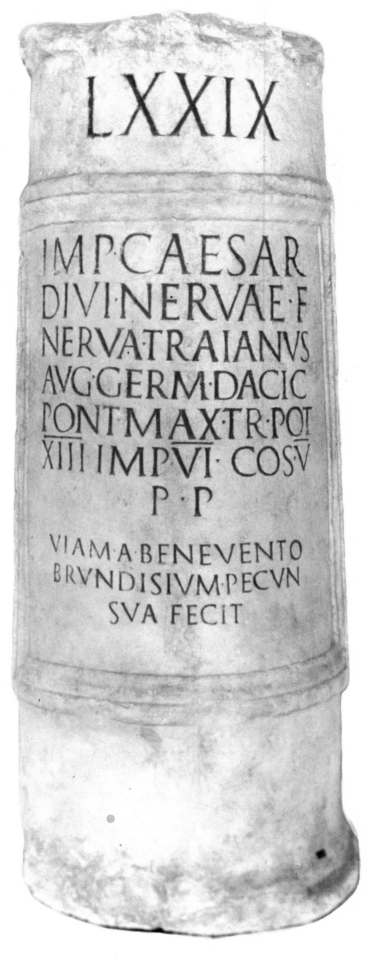

Milestone on Trajan's Via Appia, which linked Benevento with Brindisi, thereby shortening the old route of the Via Appia. The milestone registered the fact that Trajan built the road at his own expense. (Museum of Barletta).

246

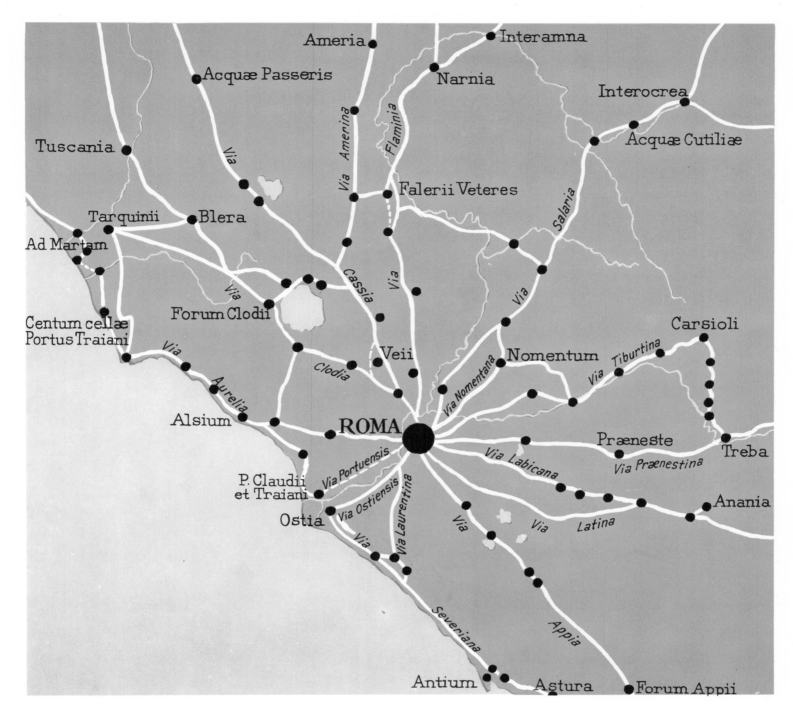

Diagram of the more important routes radiating from Rome and leading directly or by branch roads to the principal cities and ports of the peninsula and the provinces.

To mark out a road, the Romans began by digging two parallel ditches which determined the width; then they removed the earth between the ditches until they reached a stratum sufficiently firm to support the weight of the pavement. On this they spread a uniform layer of sand and chalk (*pavimentum*) and, little by little, four further layers of various materials — the *statumen*, formed of large cut stones fixed with clay or cement; the *rudus*, made of compressed gravel and chalk; the *nucleus*, composed of chalk, sand, earth and pieces of brick, well rammed down; and lastly the pavement of pebbles or stones, the *summa crusta* or the *summum dorsum*, which was slightly convex to allow the rain-water to drain off. The total thickness of these layers varied between one and one and a half yards, but in certain cases the thickness could be three yards or even more. Sometimes, if the route ran through marshy land or in case of urgent military need, prefabricated foundations were prepared, using large wooden tables which really amounted to rapidly assembled bridges (*pontes longi*).

The Romans laid their roads in a straight line whenever possible, and avoided going round the foot of hills. They always preferred to level a peak or dig a tunnel, as Vespasian did at the Passo del Furlo on the *Flaminia*, and as Trajan did, a little later, on the *Appia*, when he avoided the escarpment of Terracino by cutting through a rock — the Pisco Montano — to a depth of thirty-seven yards.

To these works should be added the hundreds of bridges, of which numerous examples still exist in Italy and elsewhere. They were built to a degree of perfection; indeed it can be said that the architectonic rules that inspired them remained valid for twenty centuries and were only overtaken by our modern technique of reinforced concrete.

HOW THEY TRAVELLED

The peace and quiet of the Roman roads! The traveller on his placid mule, passing from one town to the next by carefully chosen stages, would always have before his eyes a long, empty road flanked by a countryside still wild and vibrant with an awesome beauty.

The small merchants who carried all their wares in the packsaddle of their mounts preferred to join up with some more imposing convoy, travelling under the escort of armed slaves, for when crossing certain rather isolated regions it was not uncommon to encounter a gang of brigands who would stop at nothing.

*The paving of the big highways, especially in the vicinity of towns and at the approaches to bridges, consisted of large pebbles and stones which formed the covering (*summa crusta*) of the layers of various materials that made up the foundation of the road. As explained in the text, there were generally four layers (Fig. 1 opposite). Occasionally the number of layers was reduced to three, in which case a backing of stone gave added stability to the upper part (Fig. 3). When the road ran through marshy land it was anchored to the solid ground beneath the marsh by using wooden bridges which in turn rested on large piles (Fig. 2).*

The Via Stabiana at Pompeii, with paving typical of the Roman roads.

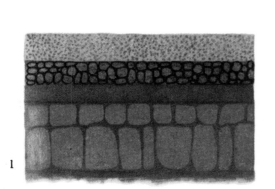

It was therefore prudent to travel in sizable groups and to have within reach the dagger that was an essential piece of the traveller's equipment. Officials and magistrates setting out on duty were always guarded by a substantial military escort, provided by the authorities of the region through which they were passing.

The voyage was made either on foot, which involved long and tedious stretches, or on the back of a horse or mule, or by using chariots and carts of different types, according to the distance to be covered and the travelling funds available.

In the bad season and for the longer journeys to Transalpine Gaul, Spain or Pannonia (now the Balkans), which involved crossing mountain passes in rain or snow, the wealthier travellers hired carriages. If one wished to travel fast, the most favoured was the *essedum*, a solid two-wheeled vehicle that may have been derived from the Celtic war-chariot. On the other hand the *cisium*, also on two wheels, was a much lighter and swifter conveyance similar to our gig, and was used for shorter journeys on the better roads. Another two-wheeler was the *carpentum*, an elegant vehicle, which like the chaise (*lectita*) was used in the towns and for getting to the big patrician villas in the suburbs. Within the walls of Rome the *carpentum* was reserved for the ladies and young girls of the imperial family, whereas the sedan chair, carried by slaves dressed in a military type of livery, was used by the rich, the senators and dignitaries of the Republic and the Empire. In the towns, wheeled traffic was forbidden during the day as a safeguard for pedestrians and in the interest of peace and quiet.

There were also four-wheeled vehicles which could carry the traveller's baggage: the *raeda*, apparently derived from a sumptuous ceremonial vehicle, which came into increasing use during the late Empire; the *pilentum*, drawn by a team of mules with tinkling bells; the *carruca*, a fast and very luxurious and comfortable vehicle which allowed the long-distance traveller to lie down and sleep. This conveyance was notable for its elaborate gilded ornamentation, which made it the outstanding carriage of the Romans.

On the other hand the *arcera* was a very slow conveyance, half way between the chaise and the carriage, covered for protection against wind and rain, ideal for carrying the elderly patrician in poor health, or a wealthy invalid. The *plaustrum* was the standard vehicle for carting the daily supplies of food from the countryside into Rome. It was a robust, rustic cart with two wheels made of massive wooden discs, and was drawn by a pair of oxen or by donkeys. The *serracum*, with its four solid low-slung wheels was well suited to carry heavy loads, such as wine-barrels from Apulia, travertine rocks or sacks of grain. The army had the *carrus*, modelled on a Celtic vehicle, which was manoeuvrable and relatively fast; also the *clabularium*, which was used for postal services in the imperial epoch.

THE POST

These were the vehicles and the roads that carried the daily traffic between the metropolis and the provinces — traffic that became ever more intense with the growth of the gigantic administration of the Empire. The numbers of those who for various reasons were compelled to travel grew to such an extent that it was found necessary to organise a transport service. In this way, permanent stations were created near the gates of the town for all kinds of vehicles which with their drivers could be hired by travellers.

In the time of Augustus the post became a definite state service. During the Republic this service was assured in case of necessity by either the *tabellarii* (messengers) or the *statores* (express couriers). These agents had to rely on their own endurance and that of their mounts.

In Augustus's time the public post (*cursus publicus*) was more or less militarized and became a regular daily service, which was facilitated by establishing staging posts (*stationes*) where the horses were changed and the travelling officials found comprehensive hospitality. These public staging-posts were administered at the

Two bridges on the old Roman provincial highways. Above: *the* Alcántara *bridge in Spain, built across the Tagus with granitic stone. (A model in relief in the Museum of Roman Civilisation, Rome).* Below: *the* Pont du Gard, *near Nîmes, as it is today.*

Cart and small boat at the tail end of a procession of young girls. Painting discovered at Ostia. (Vatican Museum, Rome).

expense of the towns in which they were established, and the couriers were initially recruited from the Imperial Guard, and later from slaves and freedmen. In practice the State alone profited from this organisation, private persons being excluded from it.

It was only later that the state provided funds for this service, commencing with Nerva for Italy, and with Hadrian for the rest of the Empire. Private persons could now use the postal service if authorized to do so by the government. The couriers, carrying messages in a large leather pouch slung from the saddle, travelled along the imperial highways as fast as their mounts would carry them. Every eight or nine miles they could rely on finding a fresh horse at the *mutatio* (relay) and when darkness fell they themselves were relieved or could rest for a few hours at the staging-post (*mansio.*) A *mansio* was to be found at the end of each day's travel; it included lodgings for couriers and travellers and was run by a *praepositus mansionis* who

had authority over couriers, drivers, grooms and soldiers of the escort. So perfect was the organisation that even veterinary surgeons could be found there.

INNS AND INNKEEPERS

Yet the huge network of Roman roads made no provision for hotel accommodation for private persons, who therefore suffered great discomfort when undertaking a long journey. There were the *cauponae*, but these were miserable inns rather than hotels. From archeological excavations and more indirectly from the picturesque and sarcastic descriptions by famous authors who had experienced these hovels, we know much about the *cauponae* and their crude and cunning owners, the *caupones*, and about the unsavoury company of scoundrels, quarrelsome drunks and foul-mouthed draymen that one might expect to meet there.

These houses had an inherently lugubrious appearance; they were nearly always evil-smelling and smoky, with dirty, uncomfortable and unsafe rooms, doubtless inhabited by hungry insects. The prospect of such a journey was enough to make a man shudder, unless of course he was lucky enough to find on the route the hospitable villa of some friend. Rich and poor alike searched desperately for some decent place in which to spend the night without running the risk of being burnt alive through the stupidity of a publican, or having one's throat cut while asleep, or one's baggage stolen. It seems that no remedy could be found for this situation despite the efforts of the magistrates. It may be that documents record only the complaints of the dissatisfied or unlucky ones, whose unfortunate travel experiences aroused the indignation and sarcasm of writers, while no one has ever spoken of those other innkeepers who may have offered the traveller, whether literate or not, a modest, clean and

Small-scale models of vehicles, reconstructed from bas-reliefs and mosaics. Above: the carrus, *used for transporting military and civil baggage. Left: the* carruca dormitoria, *for conveying passengers on long journeys. Below: a vehicle for the races, very light, with wheels set wide apart for stability. (Museum of Roman Civilisation, Rome).*

cordial hospitality. Yet this is a mere hypothesis, and cannot very well be reconciled with existing historical evidence.

TRAVELLING CLOTHES

It was only forty years ago that people going on a long journey by rail or by car donned a kind of travelling cloak that gave protection to the clothes from the locomotive's smuts or from the dust of the unpaved roads. The travelling cloak was also known to the Romans, who were essentially practical in all aspects of their public and private life.

One need only recall the traditional dress of the Roman citizen to appreciate his need for a more practical garment for travelling on foot or on horseback. The toga, with its dignified folds and straight pleats and its imposingly rich fabric, was far from ideal when mounting even the most placid mule. Consequently Roman travellers wore a short tunic ending at the knees, which allowed complete freedom of movement; for protection against rain and cold they needed only to add a hooded woollen cloak. By way of luggage they had a wallet made of leather or cloth and a net-bag; when on an important journey or for lengthy absences they took a wooden case in the shape of a trunk. Each traveller also carried a purse (*marsupium*) attached to his belt, which contained money and also his most valuable personal possessions. To complete this somewhat elementary equipment, the traveller in ancient Roman times carried a weapon, or at least a stick, which he could lean on when climbing, or use to repel stray dogs or ill-intentioned passers-by.

Map showing the principal roads of the Roman Empire. With more than 87,500 miles of well-kept and well supervised roads, Roman travellers, whether soldiers or merchants, were able to arrive in comparative safety at the most remote cities then known, from Spain to Asia Minor. Caesar travelled 800 miles in ten days; the messengers who brought Galba the news of the death of Nero took thirty-six hours to cover 360 miles on the Spanish roads. Although this was an exceptional case, it has been calculated that a traveller could without difficulty maintain an average speed of five miles per hour.

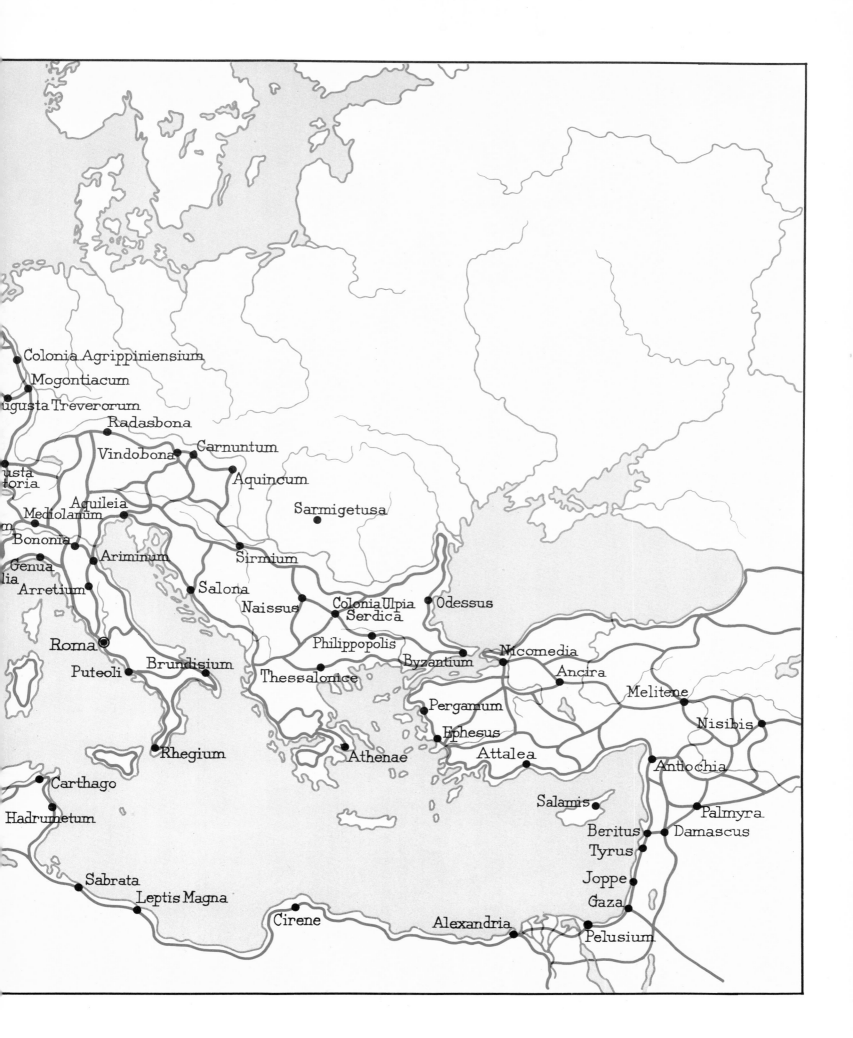

A LONG JOURNEY SOUTH

The Appia was a magnificent road. As the mule's hoofs trod the polished flagstones of the highway, the fields and thickets dropped away on both sides, and one felt proud to be a Roman.

Moving along gently, with no wish to emulate those athletic fellows who tuck up their tunics in order to walk faster, it was a pleasure to see the unfolding country, simultaneously rugged and delicate, beautiful as in no other place. The traveller was approaching Ariccia, which had nothing in common with the spectacular riches of Rome; the modest country inn would have to suffice, with its arbour and its light wine, dry and cool. Sixteen miles had been covered on this first stage, quite enough for anyone unaccustomed to long journeys.

Starting the next day on a mule already galled by the traveller's bag, Foro d'Appio was reached towards evening. This was the starting point of the canal that crossed the Pontine Marshes and ran to Terracino. Foro d'Appio had plenty of inns, but they were hovels with the usual customers and the usual thieving, insolent innkeepers.

It was already late and the travellers had eaten a meal when the servants busied themselves with finding places in the boats for their masters, while the boatmen came alongside with an air of indifference, ignoring the curses of the slaves. People began to board the flat-bottomed boats. The boatmen concentrated on steering while the mules on the tow-path pulled the boats through a night filled with frogs and cursed mosquitoes. The boatmen were in the habit of warding off bites and malaria by consuming quantities of wine or liquor. The travellers did likewise, which resulted in a cacophony of snores and songs, with violent protests from those anxious to sleep.

It was hardly possible to disembark before ten o'clock in the morning. The travellers set down their sacks and bundles, washed face and hands in the sacred water of the temple of Feronia, and having eaten, proceeded on foot for three miles, climbing towards Terracino, perched high on the bare and sun-scorched rocks. The Appia continued upwards; on the crest of the promontory it passed through Auxur, the ancient city of the Volsci. Thence the highway of shining basalt came to Fondi, thirteen miles from Terracino, where the travellers changed their carriage horses or rested their mounts. On the following day they continued towards Formies; this was a long stage; fortunate indeed were those able to muster a friend in these parts who could accommodate them in some comfortable villa, and thus avoid those smoke-filled inns, the *cauponae*, where one risked being robbed of everything.

In establishments like these you no longer felt that you were beside that marvellous highway whose entire length bore witness to the power and civilisation of Rome. For one thing, there was a clientèle of drunken draymen, gambling with dice, swearing and quarrelling, veterans of some war or other returning to their homes, but showing far more interest in drinking and yarning than in hurrying to their goal. Others who frequented the place were certain shady characters with the aim of criminals; if you encountered them on the highway, one glance at them would make you ready to hand over your travelling sack with all your money. Then there was the landlord. He would come forward sullenly to receive your orders; you had to put up with the fare that he offered you at an exorbitant price — it was pure robbery, but there was no option. As for the bed, hungry parasites were the masters there; but possibly you preferred to doze in the big room, your head resting on the table among the foul smells, the smoke and the draughts.

The next halt was at Sinuessa, the last town of Latium, near Liri. On the following day those with authority — the State officials and the heads of missions — could stop at a staging-post beside the bridge over the Savo, on the border of Campania. This boarding-house was in fact subsidized by the State, and the magistrates and public officials had the privilege of obtaining from it the essentials for themselves and their animals — salt, hay, bread and firewood.

Further stops were at Capua, and after two more days on the road, Benevento. The Appia continued to ascend and descend, with its badly quarried flagstones, its dust and mud, and worst of all, its horrible inns, where eating and sleeping progressively deteriorated and got more dangerous the more you travelled south. That is why many people preferred to go by sea.

On leaving Benevento you began to discern through the hazy distance the mountains of Apulia, scorched by the sirocco. In the summer it was quite a business to cross them without getting sunstroke. Those who could do the journey in a vehicle — a *reda*, a four-wheeled carriage drawn by mules and oxen — managed to cover twenty miles each day in reasonable comfort, apart from the jolts. But it was difficult to do the entire journey in a carriage. And you went through agonies of thirst when travelling in these lands, where water drawn from wells or stored for months in cisterns cost as much as wine anywhere else.

Of water, there was either too much or too little. In fact, if rain began to fall, the Appia transformed itself into a marsh. Moreover, after Ruvo and up to the walls of Bari it became a bad road, barely recognizable even when there was no rain. But from then on the traveller felt that his sufferings were nearing their end. The extreme point of Italy was quite close, the white ramparts of Brindisi appeared on the horizon. The journey had lasted thirteen days from the moment of leaving the Porta Capene to take the Appian Way. How on earth did they manage in the days before it was built?

(source: Horace, Satires, V)

SEA TRAVEL

To the Romans navigation, like all travel, was a necessity, not a vocation. Peasants by tradition, they were compelled by the progressive extension of their dominions and of their influence on the coasts of the Mediterranean to learn the technique of shipbuilding and the art of navigation as practised by other peoples, particularly the Etruscans of the coastlands, the Greeks and the Carthaginians.

As always, the Romans assimilated and perfected the teachings of others; as always, they equalled and in some cases even surpassed their teachers. Having defeated the great Mediterranean naval powers and eliminated them from the political scene, they then had to assume a number of responsibilities, including the onerous one of safeguarding shipping by means of costly maritime patrol operations and by establishing an effective port organisation linked with the important consular routes and inland waterways.

Along the maritime routes, no less than on the arterial highways that radiated from the golden milestone in the centre of the Forum, they created and maintained the material and spiritual unity of the State and of the Roman world, covering the dense network of trade between Rome and the provinces. Thus the expression Mare Nostrum *did not spring from any rhetorical attitude, but from the essential demands of life — demands which imposed upon the shepherds and peasants of Latium the rule of* navigare necesse est.

For their maritime traffic the Romans at first used the fleets of their Italic allies, who after being integrated in the Roman State with equal rights could regard their ships as Roman in the same way as the fleets belonging to the early coastal colonies of the Tyrrhenian Sea and the Adriatic: Ostia, Antium, Terracino, Brindisi, and later Pozzuoli, Aquileia, etc. Thanks to these fleets the Romans very soon established relations with the other Mediterranean countries that were governed by precise agreements. The first such treaty of which we know was that mentioned by Polybius; it was signed with Carthage in the first year of the Republic, i.e., 509 B.C. — a controversial date, but one generally accepted today. By this treaty Romans and Carthaginians guaranteed each other freedom to enter ports and to trade in the territories coming under their respective influences: Latium for the former, Sicily and Africa for the latter. Subsequently the treaty was renewed in the course of the fourth and third centuries B.C. Marseilles was another of the maritime cities with which Rome had close commercial relations from the earliest times. It was from this port that ships sailed for the coasts of Gaul and Northern Spain. And from Marseilles the valley of the Rhone provided access to the interior of Gaul and eventually to the Channel coast. To the east, starting in the third century B.C., the Romans in the Adriatic had to contend with the piracy of the Illyrians; but these could not prevent the spread of Roman influence in the eastern basin of the Mediterranean or interfere with Roman contacts with the Greek cities and the Hellenic kingdoms. At Delos, a free trading port in the Aegean, Roman and Italic merchants established themselves in considerable numbers from the end of the second century B.C. At Rhodes the Romans drafted the first known treaty of commerce — the *Lex Rhodia.*

Cargo boat, first century B.C. They carried goods between Rome and every other port in the Mediterranean. Unlike warships, these boats used their oars only when becalmed or when careful manoeuvring was required: they normally used only their sails. (Museum of Science and Technology, Milan).

THE ROMAN SHIP

It was from the Greeks, the Etruscans and especially the Carthaginians that the Romans learnt the technique of shipbuilding. Pliny, for instance, attributes the invention of the *oneraria*, the large transport for goods and passengers, to a certain Hippo, who came from Tyre in Phoenicia. Figures in bas-relief and mosaics give a good idea of the appearance of the Roman ships. The warships were generally propelled by oars arranged in two, three or more tiers (biremes, triremes, etc.), whereas the cargo ships proceeded under sail, using their oars only as a secondary means for short passages, or when becalmed.

The various parts of the hull were built of soft or hard woods (pine, spruce, oak) and the deck planking was covered with canvas or some other impermeable material, which in turn was lined with thin strips of lead secured by nails or iron, or more frequently bronze. The freeboard was comparatively high with a projecting

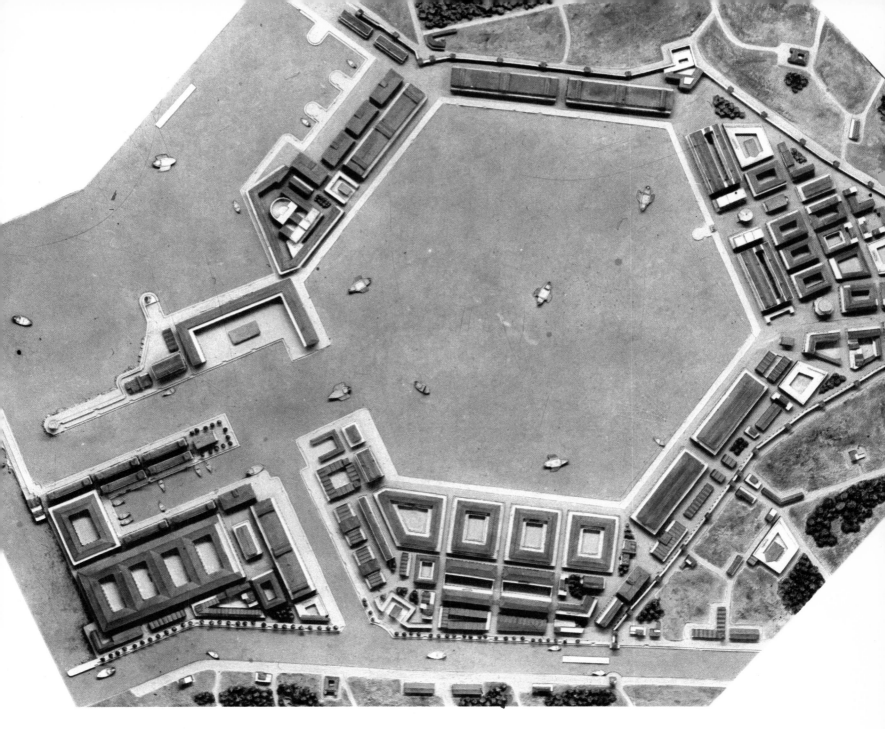

Trajan's basin in the port of Rome. The large hexagon-shaped basin, entirely dug out of the solid earth, was built to improve the safety and the capacity of the port of Claudius. (Museum of Science and Technology, Milan).

part protected by bulwarks with trellis openings, which contained the oarsmen. The prow of the ship, which was not high, frequently carried external decorations in the form of figures or symbols. On the other hand the poop was usually very high, terminating in the curved *aplustre* which was sometimes shaped like the neck and head of a swan. On each side of the poop was a rudder shaped like a spade. The helmsman (*gubernator*) was protected by a tent-like enclosure. The cargo was stowed on the open deck. If the ship carried jars or urns (*amphorae*) these were stacked in three superimposed layers, the bottom of each urn fitting between the necks and bellies of the lower ones.

The mainmast (*malus*), fitted in the middle of the deck, was quite tall and carried the principal sail, which was quadrangular or trapezoid in shape. The foremast (*artemon*) was stepped well forward in the bows, and at an angle to the vertical. It was much smaller than the mainmast, and carried a small sail. Very rarely a third mast was fitted. The sails were almost always coloured. Black denoted mourning, and sometimes the sails were marked with symbolic figures. The anchors were of iron or wood, and their stocks, made of iron or lead, could be fixed or movable.

Illustrated documents frequently show the ship with a small boat in tow, which was used for communicating with the shore when the ship could not be berthed. Cargo vessels were from ninety-six to thirty yards long, with a beam of seventy-eight to twenty-four yards. The ancients indicated the carrying capacity of their ships in terms of the total weight of liquid that could be carried in the *amphorae*. In modern terms, and having regard to the weight of the containers, it could be said that a ship carrying 3,000 to 4,000 *amphorae* had a capacity of 110 to 180 tons and a gross tonnage of 250 to 300 tons. There were also some bigger ships, of which the best example was the vessel that carried the obelisk of Caligula to Rome for the Vatican. It had a cargo in the holds of 800 tons of lentils, and the obelisk weighed 500 tons. Having completed its mission this ship was sunk in the port of Ostia (which Claudius was then building) for use as a caisson for one of the moles.

The average distance covered by these ships in a day was from seventy to ninety miles, but this naturally depended on the wind and other circumstances. Apart from special cases the sailing was mainly in daylight hours, and generally in coastal waters, so that in the evening it was not difficult to make for some inshore harbouring. In the course of time the ships ventured out on the direct routes across the open sea. Ancient documents disclose the duration of some of these voyages: from Rhodes to Alexandria, three days; from Brindisi to Antium, three days; Scipio Africanus took two days and a night to sail from Marsala to an African port south of Cape Bon.

Normally the sailing season was between mid-March and October 10th. The ships were guided by the sun and the stars, but it seems certain that the ancients had instruments similar to the modern sextant, as evidenced by the salvage in 1900 of an apparatus from a ship refloated in the waters of Ancitera (Cerigotto, between the Peloponnesus and Crete). It consisted of a clock mechanism which gave astronomical data by means of a complicated system of toothed wheels fixed to the edges of a plate carrying explanatory inscriptions. This was used for voyages from the African coast of the Red Sea to the Persian Gulf and India.

THE GREAT SEA ROUTES

The sea routes naturally coincided with the demands of commercial interests for trade and passengers. Rome and Italy gradually became the centre of considerable imports of cereals, oil, wine, marble, metal, animals for the circus shows in the amphitheatre, and precious oriental products, such as porphyry and perfumes. The merchandise arrived in the port of Brindisi, and above all in the Tyrrhenian ports of Pozzuoli, Ostia, and later, Centumcellae (Civitavecchia) and Terracino. From the port of discharge to Rome the transport was by land, but from Ostia it was also possible to proceed up the Tiber using rafts or small boats which were towed along by draught animals between Alexandria and

Figurehead of a ship in the form of a lion's head. (Museum of Nemi).

The lighthouse at Dover, in Great Britain. Built of sandstone, it was octagonal in shape and approximately thirty yards high. (Model in the Museum of Roman Civilisation, Rome).

Iron anchor with a covering of wood, which made it easier to handle when sailing on the lakes. Found at Nemi. (Museum of Science and Technology, Milan).

Greece and Carthage, between Ephesus (the principal port of Asia) and the East, and so on.

Some of the busiest routes in the Mediterranean, at least at the end of the third century A.D., were shown on a fragment of the edict on prices issued by Diocletian, which regulated the freight charges on these routes.

Outside the Mediterranean the Roman ships braved the ocean from the Pillars of Hercules along the African coast as far as the limits of Mauretania and up to the island of Mogador. The Atlantic ports of Gaul were used mainly for traffic with Great Britain.

There still exist two itineraries relating to the Red Sea and the Black Sea. The first dates from the middle of the first century A.D., the second originated with Arrianus, a writer who came from Bithynia and lived at the time of Hadrian. He listed not only the Red Sea ports, but also those in the Persian Gulf, and in the Indian Ocean up to the Bay of Bengal, where the Roman merchants met those from the Far East. These maritime itineraries, comparable to the sailing directions of mediaeval times, had their origin in pre-Roman treatises. Of these the best known is attributed to Skylax (who by tradition dates from the sixth century B.C. but should be of the fourth century). The documents contained all the information that could interest a navigator; they enabled him to identify the main points along the coast and told him where he would find ports, sheltered anchorages and fresh water. One of these itineraries was the *Stadiasmus Maris Magni*, of the Byzantine era, which however is derived from more ancient sources. Another is the *Itinerarium Maritimum*, which has survived in two fragments, one referring to the route from Corinth to Carthage via Sicily, the other from Rome to Arles. A later example is the anonymous tract of Ravenna (eighth century A.D.) which is derived from a more ancient work.

These texts and others that have since been lost provided data about the coasts of the various countries, and can be studied today in the works of the principal geographers of antiquity: Strabo, Pomponius, Mela, Ptolemy, etc.

THE PORTS

The advances in navigation, the increasing tonnage of ships and the growing density of traffic led to the enlargement and proper organisation of port installations. The Phoenicians and the Carthaginians usually established their ports in river estuaries or near promontories, or by dredging artificial basins on the shoreline. The Greeks, especially during the Hellenic period, constructed large artificial ports, of which the chief example is Alexandria; these served as models for the Romans, who further applied their own particular building methods to ensure resistance to the force of the waves and to the corrosive action of sea water. In this way they were able to build very large ports, some even facing the open sea, by providing them with moles (sometimes built in the form of arcades, as at Pozzuoli, to allow the current to flow unhindered, thus avoiding the silting of the basin) and by installing quays, mooring facilities, dockyards, stores, and lighthouses.

Until the beginning of the Empire the city of Rome's only port was Ostia, at the mouth of the Tiber. It was Claudius who built the first big port along the coast to the north of this estuary, by constructing a canal that linked the river with the sea, and by projecting into the sea two long moles which at their outer extremities were separated by an artificial island. In this way he created an enclosed sheet of water covering a considerable area (over 900,000 square yards). But Claudius's works proved excessively exposed to the elements, and Trajan established a new port farther inland, which was hexagonal in shape and covered about 450,000 square yards. It was Trajan, too, who built or enlarged the ports of Centumcellae and Terracino, which could be said to complete the port of Ostia. Nero in his day had improved the port of Antium, and to him can be attributed the first big harbour works at Leptis Magna in North Africa which were later developed and perfected by Septimius Severus.

At the entrance to every port, which at night was barred by chains, stood the lighthouse; whenever pos-

A cargo ship in port. Near the poop is the large oar which was used as a rudder; a pinnace is attached to the ship by a rope. (Mosaic in the Quirinal: Antiquarium Communale, Rome).

sible it was built on high ground. Both the name and the type of this edifice have their origin in the Pharos of Alexandria in Egypt.

The Roman lighthouses, familiar to us through drawings or ruins, consisted of square or polygonal towers rising to several floors and capped by a flame, whose light by night and smoke by day provided a guide for pilots. One famous lighthouse was that of Gesoriacum (Boulogne-sur-mer). It stood sixty-two yards high with twelve floors, and was built by Caligula.

RIVER AND LAKE NAVIGATION

For the convenience of shipping seagoing traffic was combined with traffic on lakes and rivers. All the big rivers were busy with vessels mainly engaged in carrying merchandise. The boats for traffic on the inland waterways were designed on the same lines as those plying the open sea, but they had a flatter keel and sometimes carried two additional rudders in the bows, which made them more manoeuvrable. There was much variation in the type of vessels. The Romans undertook long passages only for purposes of study or service. Every cultivated Roman aimed at visiting at least once in his lifetime Athens, Alexandria, Ephesus and Rhodes.

Military commands and provincial government often required Romans to travel to the east or the west, which sometimes meant that a sea passage could not be avoided. In such cases the return to the homeland was an occasion for joy and happiness that called for a thanksgiving to the gods, as instanced by Catullus returning from Bithynia, when he offered them the vessel that had brought him back to Italy, the *phaselus* that he gratefully described to his friends in one of his more exquisite compositions.

A SEA VOYAGE TO THE EAST

Some of the ships lay at anchor in the middle of the harbour, while others were berthed along the quay to load their cargoes. The background was filled by Brindisi, sprawling more like a large provincial market town than a city. But what distinguished the place from other towns in the interior were the masts, the hulls and sails, and those bearded seamen who before boarding their ships passed the time of day in the dark taverns, drinking, gambling and brawling.

The ship should have sailed early the next morning. The traveller had already brought his baggage on board, and the captain had assigned him a place to sleep near the poop and next to the pilot's cabin; he had shown him his bunk — a luxury compared with what the other passengers could expect.

Next morning everything had changed. The strong northerly wind that frequently blows on the coasts of Italy worried the crew of a near-by *quadriremis;* they were busy doubling the hawsers, lest this violent wind, tearing along the canal between the harbour works, should multiply the force of the waves and pound the large warship against the jetty. The ship was due to take the new proconsul to Sicily, but already orders had been received to postpone sailing.

Strong hawsers had also been secured to the small cargo ship, which being in ballast displayed its chubby sides above the water, revealing a veritable flora of incrustations that had proliferated over the years.

The sailors glanced anxiously at the lowering sky and hardly bothered to answer the traveller. But he had already gathered that there could be no question of leaving for some days. So he decided to wander through the town with its strong smells of sea and fish; he came to the fishermen's quarter where the nets were spread out to dry; he stopped to watch the rope-makers as they spun the large cables of tarred hemp, the carpenters and joiners as they put the finishing touches to a fine ship whose slender hull ended in an elegant poop shaped like a swan's neck. Later he relieved the tedium by strolling into the country, where the harvest was already ripening amidst olive trees as broad and tall as oaks.

After two days he returned to the port in the hope of sailing, as the wind had abated. But he learnt that the ship would not weigh anchor even on that morning, for the sailors, who had got drunk the previous night, were sleeping it off. It was otherwise with the *quadriremis;* she had got under way and was standing off under her large square sail, which seemed blue in the light haze.

The pilot watched this ship with regret, furious that the conduct of his men had prevented him from putting to sea. He was afraid that at this unpredictable season the wind might vanish altogether. But it began to freshen, and at about dinner-time he went to rouse the crew, who started work still reeling about half-asleep.

So the ship departed in the early afternoon, escorted by a flight of seagulls which abandoned her only when far from port. The crew, surly and quarrelsome, made a sinister pretence of wanting to get the mast down and furl the sails. On the poop the pilot operated the two oar-shaped rudders which trailed in the ship's wake where the pinnace was bobbing about at the end of the tow-rope. Already one or two sea-sick passengers had leaned over the bulwarks, their faces pale and dripping with sweat.

Slowly the Italian coast receded and soon the ship found herself alone on a green-blue expanse of sea. A light breeze filled the sail; the mast and yard groaned under its vigorous thrust.

It was a calm night. Four near-by sailors were throwing dice at this late hour, swearing and laughing noisily.

As he could not sleep, the traveller got up to speak to the pilot, who kept his eyes on the stars while steering the ship towards Greece.

Waking at dawn, he noticed that the ship had stopped. Yet no port was in sight, nothing but the sea all around. An unforeseen calm had interrupted the voyage. On this fine morning some were singing, while others, leaning over the bulwarks, attempted to harpoon the fish that leapt to the surface, or hooked their prey, which struggled violently. Sea-birds settled on the mast and almost at once a skilled hunter captured them with a snare made of plaited reeds coated with glue. The down barely fluttered in the heavy air, and the big feathers that fell in the water were soon scattered by the eddies on the surface.

But these pleasures were soon over. Gradually the wind revived in the form of a fresh breeze that held the sail and made it clatter gaily. Then the wind rose and raged, beating the sea into foaming waves and giving the ship a new vigour. The first of the Greek islands appeared over the horizon, while threatening dark clouds suddenly gathered from every quarter and brought a heavy downpour. The icy sea at once became leaden.

The crew took up their stations; the sail was furled, but the squalls changed direction so frequently that the pilot was at a loss to know how to handle the vessel, which rolled and tossed violently. Yet this was not the biggest danger. Darkness had enveloped the ship so that the helmsman could not see the bows. Now the few passengers all made a rush for the poop, ready to slide down the rope to the pinnace.

But the tornado ceased as suddenly as it had started, and after a few hours the seas subsided. The coast was now quite close, and the pilot headed for the port without further danger.

(source: The Golden Ass by Apuleius)

THE ARTS UNDER AUGUSTUS

There was little true originality in the art of the Augustan period; yet it was far from being a time of purely academic imitation. It is more accurate to describe it as a period of profound change in both taste and technique. To appreciate the real feeling of this particular moment of Roman history and in particular to understand certain features of artistic expression under Hadrian and the Antonine emperors, it is essential to look at Augustan art as it is manifested in its often fragmentary bas-reliefs, or its silver coins, or in its attitude towards Greek art. These point the way to the great art to come. If Augustan artists looked back into the past, what they took from it was re-expressed more skilfully and with an evident originality, as in the frescoes in the House of Livia on the Palatine.

For this reason if for no other, the period must be judged as one of genuine adventure and achievement, for the abounding energy of new imperial Rome found one of its finest expressions in the new artistic developments.

Augustan art has often been considered as simply a revival and a continuation of a certain type of Greek art, elegant but cold. This is not to say, though, that it is identical with neo-attic art — art deriving from Attica, undoubtedly the most typically Greek, artistically speaking. To confuse the two would prevent the true appreciation of an art which, though inspired by the great Greek tradition — as indeed Augustus encouraged it so to be — even so possessed its own significance, and was, in any case, far more complex than the simple term « neo-attic » would suggest.

In the second half of the first century B.C. there were so many different styles of artistic expression, all clearly definable but arising from several sources of inspiration, that a final and all-embracing classification is difficult. Academic, cold, Augustan, classic, are terms which do not adequately define the value of art forms representing a very original synthesis of Hellenistic and classical themes.

ARCHITECTURE

It is Suetonius who makes Augustus claim that he transformed Rome from a huddle of brick-built houses into a city of marble. The exaggeration is understandable and even acceptable, for during the first century B.C. an active and dynamic vision of the city and of public buildings in particular spread through all the cities in Italy and even beyond. Vitruvius did more than anyone else to establish certain fairly precise rules relating to the laws of architectural construction (his basilica at Fano is a typical example) and he was able by great efforts to hasten a building reform which was to reach every sphere of contemporary civilisation. It is also true, however, that the basic elements of architectural structures in the age in question came out of the previous republican era and notably out of the second century and the first half of the first century B.C.

Ever since the time of Sulla (ruling 86-78 B.C.) two particular features of building construction had been established. First the use of stone, especially tufa and travertine, in a very simple, plain manner, displaying Greek influence in the architectural order. Second, an entirely new feature — the use of bricks, and later cement facings, as a decorative element. The sanctuary of the goddess Fortuna Primigenia at Praeneste is an excellent example of the transition period typical of the art of the Republic. The arrangement on several terraces with ample stairways and grandiose arches was clearly related to the great Hellenistic cities and sanctuaries of Asia Minor, but the use of new building techniques using the so-called *opera incerta* and especially *opus reticulatum* (both described at the beginning of this book) allowed the introduction of openings, perspectives and foreshortenings which had never occurred elsewhere. This architecture of the end of the second and beginning of the first century B.C. managed to convey by its use of Hellenistic forms the feeling of newness and originality. This was reflected in the taste of both public and architects. A new feature was the round temple standing on a plinth, with an entrance flanked by two tall windows like the Corinthian temple at Tivoli. The high plinth has a feature already existing in Etruscan temples which was carefully preserved in their republican and Augustan coun-

The Temple of the Sibyl at Tivoli.

terparts. But alongside this feature which was in a sense archaic and local, the Augustan architects liked to use facings of precious and coloured marbles, decorative motifs in coloured vitreous paste, gilded wood and cloth.

The arch was a typical feature of architecture of Italo-Etruscan origin. Many cities used the arch as an entry to the town, on the model of the cities founded

266

by Alexander's generals, the Diadochi. In the late republican period the outside walls of buildings were often decorated with a series of arcades of a different architectural order, a precedent for a device which would later appear in the Colosseum. The theatre of Marcellus had already confronted the problem of arcaded tiers used for a façade which was to become a common feature of many buildings from the construction of the Colosseum onwards.

But the basic architectural feature of the late republican era which began with Caesar was the Forum plan — great open spaces surrounded by their porticoes. The Forum of Caesar, which involved the important and costly demolition of a whole district of poor houses on the northern side of the old Roman Forum, consisted of wide-arched colonnades in the rear, the Basilica Argentaria, a great wide square and a Corinthian-style temple in white marble dedicated to *Venus Genetrix*, the protecting divinity of the Julian *gens*, built all of white marble. The idea of assigning a Forum to the private cult of the reigning family and of enlivening the square with buildings of practical and public usefulness was familiar to the Hellenistic world, but the concept of worshipping the divinity of the actual family was particularly Roman, and Roman too was the idea of combining that cult in a public place with the cult of a state divinity.

In the centre of the esplanade, the lavish use of white marble from Luni in the central temple contrasted sharply with the severe travertine, tufa and peperino used for the arcaded shops which surrounded the piazza. The Forum was inaugurated during the night of September 24-25 in 46 B.C.

The first half of this century is remarkable for the very wide use of marble in Italy and in all the provinces of the Empire. The extensive quarrying of the Luni marble is proof of the great luxury of the buildings which led Caesar to take measures preventing exaggerated decorative use of building materials, precious stones and wall paintings. The various triumphal processions favoured extraordinary displays of wealth. The image of the triumphant hero was carried in procession: when Pompey celebrated his triumph over Mithridates, his portrait was studded with pearls. The triumphs of Lucullus and Caesar were also excessively luxurious. The Emperor Augustus took especial interest in architecture: in his reign it not only gave the city a new appearance, but was used to develop a new town plan. The twelve great regions or districts of Rome date from Augustus. He was very proud of this, and in his will mentions it among the worthwhile things he had done. His reconstruction of part of the Suburra district was intended by Augustus to be a reminder in the shape of a large architectural unity of his laws and the new constitution of the State: this unity was the Forum of *Mars Ultor*. The available space was not large. The architect tackled the problem with a somewhat shortened temple provided with a very wide flight of steps and a great portico which served as a sort of mausoleum with statues of all the great figures of Roman history, from those who were almost legendary to those who had contributed more recently to the grandeur of the Empire, like Marius and Pompey. On the plinths of the statues were inscribed eulogies, so that future generations might know of their famous deeds which Augustus himself admired respectfully and passionately.

Architecture does indeed owe Augustus a debt for the technical impulse he gave to it. He embellished and enlarged the aqueducts of Rome, especially that

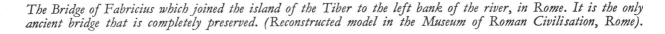

The Bridge of Fabricius which joined the island of the Tiber to the left bank of the river, in Rome. It is the only ancient bridge that is completely preserved. (Reconstructed model in the Museum of Roman Civilisation, Rome).

of the *Aqua Marcia;* and his engineers restored and re-built several bridges, such as the *pons Fabricius,* originally built in 62 B.C., exemplifying construction techniques which would be perfected with the passage of time; the bridges at Narni, and the triple-tiered arches of the Pont du Gard. In the Narbonnais in Southern Gaul, the Maison Carrée at Nîmes (*Nemausus*) is an elegant example of sober temple architecture, the portico acting as façade on top of a podium, reached by a flight of steps, and the Corinthian columns of the vestibule (*pronaos*) supporting the main sanctuary (*cella*). This temple was built between 19 and 12 B.C.; its architectural composition displays the same Hellenistic forms we find in the so-called temple of Vesta in Rome (which was most probably dedicated to Juventus or Hercules), and in the rectangular temple of the Boarian Forum probably dedicated to Portunnus and designed on the same plan as the Maison Carrée. The temple at Nîmes, like the old Pantheon in Rome, the nearby baths, the Forum and theatre at Arles and the temple and Forum at Vienne, were all due to the intelligence and foresight of Augustus's great general, M. Vipsanius Agrippa. Between 28 and 19 B.C. Augustus sponsored a number of buildings in Rome, and then in the provinces he promoted an architectural style even more Greek in appearance, but retaining at the same time a very Italian use of large podia, bricks and extensive use of local stone and marble.

Among arches, from the early years of the Empire, the simple and austere examples at Aosta, Rimini and Ancona are memorable. They represent an attempt (the least successful at Rimini) to marry a Hellenistic type of structure to the Italo-Etruscan architrave. At Rimini the combination of human or animal heads on the architrave and classical Corinthian columns is not especially successful, but at Aosta the breadth of conception and the exquisitely simple relation between the Doric architrave and the Corinthian elements reveal a greater harmony of forms and a far greater technical experience. In the arch at Susa, where the bas-reliefs on the architrave illustrate local events, vaulting and columns blend perfectly.

But whilst in Rome as in the provinces there was great variance both in architectural inspiration and technical craftsmanship, each has perfect expression in the Julian memorial at St. Remy (the ancient *Glanum*),

Frieze from one of the altars of the Temple of Neptune in Rome, consecrated by C. Domitius Enobarbus. The frieze represents the sacrifice of a bull, a sheep and a pig: the suovetaurilia. *(Louvre, Paris).*

where the bas-reliefs, underlined with projections, evoke hunting scenes and events in the lives of those commemorated there. The whole concept reveals a strong influence from visual imagery and Hellenic inspiration. Above a large quadrangular plinth, whose walls carry these unusual scenes in relief, there is a sort of four-pillar or four-fronted arch which came back into fashion in the second century A.D. and which resembles the Hellenistic arches of the Diadoch period, after Alexander the Great. The technique of the reliefs makes this one of the most extraordinary monuments of the end of the first century B.C.

Augustan architecture takes its structural inspiration from two great creative sources, Hellenism and the Italo-Etruscan tradition. It is sober and harmonious and generally restrained in the use of precious marbles, even if the variety of them employed in certain enclaves like that of *Mars Ultor* must have created a curiously colourful effect. All in all it reflects considerable economic prosperity and a combination of the practical necessity from which it sprang, with a harmony superior to that of the classic tradition.

SCULPTURE

In dealing with Augustan sculpture it is necessary to go back in time to a period prior to Augustus's inauguration after the battle of Actium in 31 B.C. If an appreciation of Roman imperial sculpture is to be reached one work above all must be studied: the bas-reliefs on the so-called altar of Domitius Enobarbus.

Dating this monument has caused controversy, but 70 B.C. seems the most likely. The sacred rites recorded in the purification ceremony — the *lustra censoria* — for the year 70, names the censor L. Gellius Publicola. The reliefs preserved at the Louvre portray a magistrate receiving a report. He is surrounded by some figures and soldiers with long shields. Next comes a ceremony at the altar of Mars, at which the god himself, fully armed, is present. On the right of the altar is the veiled figure of the official in charge of the sacrifice, which may be one of the two censors in office that year. The sacrificial procession conforms to the usual ritual of the three victims (the so-called *suovetaurilia*), the bull, the ram and the pig. Three soldiers, one on horseback, close the procession. The

35

other part of the relief has a different decorative purpose. Here is no historical and concrete tale such as the Romans loved, but the galloping chariot of Amphitrite and Neptune drawn by their Triton sons. This clearly derives from a Hellenistic source and may even be inspired by the famous *thiasus* or Bacchic dance made by Scopas for some Asiatic city. This work, with its two very different stylistic parts, displays clearly the features which are found again in the *Ara Pacis Augustae*: one side unmistakably derived from Hellenistic models, the other an imitation of scenes which must have frequently appeared in paintings made for the triumphs, and reflecting that vivid narrative sense so evident in the official monuments of Rome.

The *Ara Pacis Augustae* is of considerable value on two accounts: the perfection of its preservation and the importance of the scene it illustrates. But even before this monument there is evidence of an intimate collaboration of Greek tradition and Roman taste in the work of two artists. The first is Pasiteles, a Roman citizen from one of the ancient Greek settlements in Italy, known to have published books about his art. He seems to have been a cultivated man, and as an artist, was inspired by the southern Italian terracotta tradition which had reached great technical perfection. Pasiteles represents the artistic affinity which linked Rome and Magna Graecia at this time. His true personality escapes us because we have none of his original works. The evidence available describes his special skill in working precious metals on which he depicted scenes from nature of realistic inspiration like those reliefs of Hellenistic origin often met in the Augustan and in the Julio-Claudian period.

A different artist was Arcesilaus, sculptor of the statue of *Venus Genetrix* for the triumph of Caesar. Although many literary fragments describe his superb talent, they do not help us to identify any of his work. The group showing a centaur stealing a nymph now in the Vatican, reveals its Hellenistic origin in what one might perhaps now term its slightly baroque conception, and this can also be seen in the decorative parts of the so-called Altar of Ahenobarbus. It seems not improbable that this work can be attributed to Arcesilaus. The group of the lioness surrounded by dancing cupids seems an echo of a light and elegant style which comes straight from the schools of Pergamum and Alexandria. This tendency to take inspiration from different schools must have also been fashionable in Magna Graecia, where Arcesilaus was born.

Other artistic personalities like the sculptors Menelaus, author of a group of Orestes and Electra, and Stephanos, belong to the neo-attic tendency mentioned earlier, a tendency which has led some to judge Augustan sculpture cold and academic. These neo-attic sculptors in fact imitate in a remote and insensitive way the statues of youths (*Kouroi*) and young women which have been known since the fifth century B.C. As sculptors they do not represent the taste of the age. That taste was really demonstrated by a harmonious fusion of the Italo-Etruscan current with the Hellenistic current from the schools of Pergamum and Alexandria.

A further contribution to our knowledge of Roman republican art of the first century B.C. lies in the very interesting fragment of a frieze from the Basilica Aemilia, which must have been part of the decoration on the architrave. The date is still the subject of discussion, but it probably belongs to the period between 55 and 34 B.C., when the basilica was restored. The scenes come from Roman history: the story of Romulus and Remus, Tarpeia peering out from the heap of shields thrown at her, the rape of the Sabines. The episode depicting the building of the walls of Lavinium, however, derives from the Trojan-Latin legends and can be compared with the paintings on the Esquiline. The artistic origin of these reliefs has recently been studied and published. The pastoral scenes recall the Hellenistic country tradition. But the figures of soldiers and some of the workmen's heads in the building scene are clearly inspired by the pre-Augustan Roman tradition. There is a fine workman's head looking over from the wall which is in the well-known popular tradition, frequently found in Roman portraits of the first century B.C. The fact that the figures are crowded together in places in a rather disorderly fashion is not an evidence of inexperience on the part of the artist but rather of a somewhat eclectic taste which is apt to lead to untidy composition. The artist combines the Roman bas-relief with a profound classical background, and his work in this frieze is typically Augustan in its assimilation of Hellenistic and classically-minded art with popular and Roman currents.

Attention has recently been drawn to the eclectic character of certain designs on coins of the late republican period: scenes of sacrifice in which a consul carries the offering up the steps of the temple of Jove Capitolinus, fights between two gladiators, scenes showing voting and assignments of land, the goddess Roma symbolically represented as an Amazon shaking hands with Italy in the guise of the goddess of plenty. Buildings are sometimes shown on coins from the first century B.C. and undoubtedly this is the origin of the practice of depicting architectural items on the historical bas-reliefs of the imperial period.

The most remarkable monument from the end of the first century B.C., the *Ara Pacis Augustae* breathes a quieter and more restrained classicism. It had been given approval by vote in 13 B.C., on the return of Augustus from Gaul and Iberia, when a long period of peace and political stability seemed likely at last, after a century tormented by the revolts and internal struggles arising from the civil wars. The great monu-

ment was Hellenistic in form and structure, but typically Roman and Augustan in its realisation.

An almost square enclosure built of Luni marble slabs decorated with delicate and extremely vivid reliefs surrounded the altar, which was altogether Hellenistic in concept. On either side of the two doors which opened towards the Via Flaminia to the west and to the Campus Martius on the east were scenes of purely Roman mythology, the miraculous birth of Romulus and Remus, Aeneas sacrificing to Laurentius, an assembly of divinities including the goddess Roma and the symbolic *Genius Populi Romani*, as well as the famous *Itala Tellus* scene, in which the ancient goddess of marriage is accompanied by two *Aurae*, one the symbol of a swan's aura and the other in the form of a nymph astride a sea monster. The central figure of this relief represents the Great Mother of all the produce of the earth (*magna parens frugum*) who is nursing two

Head of Venus Victrix. (National Archaeological Museum, Naples).

small boys while around her blossom all kinds of plants and flowers. Below a bull and a ram represent examples of peaceful flocks. There are trees and greenery everywhere and the wind billows out the women's garments giving them the form of a shell. The wealth of fruit in the lap of the central figure is certainly symbolic. All this may seem far from reality, but imbued with a quiet yet powerful vibrance it expresses the purest pastoral poetry, even if the language is that of the Hellenistic East.

The insides of the panels are decorated with carved garlands of greenery, fruit and flowers recalling vividly that solemn ceremony when the altar was consecrated and they hung on the scaffolding in all their freshness. These garlands for which Augustan artists showed such a predilection come of course from Pergamum and from the Greek craft tradition. They were popular not only for the solemnity they added to sacred occasions, but also for their purely decorative value. The silken fragility of the acanthus leaves seems to give delicate support to the scenes resting upon them. The elegant nature displayed here has nothing realistic about it. It belongs to the refined and decorative world of the art of Pergamum. In the Augustan Age these stems of acanthus and the garland themes fit excellently with the decorative spirit of the time.

The great historical frieze on the *Ara Pacis* representing the Julian *gens* preceded by consuls and lictors is clearly inspired by the Panathenean frieze designed by Phidias on the Parthenon, but whereas there the celebration was the city's, and all social groups took part in the procession so that the entire Attic population might be included in the most important ceremony on the Acropolis, in the *Ara Pacis* frieze the people who gather round the supreme magistrates and the emperor witness a ceremony which celebrates a person and a whole family and therefore exalts an entire dynasty.

There are certain disharmonies in the style and some curious technical imperfections arise from the

Detail of the Ara Pacis: *Procession of priests and senators.* Above: *some friezes.*

attempt to include as many people as possible in the frieze. Only in the *Ara Pacis* do we find the imperial family, incarnating the ideal of a new city and national community already sanctioned by the political situation, closely wedded to that traditional Roman religion of which Augustus was the jealous and severe custodian. This religious element which is expressed in the mythical scenes on either side of the two entrances, reappears in the little frieze round the real altar, in between decorative griffins and scrolls in the Hellenistic tradition. However, the scenes of the sacred ceremony are carved in a different style from that of the frieze, a sharper and more popular style, one which will henceforth be found in all the sacrificial reliefs on Roman monuments such as commemorative and triumphal arches.

This is the age in which the Roman historical relief took the first steps in its astonishing evolution. Possibly not enough attention has even been paid to those scenes of the *lustratio* or purification by sacrifice on certain altars like those of the Vicomagistri, in the Uffizi, or on the plinth at Sorrento or to reproductions of certain statues of divinities which were on the Palatine in the temple of Apollo splendidly restored by Augustus. These all contribute to the flourishing development of the bas-relief. In the embossing of the wonderful silver chalices of the Boscoreale and Hildesheim treasures there is little trace of the Hellenistic tradition of decorative relief work, with its conventional themes. They show instead the typical Roman tendency towards the narrative in art, which appears even in the most detailed jewellers' work, a tendency which reveals itself in a careful choice of human scenes as decoration. Even in their later Hellenistic age the Greeks preferred mythological scenes. In Roman jewellery the craftsman would always involve any symbolic figure he used in a historical scene, in order to establish a connection with living reality. In the Boscoreale chalices the emperor receives the homage of the defeated

Cameos of the Augustan Age. (Kunsthistorisches Museum, Vienna).

barbarians; yet there are also statues of Victory and statues of the provinces — a symbolism also found on coins and frequently in bas-reliefs from the second century onwards.

Symbolism is predominant on the great Augustan cameo at Vienna. On the surface of the great onyx the figure of the inhabited world (or *Oikoumene*) and that of the earth-goddess *Tellus*, who with twins in her arms represents both the earth and its fertility, stand beside the emperor along with Oceanus and the seas in general. If we compare this pronounced symbolism with the slab of the *Tellus* on the *Ara Pacis*, we discover how much ground has been covered — the sculptors of the *Ara Pacis* were more spontaneous and lively. But even here, as in the coins, the historical realism is keenly felt and applied. The dramatic sense of events is visible in the example of this cameo in the conquered barbarians and the trophy raised to celebrate the victory of Tiberius over the Germans.

As for the portraits of the Augustan Age, a certain realism and violence which was peculiar to the first century B.C. especially in tomb sculpture, becomes milder, more balanced, intimate and natural. The women no longer appear with sharply carved and harsh features; the old men with taut skin etched with deep lines, so frequently encountered in the first half of that century, now appear with serene dignity, far removed from the death masks formerly carried in funeral processions.

The idealisation of facial traits in portraits — a Greek practice — gradually combines with the Italian tradition of the realistic portrait which tries to reproduce the subject's features as closely as possible. Thus the portrait of Cicero, so much inspired by Greek models as to be confused with that of Menander, could never be a product of the Augustan Age.

The evolution of the portrait is best illustrated by the development of that of the emperor. It is a very long step from the portraits of Augustus on the silver coinage of 31-27 B.C. to the statues found at Prima Porta and in the Via Labicana. Not only is the subject naturally much more mature, but a quite new conception of the emperor's image is apparent. The young face on those coins has hard features and the tousled hair frames the face rather heavily. In the portrait found at Fondi, now in the Naples Museum, the hair is even more untidy and the technique recalls terracotta work. As time goes on, the portrait becomes more

harmonious and more like the classical Greek portrait. This classical tendency is obvious in the portraits at Arles, in the Capitoline Museum at Prima Porta, while the heads found at Pergamum and on Samos bear a more recent Hellenistic influence, and the latter recalls the work of the greatest Greek sculptor.

At this point the Augustan portrait began to take on a truly official significance, as can be seen in the portrait of the emperor as a child, dating from A.D. 2, where the face takes on that official court look, which all the Augustan and Julian-Claudian emperors were to wear during the first half of the first century A.D.

In the Prima Porta statue, Augustus wears the toga, a reminder of the official fashion. It is an important statue in any study of the new classicism of the age. The emperor wears a cuirass; in his left hand he carries the sceptre and his toga is gathered on that arm and the right arm is raised in a typically oratorical gesture — familiar to us from the famous bronze of the Florentine Orator, and typical of the Italic tradition from the beginning of the first century B.C. The stance of the figure is clearly inspired by the Greek sculptor Polycletus: the left leg set slightly back from the right in a position known as decussated, because the parts assume the form of a cross as in the Greek letter X. In this case the movement is somewhat inhibited by the presence of the cuirass. A further Greek element appears in this rather late work: the Hellenistic style. It is found not only in the dolphin which appears on the plinth, but also in the small cupid near the right leg, holding up its arms. The cupid is obviously symbolic and refers to the emperor's alleged descent from the goddess Venus. In the context of such solemnity, the allusion to the divine origin of Augustus is — if one can borrow a piece of modern terminology — almost baroque or rococo and has a significance which would have been meaningless to a Greek of the fourth or third centuries B.C. This work therefore contains three fairly evident artistic trends, one derived from the Italic-Etruscan tradition (the right arm extended), one from the Greek classical figure (the decussated position), and the third, Hellenistic, inspired by art (the cupid). It is the fusion of the three that makes the statue achieve that classical harmony which goes by the name of Augustan.

The decoration on the cuirass is important for an understanding of this style. The figures on it, very typical of Augustan art, correspond to those on the cameos in Vienna and in Berlin. At the base is Tellus or mother earth nursing the familiar twins; on the left Apollo rides his griffin, and on the right Diana is mounted on her stag: these were the protecting divinities Augustus favoured; in fact Augustus was often identified with the Apollo figure. At the top centre is the personification of the heavens, Caelus; on the left, the Sun in his chariot; on the right Aurora — and above her a goddess (possibly Venus Lucina) bearing a torch. On the right and left of the central scene are two personifications: on the right the Danubian province characterised by the boar's head she holds, and on the left, on the right side of Augustus, the province of Germania. Two figures standing in the centre represent, on the right, a barbarian carrying the legion's insignia with an eagle on top, and on the left a Roman officer, with a wolf beside him, who is about to shake hands with the barbarian. The latter is holding out the standard towards Augustus as though to signify that the return of the legion's insignia is due to Augustus (and indeed in 20 B.C. Augustus did secure the return of standards lost to the barbarians when Crassus was defeated in 53 B.C. and Mark Antony in 40 and 35 B.C.). The concentration of so many themes in one

Caesar Augustus. (Vatican Museum, Rome).

Friezes from the House of the Vettii in Pompeii.

statue and its clearly religious nature make it likely that it was done after the emperor's death, so that it could date from A.D. 14, in which year he was named *Divus Augustus*.

The other statue of Augustus from the Via Labicana is likewise posthumous, and was made in the reign of Tiberius. Here he is not presented as a new Mars, but as *pontifex maximus*, his toga drawn in a veil over his head; the shape of the toga confirms this late dating. The contrast between the pale, emaciated face, which was carved separately, and the rich and glorious drapery that enfolds the body make this statue a work full of spiritual power, and uncommonly effective from a pictorial point of view. Technically also the work shows the marked refinement which the sculptors of the Tiberian age had achieved. From the age of Tiberius to that of Claudius, official imperial art increasingly tended to emphasize the symbolic in its portraits. In the apotheosis of Augustus at Ravenna, and in the carved procession of the magistrates in the Vatican Museum (which probably belonged to the Ara Pietatis Augustae started in A.D. 43), the Augustan influence of the Ara Pacis is never far distant, but there is increasing use of symbolism aimed at presenting the Augustan Age as one of perfect peace.

Alongside the great examples of official sculpture at the end of the first century A.D. and at the start of the second, there was much fine artistic craftsmanship in the fields of terracotta bas-relief, and gem and cameo cutting. The art of working in terracotta was used on the so-called Campanian slabs which decorated the upper part of public and private buildings like a frieze. They were inspired by Greek themes, dictated by the neo-attic taste of the time, and they often portrayed mythical episodes, those connected with Dionysus being very popular, or purely decorative figures and objects. Frequently archaic models are imitated, but always in an elegant and delicate form.

PAINTING

Augustan art was also subject to Greek influence in its painting, though in this case, it came through the filter of Hellenism; here, too, there were popular themes of various origins.

In the first century B.C. in Pompeii and in Rome the taste for decorative wall paintings had become fairly widespread: examples of it are familiar through the surviving paintings in the House of the Griffin on the Palatine in Rome, the House of the Faun in Pompeii and similar work on the island of Delos, all dating from around 69 B.C. The first wall paintings imitate marble slabs in every detail and colour. This early style did not last long, either because Greek artists arrived in Italy in the course of the many contacts between the Roman and the Greek world and changed existing tastes by the lessons they taught there or because Italian painters wanted to imitate Greek wall paintings. Certainly around 50-40 B.C. the grand houses began to be decorated in a different style, taste changed, and, even if the fashion for painting architectural frameworks on the walls remained, scenes with people were inserted in between them. This is what happens in Pompeii in the Villa of the Mysteries which is called after the chief scenes in the paintings. They have a unique theme and are still standing in an *oecus* or sitting room next to the bedroom. These scenes cannot be considered Augustan at all. They are typical in subject and style of neo-attic painting. This kind of painting was fairly common in Rome and in the provinces in the first century B.C. The scene is spread across several large panels and shows various stages in a Dionysiac rite, into which a character, probably a bride, is being initiated. The manner of portraying the different figures, the obvious references to classical works of various periods, the curiously unequal quality of the work-

House of the Vettii. Wall painting of Apollo's victory over the python.

Villa of the Mysteries, Pompeii. Wall painting of the unveiling of the adept Vannus.

Venus and Cupid. (Wall painting. - National Archaeological Museum, Naples).

manship are all typical of the real character of the period. The artists who painted the Esquiline frescoes as well as those of the House of Livia on the Palatine are different in both conception and execution. The scenes from the Esquiline are based on the traditional story of the Odyssey and are true examples of Hellenistic painting. But the artist of the Villa of the Mysteries took his story from themes used by the neo-attic painters and reproduced it in neo-classical terms, deriving from the work of the sculptor Lysippus.

In the Esquiline paintings, the human figure is not of any importance and serves, as in French impressionist painting, simply to provide some colour splashes in the natural scene. The artist who painted them had certainly found inspiration in the great wide landscape paintings of Hellas, and the Greek inscriptions which form captions for the various characters in the scenes showing Ulysses among the Laestrygones confirm this.

The idea of a figure as a mere patch of colour in a landscape, the blurred outlines of natural objects, the mistiness among the rocks and woods in this painting, are all typical of certain modern tendencies and are therefore immensely interesting.

The so-called architectural style is found mainly on certain walls in Rome, Pompeii and Herculaneum, where it is used as decoration in lively scenes with buildings in perspective. The decorative use of accurately painted marble panels is still in fashion, but

Spring or Flora. (Wall painting from Stabia. - National Archaeological Museum, Naples).

mainly as a base for mythological events in the lives of Theseus, Heracles, Achilles, Odysseus and the Hellenistic pastoral world. High up there are little panels containing still life or landscapes in perspective, often seen through painted open shutters, as though the wall were an external one. Sometimes, instead of mythological subjects, there are buildings on various planes which recede in perspective; these are of considerable interest to the historian of architecture, and throw light on present problems of foreshortening and space in urban architecture.

The paintings from Boscoreale, now separated and scattered in museums in Naples, New York and Mariemont in Belgium, can still be studied with ease because they are well preserved. The panels have often been considered as expressing the rules of Vitruvius applied to scenic stage painting, which Vitruvius attributed to the painter from Asia Minor, Apaturius of Alabanda. Whether they stem from the theatre or not, they reveal an intensive geometric study of spatial effects, and show unusual competence in perspective drawing.

The same technical competence is evident in the little top panels seen through fake shutters, with their streets full of foreshortened houses and porticoes, just like a Renaissance chest with a landscape. In Livia's House on the Palatine and houses in the same style in Pompeii there are several strips in grisaille depicting oriental landscapes or identifiable scenes from the banks of the Nile, a fact which speaks not only of contacts with the East but also of direct collaboration with Egyptian craftsmen. At that particular moment at the end of the first century, Egypt, with all its Hellenistic culture, undoubtedly had great artistic influence on Roman and Campanian craftsmanship. Politics and dynastic problems were responsible in part, since the new Pharaoh was pro-Roman. In the later architectural style of painting, the decorative and figurative elements part company. The latter uses a language that is not always of high quality and which must be related to a type of Hellenistic painting now lost. It is impossible to judge these Roman and Pompeian painters, for what they copied has been lost. All that can be done in these mythological scenes is to notice the different personalities of the imitators. The same myth — that of Theseus being a special favourite — might be treated several times with skill, imagination and a wealth of colour, but sometimes it appears as a tired and unintelligent copy.

Some basis of judgment on the painting of the Augustan Age has often been sought. How far can it be called Roman and how far is it really permeated by Hellenistic culture? So far there is no agreement. Some scholars emphasize the artistic value in their own right of certain scenes painted on the walls of Roman and Pompeian villas, regardless of their origins and sources. But they cannot be judged apart from

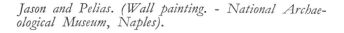
Jason and Pelias. (Wall painting. - National Archaeological Museum, Naples).

The Laestrygones prepare to attack Ulysses. (Wall painting. - Vatican Museum, Rome).

Sacrifice of Iphigenia. (Wall painting. - National Archae-ological Museum, Naples).

these: and although we know the figurative Hellenistic world only indirectly, since the masterpieces of the Theban school of the fourth-third centuries and those from Pergamum have not survived, some concrete evidence is available from the works of contemporary craftsmen on the Alexandrine steles on tombs, or the Theban steles in Boeotia and Volos. In these, style and themes can be seen and judged. Thus the paintings of the necropolis at Shiatbi in Alexandria, where the frescoes show little gates leading to luxurious gardens (possibly to portray the surroundings of the dead) are the forerunners of the architectural landscapes of Boscoreale. It might well be that the famous garden painting of the Villa Livia at Prima Porta (now in the Terme Museum in Rome) is inspired by the same source; although executed differently it still has the same

splendid abundance of plants, fruits and flowers and is undoubtedly the masterpiece of painting from the beginning of the first century A.D.

Here too, then, it is better to recognize a deliberately eclectic taste in these wall paintings, in which themes taken from Egypt, Pergamum and Hellenistic Greece are freely used. Since the great Augustan families could not always obtain original wall paintings, the fashion among them was to put in here and there on their walls famous mythological scenes which were close to Hellenistic culture, sometimes reducing them in size, or cutting them ruthlessly out of other scenes and trusting entirely in the skill of the copyist. There was a certain Ludius or Studius who, according to Pliny, seems to have had particular ability in creating paintings of seascapes, ports and coastal towns, woods, etc., such

Head of unknown Roman, from the republican age. (Uffizi Gallery, Florence).

Above: *Maecenas. (New Museum on the Capitol, Rome).* On the right: *Bronze head of Augustus. (British Museum).*

as frequently figure in single tone painting, yellow or white, in the Farnesina, the Villa Livia on the Palatine and in Pompeii. Such painting must have been inspired by the Neapolitan coastline, as well as by the conventional and fashionable views of the banks of the Nile.

Even those who have most objected to the idea of an original Roman school of painting have admitted that some of the more popular themes do show a specifically Roman taste. They developed quite apart from the Hellenistic trend and show such things as processions in honour of divinities like Cybele at Pompeii, or fights between the Pompeians and the Nucerines; they reveal a Roman taste and are nearly all typical of the sculpture of the provincial Italian municipalities, like the bas-relief of a funeral scene at Amiternum, a sacred scene of Republican date at Ostia, or the bas-reliefs in the Uffizi showing Roman shops. In their third and fourth styles which go beyond the first century B.C. and extend right into the Flavian period the Pompeian painters are no longer inspired by the vast mythological subjects familiar to Hellenistic painting, but engage in bold decorative fantasy. In his day Vitruvius had criticized this kind of art as lacking logic and harmony. Colonnades with slender stems for pillars, extravagant arabesques drift down walls in mad unreality, decorative taste has become altogether capricious; but why should we be scandalized when so many other art forms have been far more excessive? The painters of the end of the Augustan Age and the Julio-Claudian period had a fairly elegant and refined, if freakish, taste with a rich freedom of imagination which has sometimes been compared by critics with that of the Napoleonic era except that all these fantasies did not yet include worship of the emperor and the personality cult that was to begin after the death of Augustus.

MUSIC AND DANCING

The earliest Roman music seems to have been both popular and religious, consisting mainly of funeral music and religious chants, drinking songs and satirical couplets. Little is known of its early history, and the first intimations come when Roman civilisation encounters the arts of Greece.

For the Greeks music and dancing were a symbolic representation of the universal harmony in which they believed. Divine rites, science, philosophy, the theatre and poetry were all intimately connected with music and dancing, and all together formed an integral part of civilisation and education.

But this kind of musical mystique had degenerated a good deal by the time Rome came into contact with the Greek world. The study of the musical arts in the Alexandrian period had become an outworn tradition, and empty virtuosity had crept into public performances.

The gaiety of the Greek music and dances which first reached Rome provoked negative reactions in the austere atmosphere of the Republic. In the middle of the second century B.C. Scipio Aemilianus, a protector of literature and the arts, severely criticized the new music and dancing courses which people were taking. Later Sallust wrote of a grand lady of the Roman aristocracy (actually the mother of Brutus) who played the lyre and danced with more skill than was seemly in an honest woman. But this kind of complaint and insinuation could not arrest the development of a fashion which began to spread rapidly. Under the Empire it ceased to be a matter of moral prejudice especially when the emperors, who were considered as human embodiments of an almost divine nature revered by most of the population, boasted of being competent amateurs. For this, Caligula, Britannicus, Titus, Hadrian, Commodus, Heliogabalus and Alexander Severus were praised by their biographers. Nero went so far as to claim a professional's skill.

The wealthy and the aristocratic, in imitation of the prince, not only tried to reveal some talent of their own, but went so far as to keep whole private orchestras of young slaves (*pueri symphoniaci*) who accompanied them when they travelled and played at their banquets. At Trimalchio's Feast which was apparently written in Nero's reign everything happened to the sound of music from the carving of the meat to the cleaning of the hall. Exotic dancers, often from Africa and the East, and dancing to the rhythm of their tambourines or to castanets, performed at these banquets.

A few of these artists who were able to perform « special dances » achieved a high place in society, and were able to charge high fees both for performances and lessons. They became favourites of the men and were adored by the women: even Vespasian, who was noted for his avarice, took no account of cost where artists of this kind were concerned.

This search for talent and novelty and the worship of the star performer gradually produced a decline in the study of music as a liberal art or as an integral part of education. Dancing and singing still formed part of general instruction but they played a lesser role, and only choral singing seems to have retained a certain prestige. As instruments grew more and more complicated amateurs found it correspondingly difficult to play them.

In ancient Greece there had been two chief instruments, the lyre, a small harp with seven strings, and the *tibia* or *aulos*, which resembled the modern oboe. The *syrinx* or pan pipes formed of seven or eight reeds of different lengths were used only for pastoral tunes and shepherds' dances.

Even in the reign of Augustus, Horace sadly compared the plaintive *tibia* of former days with its contemporary equivalent which, he said, sounded like a trumpet.

The lyre too changed and developed into the concert « zither » which sometimes reached huge proportions; the organ, which was already an orchestra on its own, was soon able to dominate the hubbub in the vast amphitheatre by its volume of sound. In time it became really monumental and was operated by cascades of water. Cassiodorus compared it in his day to a tower.

It is clear that this uncontrolled and tasteless search for the outsize would kill Roman music — which indeed it did. Its noisiness, its sensuality and its connection with a choreography of poor quality could not but trouble the Christian ethic. So in the fourth and fifth centuries the Fathers of the Church decided upon a radical condemnation of the use of songs and musical instruments in church services. But the condemnation did not last long for by the end of the fourth century Saint Ambrose had created the sacred music which bears his name, and which was naturally inspired in part by the secular music of his day.

INDEX

INDEX

INDEX TO CONTENTS

CHRONOLOGY

B.C.

753 Traditional date for the founding of Rome by Romulus and Remus.

510 Expulsion of Tarquinius Superbus, the last king of Rome, by Lucius Junius Brutus, who becomes consul in 509.

451 Codification of the Twelve Tables which form the basis for the development of Roman law.

396 Beginning of conquest of the Etruscans at Veii.

390 Rome sacked by invading Celts.

366 First election of *praetor urbans* to supervise the administration of justice.

343-341 First Samnite War.

328-304 Second Samnite War. Romans suffer disastrous defeat at the Caudine Forks (321.)

275 Final defeat of Pyrrhus, King of Epirus, called in to support Rome's enemies in southern Italy.

262-242 First Punic war, ending in the defeat of Carthage.

241 Rome acquired Sicily and (238) Sardinia.

218 Second Punic war starts. Hannibal crosses the Alps with his elephants.

217 Hannibal defeats Flaminius at Lake Trasimene.

216 At Cannae, Hannibal inflicts on Rome the worst defeat they have ever known.

202 End of second Punic war when Scipio defeats Hannibal at Zama. The Romans acquire Spain.

149 Death of Cato the Elder.

147 Annexation of Macedonia.

133 Death of Tiberius Gracchus, the great reformer and founder of the Popular party.

133 Destruction of Numantia (Spain) by Scipio Aemilianus; Rome subdues all opposition in Spain.

133 Pergamum bequeathed to Rome, forming the province of Asia.

125-121 Final defeats of the tribes of southern Gaul allow Rome to form the province of Gallia Transalpina or Narbonensis.

121 Death of Gaius Gracchus, brother of Tiberius and upholder of his policies.

112-106 War with Jugurtha in Numidia.

104-101 Marius holds consulships and defeats the Cimbri and the Teutons.

91-87 Allies' war.

88 Sulla's march on Rome at the head of the legions starts period of violence and civil war.

86-78 Constitution of Sulla.

63 Cicero (106-43 B.C.) as consul upholds constitution against the consperacy of Catiline.

60 Pompey, Caesar and Crassus form the first Triumvirate.

59 Caesar becomes consul and wins Gaul as a new province.

55-54 Caesar invades Britain.

48 Caesar defeats Pompey, now his rival, at Pharsalus.

44 Caesar made dictator for life. Murdered by conspiracy headed by Cassius and Brutus.

43 Antony, Octavian and Lepidus form second Triumvirate. Cicero put to death.

42 Cassius and Brutus defeated at Philippi.

31 Antony defeated by Octavian at Actium.

29 Virgil begins to write the *Aeneid*.

27 Octavian receives the title of Augustus and a ten-year tenure of power; the Republic is officially restored.

23 Augustus given complete control of the state for life. This marks the end of the Republic.

A.D.

8 The poet Ovid exiled to Tomis on the Black Sea.

14 Tiberius becomes emperor.

17 Livy dies, having completed forty-two books of his *History of Rome*.

37 Caligula becomes emperor.

41 Claudius made emperor by the Praetorian Guard. During his reign Mauretania (42), Britain (43), Syria (43) and Thrace (46) were added to the Empire.

54 Nero becomes emperor.

64 A great fire destroys Rome and rumour attributes the deed to Nero. Nero in turn makes the Christians the scapegoats.
Boudicca's revolt in Britain (61) heralds a period of open opposition to Nero: Judaea (66-70), Vindex in Gaul (68) and Galba in Spain (68).

65 Death of Seneca the playwright, also Nero's tutor.

69 The year of the four emperors: Galba, Otho, Vitellius and Vespasian.

70 Capture of Jerusalem and destruction of the Temple by Titus, Vespasian's son.

77 First publication of the *Natural History* of Pliny the Elder.

79 Titus becomes emperor.

81 His brother Domitian succeeds him. His reign ends in a period of terror (93-96.)

96 This year marks the beginning of the period called « the reigns of the five good emperors » (96-180,) the culmination of which was regarded by the historian Gibbon as the happiest ever known to man. The first emperor was Nerva, followed by.

98 Trajan.

101-106 Wars in Dacia end in its annexation and forming of the Danube province.

117 Hadrian, adopted by Trajan, succeeds to the throne.

122 Work starts on Hadrian's Wall on the border between Scotland and Britain.

138 Antoninus Pius, proposed as his successor by Hadrian, becomes emperor.

161 Marcus Aurelius, the last of the good Antonine emperors and outstanding Stoic philosopher, becomes emperor.

180 His son, Commodus, becomes emperor, reverting to the dynastic principle of succession.

193 Accession of Septimus Severus.

211 Accession of his son Caracalla.

212 Caracalla decrees that all distinction between Italians and provincials shall be abolished so that the Empire shall be a commonwealth of equal citizens.

284 Diocletian becomes emperor and makes the first real and effective attempts to save the Empire from disintegration.

306 Constantine proclaimed Augustus at York.

313 Edict of Milan allowing Christians to worship openly. Constantine becomes a Christian.

330 Foundation of Constantinople, the new capital of the Empire.

361 Julian, called 'the Apostate', antagonistic to Christianity, becomes emperor.

395 The two sons of Theodosius (379-395) divide the Empire into two parts, east and west, henceforwards to be ruled separately.

Museum of Roman Civilisation, *Rome*
Vatican Museum, *Rome*
Lateran Museum, *Rome*
Capitoline Museums, *Rome*
Torlonia Museum, *Rome*
Terme Museum, *Rome*
Museum of Villa Giulia, *Rome*
National Roman Museum, *Rome*
Communal Antiquarium, *Rome*
Vigna Codini Columbarium, *Rome*
Villa Torlonia, *Rome*
The Louvre, *Paris*
Museum, *Epinal*
Museum of Art and History, *Brussels*
Wallraf-Richartz Museum, *Cologne*
Antiken Sammlung, *Berlin*
Museum, *Berlin*
Archaeological Museum, *Aquileia*
National Museum, *Vienna*
Museum, *Budapest*
Museum, *Pettau*
British Museum, *London*

Museum, *Tripoli*
Uffizi Gallery, *Florence*
National Archaeological Museum, *Naples*
Archaeological Museum, *Parma*
Museum, *Guelma* (Algeria)
Archaeological Museum, *Florence*
National Concordiese Museum, *Portogruaro*
Museum, *Nemi*
Museum, *Barletta*

and further:

Excavations at *Pompeii*
Excavations at *Herculaneum*
Bas-rilief on the Arch of Trajan, *Benevento*
Church of Santa Bibiana, *Rome*
Baths of Caracalla, *Rome*
Orbe, *Switzerland*
Map of Ancient Rome at Porta San Silvestro, *Rome*
Church of San Lorenzo outside the Walls, *Rome*
Church of San Vittore, *Ravenna*

THE WORLD OF ANCIENT ROME has been produced in collaboration with SCALA - Istituto Fotografico Editoriale of Florence and the firm of FRATELLI ALINARI, Florence

Collaborators in the reproductions and in the printing of the volume: OFFSET and TIPOGRAFIA BONA.

The paper was provided by CARTIERE DEL GARDA, Riva di Trento.

The binding was done by the binders L. DEGLI ESPOSTI, Bologna.

PRINTED IN FLORENCE
AT STABILIMENTI GRAFICI BEMPORAD MARZOCCO
JULY 31 1967